D0219544

Macau
The Imaginary City

Macau
The Imaginary City

Culture and Society,
1557 to the Present

Jonathan Porter

Westview
PRESS

A Member of the Perseus Books Group

New Perspectives on Asian Studies

Photos by the author except as noted.

Excerpts from *Invisible Cities* by Italo Calvino, copyright © 1972 by Giulio Einaudi, editore s.p.a., English translation copyright © 1974 by Harcourt Brace & Company and by Secker & Warburg. Reprinted by permission of Harcourt Brace & Company and by Reed Books Ltd.

All rights reserved. Printed in the United States of America. No part of this publication may be reproduced or transmitted in any form or by any means, electronic or mechanical, including photocopy, recording, or any information storage and retrieval system, without permission in writing from the publisher.

Copyright © 2000, 1996 by Westview Press, A member of the Perseus Books Group

Published in 2000 in the United States of America by Westview Press, 5500 Central Avenue, Boulder, Colorado 80301-2877, and in the United Kingdom by Westview Press, 12 Hid's Copse Road, Cumnor Hill, Oxford OX2 9JJ

Find us on the World Wide Web at www.westviewpress.com

Porter, Jonathan.
　　Macau : the imaginary city / Jonathan Porter.
　　　　p.　　cm. — (New perspectives in Asian history)
　　Includes bibliographical references and index.
　　ISBN 0-8133-3749-6 (pbk.)
　　1. Macau—Civilization.　I. Title: Imaginary city.　II. Series.

DS796.M2P66　2000
951.26—dc21
96-047016
CIP

The paper used in this publication meets the requirements of the American National Standard for Permanence of Paper for Printed Library Materials Z39.48-1984.

10　　9　　8　　7　　6　　5　　4　　3　　2

Contents

Illustrations

Acknowledgments

This book had its genesis when, as a teaching assistant to Woodbridge Bingham's course on Eastern Civilizations at the University of California at Berkeley, I saw some slides shown by Professor Bingham of a city that seemed to exist from another time. I knew then that I would have to go there.

Macau, the place and its people, have captivated me, almost in the literal sense of the word, since I first visited Macau almost thirty years ago. The writing of this book has been a prolonged effort to acknowledge that captivation and perhaps, partly unconsciously, to escape it. If that very personal obsession with Macau has emerged in this book, I have not attempted entirely to suppress it.

I owe an incalculable debt to the anonymous (to me) but not faceless people of Macau—people I passed in the streets, encountered sitting reflectively at the ends of narrow alleys, jostled in the market, accosted in the shops; children playing in the schoolyards and parks; friendly and helpful custodians of temples; men attending their pet birds in the gardens. Without them this book would not be. A good part of this book was written while sitting on the balcony of the old Bela Vista Hotel. Surely I must also acknowledge the benign influence of that fine old building.

The staffs of the Arquivo Historico de Macau, the Sir Robert Ho Tung Library, and the National Library at the Leal Senado were courteous and helpful. Monsignor Manuel Teixeira, always generous to visiting scholars, guided me through the Catholic institutions of Macau. I am grateful to Joanna Kaestner of Albuquerque for supplying me with a copy of the manuscript journal of Edward E. Fuller. I am also grateful to Noelle Sullivan and Liping Zhu for their research assistance.

Stephen Mackinnon, Robert Kern, Paul Hutton, Jerry Bentley, and William H. McNeill read various versions of the manuscript and offered their criticism and encouragement. Although I may not always have been successful in following their advice, their interest and suggestions for improvement gave me the confidence to continue. To Virginia Scharff, my friend and colleague, I acknowledge a special debt of gratitude. Her sympathetic yet demanding reading of the manuscript made me see things in new ways. If I have failed to live up to her expectations, I have gained immeasurably from her suggestions. I wrote most of this book while serving for nine years (1986–1995) as chair of the History Department at the University of

New Mexico. If it had not been for the unflagging support of Yolanda Martinez, the department administrator, through all those difficult years, I would not have been able to complete this work. I am grateful to the University of New Mexico for a sabbatical leave in the fall of 1988, when I could work on the book for an uninterrupted period.

I also want to thank the New Perspectives on Asian History series editors Edward Farmer and Ainslie Embree; Peter Kracht, Westview Press Senior Editor; as well as project editor Shena Redmond and copy editor Joan Sherman.

My greatest debt is to Zoë, who has been since our first visit to the city an ever-present and resourceful companion in our discovery of Macau. Thanks to her, the memory of our very first visits to Macau, when we stayed at the much-beloved old Pousada de Macau—only four rooms and one of the best restaurants in the Far East—next to the Government House on the Praia Grande, is still fresh.

It will be apparent to the reader that this book took shape and was written over a period of many years. Macau today is a different place than it was twenty or thirty years ago, when I first visited the city. Much of the isolation of Macau, its island-like quality and with it much of its peculiar charm, has been eroded by the rapid economic integration of the enclave with the neighboring mainland—itself rapidly developing—in the past decade. Even so, I have been pleased that very recent first-time visitors to Macau have relayed to me some of the same fascination with the place that I first experienced there. This book is dedicated to that particular but elusive experience that is Macau.

Jonathan Porter

Preface

By the end of 1999, when the territory is handed back to China, Macau will have been occupied and governed by the Portuguese for 443 years—almost half of the closing millennium. Those five centuries encompass one of the most epochal movements in human history: the expansion of European peoples around the globe. It was a movement driven by diverse motivations, having many dimensions, and holding vast implications, many of which continue to shape the world at the close of the millennium and into the next. The effects of this expansion and the dominance of European peoples over Asians, Africans, and other peoples were both benign and malign, constructive and destructive, noble and ignoble. Arguments over these effects probably will never be resolved because both those who were the subjects of the expansion and those who led it have been thoroughly transformed by the process. But one thing is indisputable: The interaction of peoples and their cultures, institutions, and technologies has been the salient legacy of this epoch. Macau is one place where that cross-cultural interaction occurred over almost the entire period of expansion and contraction of European dominance in Asia.

Known imperfectly to Europeans through the narratives of such early travelers as William of Rubruck, Odoric of Pordenone, and Marco Polo, China was the original goal of the first mariners who pushed hastily onward from their early destinations in India and Southeast Asia. The Portuguese first reached the China coast by sea in 1513. After clinging to tenuous footholds for the next several decades, they settled permanently at Macau in 1557. Thus Macau became the first continuously occupied European settlement in China and finally became the last European territory in Asia.

Perhaps that fact alone imparts to Macau a sufficient symbolic significance as the first and the last. Macau's separate historical identity could reasonably be expected to end with its return to China, reabsorbed into the larger historical process from which it was once detached. Macau was never, after all, a place of such importance in the ebb and flow of East-West relations as Canton or Shanghai. But it was, as I have tried to show in this book, for so many centuries the threshold of a cross-cultural exchange that peculiarly reflected the changing characters of the two very different worlds that met there.

Yet just as the significance of the protracted encounter at Macau, as it evolved over time, varied according to each side's perspective on their encounter, so also the resumption of the exercise of Chinese sovereignty over

Macau holds different meanings for China and Portugal. For China, which has felt the bitter sting of national defeat and humiliation at the hands of the Western powers since the mid-nineteenth century, Macau is one of the "lost territories" (also including Hong Kong and Taiwan) whose restoration to the motherland will make the nation whole again. Macau in Western hands was a symbol of China's imperfect sovereignty, and with the return of Hong Kong and Macau (and ultimately Taiwan?) part of China's national honor is restored.

But curiously it was not always thus. Nationalism and its concomitant sense of national sovereignty is a modern phenomenon. Ironically the People's Republic of China has appropriated the imperial mantle of the Manchu Qing dynasty, which its founders once excoriated as even more condemnable than the Western oppressors who victimized the dynasty. Although the Qing asserted its claim to territorial jurisdiction over Macau, it did so in the name of a larger concept of a cultural imperium that could accommodate the presence of foreigners' limited and local political arrangements as long as those foreigners did not disturb the cultural and social stability and harmony of the Chinese world. And before the Qing, the Ming, whose local officials had granted the Portuguese a lease to occupy Macau as a convenient trading base to the benefit of both sides in the pursuit of local commerce, were not much troubled by modern legalistic notions of territorial sovereignty as long as the occupants comported themselves with due respect for Chinese ways. The contemporary Chinese attitude toward Macau, therefore, is largely the product of a relatively recent political agenda.

To a much lesser extent, China has an economic interest in Macau as a source of foreign exchange revenue through export production and investment. China has invested heavily in Macau's infrastructure, commercial, and industrial development, and as a free port like Hong Kong, Macau offers China convenient access to the global economy. For this reason the Macau Basic Law, the constitution that governs Macau's existence as a Special Administrative Region of the People's Republic of China after 1999, stipulates that the socialist system and policies shall not be practiced in Macau and that the previous capitalist system and way of life shall remain unchanged for fifty years.

For Portugal, Macau has a very different meaning. Macau is the distilled legacy of the heroic, epochal phase of Portuguese national history, a memorial to Portugal's past greatness. The Portuguese seaborne empire long ago collapsed and fragmented into a few dispersed colonial possessions of which Macau was the very last. The positive legacy of that epoch, as construed by the Portuguese, was the diffusion and interaction of cultures made possible by the agency of Portuguese maritime expansion, commerce, and settlement. In the heyday of the Portuguese empire, elements of European, African, Indian, Southeast Asian, and Chinese cultures interacted in complex encounters. This interplay of cultures was Portugal's contribution to world cross-cultural understanding. Ironically, Macau, at once the most autonomous and the most loyal of Portuguese overseas territories, has become the last tangible monument where that legacy still lives in the diversity of its contrasting cultural elements and institutions and in its role as a gateway between China and European and Latin peoples.

So for the Portuguese, Macau evokes a nostalgic sense of national pride, which they are anxious to see reaffirmed and vindicated in the amicable passage of Macau to Chinese possession. While for the Chinese the return of Macau erases a past violation of national honor, for the Portuguese it hopefully commemorates a great national achievement. As for the future, Macau itself, its history and culture, is largely meaningless to China, but it is paramount for Portugal. Conversely, Macau's contemporary function, its economic institutions and resources, is of little interest to Portugal, but it is of considerable benefit to China.

Thus we find in Macau a curious juxtaposition of economics and history. On one side are modern commercial development and financial energy rushing almost blindly onward; on the other side are the remnants and mementos of traditional culture preserved with increasing desperation in the face of extinction threatened by the first. Macau has become two cities interpenetrating each other as one. But it is not always certain which is which, or where to draw the line between them. One is a compact city of commerce and finance inhabited by bankers and bureaucrats, merchants and entrepreneurs, gangsters and unskilled laborers. Here are the glass-walled banks, imposing office buildings with pretentious names, rectilinear apartment blocks, the somber grey post office, the modern ferry terminal, the new airport, the crowded street markets. And everywhere, filling the interstices of the city, the automobiles, circulating endlessly yet seemingly with nowhere to go.

The other city is made up of fragments, some old and venerated, like the displays of a history theme park for the edification of the curious public, others new and contrived like the flashy entertainments and concessions of an amusement park. Here are museums and gardens guiding visitors through Macau's colorful history; restored districts and streets where the façades of old buildings evoke the scenes of a century ago; old churches and temples attesting to the confluence of cultures that shaped the city; modern monuments catering to the contesting claims of cultural diversity—a statue of Guan Yin, the Buddhist Goddess of Mercy, facing the shore of the outer harbor; another towering statue of Mazu, Macau's patron goddess of seafarers, gazing at the mainland from the top of a hill; and a modernistic monument to intercultural communication and understanding, incongruously anchoring an immense predatory commercial development on reclaimed land. There is the neon-glitter of the casinos with their atrociously decorated velvet and satin VIP rooms, and the frantic noise and spectacle of the races—the Dragon Boat races in the

Spring and the Grand Prix car race through the streets in the fall. And rising in sweeping undulations on spidery pylons, the bridges, like roller coasters connecting parts of the two cities. This other city is inhabited by tourists, gamblers, and prostitutes; souvenir vendors and casino workers. Tourists come in growing numbers to view the well-preserved historical sights and the picturesque streets, visit the monuments to the city's culture, gamble in the casinos, and play the horses; revenue from tourism and services now exceeds that from exports, and tourism is the biggest employer.

One is a serious city; the other is frivolous. Although they seem to coexist harmoniously, the visitor might be forgiven for assuming that the first city is the real city of substance and that the other city is merely an artificial façade living tenuously in the shadow of the first. But the visitor would be wrong to conclude that it is the solid city of banks and offices, industry and finance, that will endure, and that the insubstantial city that lives within it will gradually fade away, leaving only the banks and offices and automobiles. Either city is incomplete without the other; in Macau the frivolous and the serious are one and the same. One cannot be differentiated from the other because Macau itself is a kind of museum where the serious and the frivolous long ago converged. Thus to engage Macau in any but the most casual way demands, as in a museum, that one invoke the imagination for what lies behind the façade, beneath the hard surface of concrete and glass and steel. It is only that effort of the imagination is becoming ever more difficult.

Jonathan Porter,
1999

The Imaginary City
Departures

"From now on, I'll describe the cities to you," the Khan had said, "in your journeys you will see if they exist."

But the cities visited by Marco Polo were always different from those thought of by the emperor.

"And yet I have constructed in my mind a model city from which all possible cities can be deduced," Kublai said. "It contains everything corresponding to the norm. Since the cities that exist diverge in varying degrees from the norm, I need only foresee the exceptions to the norm and calculate the most probable combinations."

"I have also thought of a model city from which I deduce all the others," Marco answered. "It is a city made up only of exceptions, exclusions, incongruities, contradictions. If such a city is the most improbable, by reducing the number of abnormal elements, we increase the probability that the city really exists. So I have only to subtract exceptions from my model, and in whatever direction I proceed, I will arrive at one of the cities which, always an exception, exist. But I cannot force my operation beyond a certain limit: I would achieve cities too probable to be real."[1]

The city becomes rapidly smaller as it recedes in the distance. The bridge, the casino, the hydrofoil terminal, the lighthouse on the hill blur through the thickening sea-haze, and the city assumes an undifferentiated blank whiteness before it finally vanishes, lost to sight against the low green and yellow mountains of the coastal islands. Straining to catch that last fading image . . . Was it ever there? Was it, after all, only some dreamy illusion, a figment of the imagination conjured like a vision in the overwrought mind of a determined explorer seeking the new world of magical cities he knows must exist some-where?

Yet as I watch the imaginary city vanish so quickly, I recall, behind that white facade, other images—of color, and noise, and smells; of people, and houses, and narrow streets, and strange signs; of dark temple doors, and busy, crowded bazaars. Does it matter to the people who live there that their city is only imaginary? When their image finally fades, do they cease to exist, does their movement end, as if frozen in time, until, when I return some day, they awaken again and resume their interrupted movement oblivious that anything had happened?

৴ৼ   ৴ৼ   ৴ৼ

For many people who have encountered it, whether at length or only briefly, Macau is a very personal experience. There is some quality in the place, something unusual yet elusive, that makes a deep impression on the imagina-tion. But what that quality is, I cannot say precisely. It is as if the city were not entirely real or, rather, not of the real world. Perhaps that is because it belongs, in fact, not to one but to two worlds. Yet there are other cities where different worlds meet that nevertheless convey no such illusory qual-ity. Macau so often seems dreamlike, as though it were sustained partly by the effort of some powerful imagination. This is not because it is such an idyllic place, a peaceful, perfect paradise. It is dirty, noisy, grimy, crowded, often ugly. But if it is all these things, it is also more—in its midst are ele-ments of serenity, peace, charm, fascination.

It may be that Macau's dreamlike quality arises from its small size and its isolation. Physically, it is confined within the perimeter of the bays sur-rounding it, making it virtually, if not actually, an island. Moreover, politi-cally and socially isolated from the surrounding mainland, it could not spread as other cities have done to the surrounding land. Economically, it has been isolated by the shallowness of its harbor and channels from the mainstream of the modern commercial world. Finally, it has been isolated as much in a historical sense as in a geographical one, abandoned as a historical fossil, passed over by the great modern movements of historical change in the two worlds to which it has belonged.

So it is possible, in a sense, to easily encompass the city in one's mind. Few, if any, other cities that deserve the name can be so readily compre-hended by the imagination. In the process, however, the city may come to seem a mere product of the imagination.

Imagination and the experience of place are linked. A place like Macau possesses an accumulated energy that shapes and gives expression to its his-tory and experience. If it did not have this energy, it would become a dead place, merely an incoherent collection of physical properties and features without a collective life of their own. "A place is dead if the physique does not support the work of imagination, if the mind cannot engage with the experience located there, or if the local energy fails to evoke ideas, images, or feelings."[2] To discover a sense of place, then, is more than an effort in physical analysis and static description; it is to imagine "expressive space."

Macau has endured for more than four centuries. Yet it is a fragile city. Now, the peculiar character of Macau is rapidly being obliterated by new, nondescript, imitative, characterless neomodern cultural styles imported from Hong Kong and abroad. Every year, every month, some of what made Macau remarkable and extraordinary disappears forever. Finally, the ineffable quality that characterized Macau truly will belong only to that city dwelling in the imagination; only the dead city of fact will remain.

⚘　⚘　⚘

Macau may be viewed from a variety of historical perspectives. One of these might focus on the city as an artifact of the history of Western political and military expansion and its impact on Asia. This view tells us much about the balance of political power and its changes and about cultural interaction mediated by such power.[3] A second perspective focuses on the growth of commerce and East-West trade and the role of Macau as a trade emporium in a hemispheric exchange of commodities in which cultural exchange was again involved.[4] A third perspective comes from the history of missionary evangelization as an extension of the Christian crusade and the role of Macau in that movement in Asia.[5] From still another point of view—that of urban history and sociology—we may seek to understand Macau as a city, in particular a colonial city, in a typology of cities including commercial entrepôts and colonial port cities.[6] And then Macau may be seen as an overseas Chinese community exhibiting a wealth of Chinese popular culture on the colonial periphery of China.

I have been influenced in my attempt to understand Macau by all of these views and perhaps by other unconscious ones besides. Since I first encountered Macau in 1967, my growing fascination with the place drew me back on many occasions, in different seasons and for varying lengths of time. This book is not in any sense a conventional chronological narrative history of Macau from any of the individual perspectives suggested previously.[7] Such approaches fail to comprehend, I believe, the extraordinary phenomenon of Macau both as a place and as a process—in space and in time. From its inception as a settlement, Macau has been the scene of a continually changing cultural intermixture. A finite place encompassed this interaction. But to treat the city as a sort of exercise in urban history is to raise perplexing questions of definition: What kind of place and what kind of city is Macau?

The traditional commercial emporia of the Indian Ocean and the South China Sea grew on the foundations of a long history of maritime commerce and its connection with continental trade routes prior to the European era. Like Canton or Bangkok, some of these cities were located at the junction of a major river with the coast, providing access to upriver trade routes. Others, such as Calicut and Surat, were also nurtured by indigenous economic and political conditions and access to agricultural and other raw materials and the manufactured commodities of the interior regions. Or, like Malacca, Hormuz, or Aden, they were poised on a strategic passage that could be exploited by local powers.[8]

Following the invasion of the European peoples in the sixteenth century, new trading ports, including Bombay and later Shanghai, were born on the sites of previous non-European settlements or were established where no towns of consequence had previously existed. All of these cities were central places that owed their importance to economic conditions of long duration.[9]

Macau was different. It was located in an eccentric position relative to Canton and the trading network focused there. It was not nurtured, except perhaps in an exclusionary sense, by the economic and political conditions of the region. No prior emporium existed where Macau grew on the fringe of the South China coast. Macau was not a central place—indeed, although its early prosperity derived from its strategic location on the trade route from Goa through Malacca to Japan, its access to nearby Canton and the China market was what made it important.

What set Macau apart from other colonial port cities of Asia, then, was that it belonged neither to the class of numerous small traditional Asian ports that preceded the establishment of Western hegemony nor to the few preeminent Westernized colonial emporia that emerged in the nineteenth century. Nor was Macau positioned on an evolutionary continuum from the first type to the latter. Rather, it lay to one side of that development, borrowing something from the pattern of traditional Asian ports but never emerging to become one of the great Western colonial emporia. Like the smaller Asian ports, Macau was suited to access the trade of a limited hinterland as an entrepôt in the traditional maritime trade network, but it was inadequate for exploiting the large-scale production for export from a vast inland region, requiring large ships and deepwater port facilities, that emerged later.[10]

Macau was built by Portuguese traders, and its administration was modeled on that of Portuguese cities and on the Estado da India, sanctioned by Goa or Lisbon. Its culture was dominated by its Portuguese settlers and sojourners. Yet it became—and never ceased thereafter to remain—a Chinese city as well. Chinese sovereignty was never definitively surrendered and was frequently and periodically exercised, generally with Portuguese acquiescence. Ultimately, however, Macau was highly individual and autonomous, cherishing a strong sense of independence from both China and Portugal.

All entrepôt cities are founded on commercial exchange. Commerce arises where diverse social and economic systems meet, but people are the actors and mediators of commercial exchange. And where people of different cultures encounter one another, cultural exchange also occurs. Located thus on the boundaries between economic and social systems, entrepôt cities are often thresholds connecting different cultural regions. Although Macau was, in some respects, sui generis, it may be compared to other international multicultural emporia of the maritime trade system of East and Southeast Asia, places such as Malacca, Singapore, Canton, Hong Kong, and Shanghai. All of these cities were celebrated at various times for their cosmopolitanism, reflected in their attraction of people—sometimes grouped in organized communities—of various trade diasporas. In some, such as Malacca in the fifteenth century and Canton in the ninth and eighteenth centuries, complex commercial institutions emerged to facilitate and control trade among these groups. Others, especially Singapore and Hong Kong in the nineteenth and twentieth centuries, were different in maintaining much less regulated or completely unregulated free ports. Of these, only Malacca and Canton were established as foreign trade ports before the arrival of the Europeans.

Malacca was a nexus of regional commerce of the Malay Peninsula and Indonesia, as well as of Indian Ocean and South China Sea trade routes, at least a century before the Portuguese captured the city in 1511. It organized the exchange of diverse maritime, forest, and mineral products gathered from several mainland and maritime hinterlands through a system of personal alliances among commercial agents. Communities of merchants representing all of the trade diasporas of the Asian maritime system—Arabs, Chinese, Bugis, Gujeratis, Parsees, Tamils, Bengalis, Javanese, and Japanese—resided there; it was said that eighty-four languages were spoken in Malacca.[11] The city's prominence rested more on its function as a collection and redistribution point rather than on any specific location contiguous with a major cultural and political center. Because the Portuguese were flexible and did not displace the system they found in place, Malacca flourished under Portugal's control, but it subsequently declined under the Dutch, who were intent on creating an economically rationalized system. Finally, it was superseded by Singapore in the nineteenth century.[12]

Singapore replaced Malacca as the principal emporium of Southeast Asia after it was founded in 1815 by the British. Like Malacca, Singapore was not located on the periphery of a great economic and cultural center but owed its success instead to its geographic position at the conjunction of the maritime trading subsystems of the Indian Ocean and the South China Sea. Indeed, the Malay Peninsula had already been a nodal point in regional Southeast Asian trade before Singapore's founding, and the city continued to function in this respect under the unregulated free trade of the new port, where Arabs, Parsees, Bengalis, Tamils, Bugis, Javanese, and especially Chinese congregated.[13] Yet, because it was isolated on the very tip of the long Malay Peninsula (actually on an island), proximity to a continental civilization was even less important for Singapore than for Malacca, which at least exchanged products with the peoples of the contiguous regions of the peninsula. Singapore's true hinterland comprised the maritime trade networks extending east to China and the Moluccas and west and south to India, Sumatra, and Java.[14]

Canton was a gateway for trade with China on the South China Sea at least as early as the eighth century, when a large Arab merchant community dominated the port. Unlike Malacca, Canton's importance derived not so much from regional trade in extracted natural products as from its ability to provide an outlet for the manufactured products of the increasingly sophisticated economy of the South China hinterland (especially silk, porcelain, and lacquer) and access to the potentially vast China market. Although the Chinese had always sought to control foreign trade, the increasingly restrictive policies of the Ming and Qing from the fourteenth century limited the formation of organized foreign trading communities in Canton.[15] Moreover, unlike any of the other cities under consideration, Canton's status as a provincial capital and an administrative and political center inhibited its autonomy. By the mid-eighteenth century, trade was compressed into a tightly regulated monopoly imposed by the Cohong system, and year-round residence of foreigners was prohibited.

Hong Kong, a natural anchorage on the estuary of the Pearl River leading to Canton, was occupied by the British during the Opium War with China (1839–1842) and ceded to Britain by the treaty that ended the war. Organized as a free port, it soon demonstrated its value both for transshipment of goods and for access to the commerce of the China coast, while remaining completely detached from Chinese authority and control. Like Singapore but unlike Canton, it was geographically isolated, which may have enhanced its role as an autonomous enclave of foreign power in China. It was not until after World War II that Hong Kong experienced phenomenal growth as a financial and manufacturing, as well as commercial, center.

Although Shanghai was a traditional Chinese market town at the mouth of the Yangzi River before the Opium War, it was completely transformed after the 1850s when it became the leading treaty port, strategically positioned at the junction of two vital commercial axes: the Yangzi River trade penetrating the heart of China and the regional and international maritime trade of the China coast. Its international settlements became the focus of Western economic, political, and cultural influences in China. By the early twentieth century, foreign investment had fostered manufacturing industry in the city, and Shanghai became the financial center of Western imperialism in China, symbolized by its imposing banks lining the Bund.[16] Not until the Chinese Communist victory in 1949 was Shanghai's financial and industrial establishment forced to migrate to the relative safety of Hong Kong. Shanghai was vulnerable, of course, because, unlike Singapore and Hong Kong, it was not protected by geographical isolation; like Canton, it was a gateway to a vast, contiguous economic region.

If, in a general way, we compare Macau's geographical, political, and economic situation to that of these other entrepôt cities, we observe that, like Singapore and Hong Kong, Macau was located on the periphery of the continental hinterland but physically detached from it. Although that separation has largely disappeared recently in the case of Hong Kong and Macau, the locations of each of these cities were significant as much for their function as exchange points in the intra-Asia trade as for their access to adjacent hinterlands. Yet, like Canton and Shanghai, Macau was also a port of access to the neighboring economic and cultural region and to the entire Chinese world beyond. Diverse expatriate communities became permanent features of both Hong Kong and Singapore, with the Chinese emerging as the dominant community. Cultural exchange between different communities in these settings tended to be limited and shaped primarily by economic transactions. By contrast, in both Canton and Shanghai, where expatriate communities were more tenuous, cultural exchange occurred across the boundary with the contiguous society. To the extent that it shared something of these two modes of exchange, Malacca fell somewhere between them.

Although Malacca had a longer history of European hegemony than the other cities and shared with Macau the experience of Portuguese control for a time, it witnessed a succession of discrete political authorities—Malay, Portuguese, Dutch, British, Malay again—each leaving its distinctive imprint without any enduring interconnection with the others or with the wider culture and society in which it was physically located. Canton, resisting autonomous foreign resident communities, experienced cultural interaction on a much more limited basis, at least until it became a treaty port in the mid-nineteenth century. Hong Kong, like Macau, was governed by a single political authority, but it was so much more dominated by that authority that similar possibilities for cultural diversity and exchange were hindered. More insulated, it has also been more culturally bifurcated between the West and China: No creole language and no subtle gradations of culture characterize modern Hong Kong. Perhaps Shanghai, though with a much shorter history, was more like Macau than any other of these entrepôts. It was not an administrative center, and it had little commercial significance before it became a center of European trade. It was physically part of China, administered jointly by Chinese and European authority, and it possessed an extensive foreign settlement and cultural presence. Thus, it was a true boundary between different worlds across which people, Western ideas, comprador culture, economic and political institutions, revolutionary ideologies, and cultural stimulation traveled.

To compare Macau with these other cities as I have done is to minimize the peculiar spatial and temporal influences that inevitably shaped their histories and thus also their experiences of cultural exchange. But as an exercise in theoretical modeling, it is possible to construct from the foregoing considerations a profile of the cultural ecology of the entrepôt city. This profile includes, first, the *parameters* that define such a city and, second, the *indications* that may be useful to identify and distinguish such cities. Parameters include: geographic advantage of location; access and settlement by diverse peoples, groups, and communities, as well as trade diasporas; the conjunction of several diverse economies, including commerce, agriculture, extraction, and industry; political continuity and protection; the symbiosis of hinterland and periphery, usually on a maritime trade system; and a boundary or frontier between cultures. Indications include: architecture and the built environment; language and creole dialects; social customs and behavior; social hierarchies and settlement patterns; religious expressions; and technology and material culture. I will examine all of these indications as they apply to Macau.

↗   ↗   ↗

A city should be understood "as a container of presences that include ancient images and memories. These presences enter the feelings that make a town, and they help to settle a place."[17] The many and diverse influences that created Macau produced an unusual—some would say unique—cultural conglomeration, condensed in a small place. But Macau is more than a cultural repository, however diverse, or a living but static artifact of the meeting of civilizations. It has been, more or less at various times in its past, a threshold between two worlds, revealing different scenes and different opportunities depending upon which side of the threshold one is standing on. In this respect, Macau is not limited by a finite location.

All cities are places where cultural change as well as exchange take place. As cultural centers, they may have various roles depending on their origins, either to shape and articulate the traditional culture of a civilization or to mediate the conflicts of differing traditions and create new states of mind.[18]

This book, then, is an essay in cultural history. It is not a study of trade, commercial intercourse, or political relations between China and the West. These subjects have already been well treated for some periods in the works of George Bryan Souza and John E. Wills Jr. and an earlier study by Michael Greenberg, to name only a few. In attempting to comprehend Macau, I have rejected the mode of traditional chronological narrative. Rather, I have chosen to examine the city in terms of a series of images of its history and culture, both as a place in its own right and as a threshold between two larger worlds. In doing so, I have endeavored to evoke both the sense of place and the historical process that made Macau. Textual sources, of course, have been essential to this understanding of the city.[19] But I have also relied on visual and material evidence and on the constructed environment of architecture, churches and temples, and streets and markets, as well as the life that passes in them, including the mundane things that so easily escape notice simply because they are so common but that nonetheless convey the expressive spaces of the city.

The method I have adopted here is an unusual one. I have chosen a parallel thematic and topical approach, rather than the usual linear one. First, by way of introduction, I try to evoke the "mentalities" or historical styles as contexts for the encounter between the two worlds that met in Macau in the sixteenth and seventeenth centuries. Then I examine Macau as a physical place and consider the geographical and demographic context of the South China coastal region to which it has belonged. Subsequently, I explore Macau from various cultural perspectives that define the relationship of its culture and history: the built environment of its architecture, which has reflected the memory of its historical passages; the biographical history of the people who passed through Macau, in either direction, or who found in the city a resting place or a destination; the social context of popular life and culture that have imparted to Macau so much of its peculiar character; and the popular religious traditions, particularly of the growing Chinese settlement that made Macau a Chinese city as well as a European one.

I am aware that using this methodology poses a risk that the subject may sometimes appear disjointed and incoherent. But I believe there is a greater risk in approaching Macau by a conventional, linear explanatory path, for that would leave much of its innate, ineffable character unexamined. I confess that I nevertheless still find it hard to define what appeals to me so much about Macau.

> If I wished to describe [the city] to you, sticking to what I personally saw and experienced, I should have to tell you that it is a colorless city, without character, planted there at random. But this would not be true, either: at certain hours, in certain places along the street, you see opening before you the hint of something unmistakable, rare, perhaps magnificent; you would like to say what it is, but everything previously said of [the city] imprisons your words and obliges you to repeat rather than to say.[20]

one

Two Worlds
Origins: Portugal and China

Arms and noble men of valor,
Who from the western shore of Lusitania,
Across seas never before sailed,
Passed even beyond Ceylon,
And daring amidst danger and war,
Surpassing ordinary human powers,
Among distant peoples established
A New Realm, so greatly extolled.[1]

In antiquity, he who wished to illuminate virtue throughout All Under Heaven, first ordered his own state. Wishing to order his own state, he first regulated his family. Wishing to regulate his family, he first cultivated his person. Wishing to cultivate his person, he first rectified his heart. Wishing to rectify his heart, he first made his will sincere. Wishing to make his will sincere, he first extended his knowledge. Extension of knowledge lies in the investigation of things.[2]

Almost seven thousand miles separate Cabo São Vicente, at the extreme southwestern rim of Europe, from the South China coast, but the distance was considerably greater—more than fifteen thousand miles—on a sea voyage between the two places in the sixteenth century. The early voyagers sailed south and west across the Atlantic, approaching close to Brazil after they crossed the equator, then eastward around the Cape of Good Hope. After going up the East African coast to a latitude north of Madagascar, they would cross the Indian Ocean to the Malabar coast of India. From there, at Goa, Cochin, or Calicut, they sailed around the Indian peninsula, perhaps stopping on the Coromandel coast, or directly on to Malacca, on the Strait of Malacca between the Malay Peninsula and Sumatra. The final leg of their voyage took them from Malacca down through the strait, around the Southeast Asian mainland, and up the South China Sea. Following the monsoon in season would bring them to a landfall on the South China coast near the estuary of the Pearl River, flowing out of South China past the great trading city of Canton.

⚓   ⚓   ⚓

Cabo São Vicente rises more than two hundred feet above the Atlantic Ocean. Low, scrubby vegetation hugs the ground, shunning the wind; no trees are sturdy enough to grow at the end of the cape. The waves pounding the cliffs below send up long, white plumes of spray that fall back into the churning sea. Driven up long fractures in the rocks, the spray is compressed by the action of the waves and released through openings on the surface above, making deep hissing sighs like the sound from a whale's blowhole. To stand above the cliffs, feeling the force of the wind, is like being at the bow of a ship at sea.

A small harbor and the fishing village of Sagres lie just east of the point. Prince Henry, "the Navigator," arrived at this place, which is poised so expectantly on the edge of one world, to plan voyages that perhaps would reach a new world as yet undiscovered by Europeans. It is believed that this cape must have held some significance for him, perhaps to have inspired him in his endeavors, for he spent much of his life here. Certainly, its importance lies more in its symbolism than in its convenience. Here, Henry was alleged to have established some kind of school or headquarters for navigation and exploration, but its size and scope are unknown.[3] No evidence of it remains, though some recent buildings (including a church) now occupy the Sagres point. In any case, the harbor, now greatly modified by modern improvements, would have been too small and unprotected to be the base for significant expeditions.

A more important base for voyages was at Lagos, on the Algarve coast farther east of the cape. From Lagos, Henry embarked on his first expeditions to Africa and launched his voyages of exploration and trade to the west and down the coast of Africa. Until Lisbon (actually the town of Belém, nearby on the Tejo River west of Lisbon and closer to its opening to the sea) became the central embarkation point for much longer and more ambitious expeditions later in the fifteenth century, Lagos, more than any other place, was associated with the initial thrust of the Portuguese out upon the seas.

Henry was a product of the Middle Ages; in him, the themes of the Crusades, late feudal society, and the national unification of Portugal converged. Although these interests imparted many dimensions to his enterprise, a scientific curiosity impelling him to discovery was not, at least at first, foremost among his motivations.[4] Yet the logic of his activities compelled him to seek out and use knowledge of the horizons of his world and the technical means to reach and cross them. Explorers like the Portuguese were driven on not by curiosity alone but also by the impetus or momentum of their own activity, which, as for collectors, demanded that the enterprise be continued to completion or as far as it was possible to go. How could one stop at any single point along the journey when no point seemed thoroughly or clearly final?

The horizons of navigation were at first very narrow and forbidding. Cape Bojador, on the northwest African coast at the edge of the Sahara, stood at the southern limit of geographical knowledge. The coastline there was desolate and dangerous; reefs raked the towering ocean waves, and fogs obscured the shore.[5] The first captains to explore the way south had to timidly hug the shoreline, in spite of its hazards, to find and retrace their routes. Bojador could be passed only by standing out to sea to avoid its contrary currents. Later, as the vast shape of Africa became clear and better known, navigators were able to set a course far off the coast in midocean.[6] But even when the Carreira da India had become a well-traveled passage to and from the East around Africa, the dangers of the voyage were hardly diminished. Besides the problems of obtaining fresh water and nutrition on the months-long journeys, storms at sea regularly took their toll of ships and men. The Cape of Storms was as daunting then as it was when Vasco da Gama passed it in 1497.

I saw clearly an intense light, which mariners take to be holy, amidst the storm and insolent winds of the glowering and baleful tempest. No less miraculous, a thing certainly most astonishing, was to see the clouds on the sea, like a huge tube, suck up the water from the ocean.[7]

On a voyage westward in 1847, Rong Hong, a Chinese traveling from Macau to the United States, described the fearful passage in much the same way:

The tops of the masts and the yards were tipped with balls of electricity. The strong wind was howling and whistling behind us like a host of invisible Furies. The night was pitch dark and the electric balls dancing on the tips of the yards and tops of the masts, back and forth and from side to side like so many infernal lanterns in the black night, presented a spectacle never to be forgotten.[8]

Prince Henry had inherited the position of grand master of the Order of Christ, founded in the early fourteenth century after the dissolution of the Knights Templar. Endowed with their own resources, members of the order were dedicated to defending the faith and to carrying on the war against the Muslims.[9] But in any such crusading enterprise, religious benefits might be expected to bear economic advantages. The two were not seen to be inconsistent since, although wealth from plunder and trade would fall to the victors as rewards for their efforts, they would also correspondingly diminish the enemy's strength and resources. War and exploration, after all, were expensive undertakings, and as a princely patron, Henry had numerous followers and clients, as well as his household, to support. In this respect, the numerous motivations underlying Henry's activities were inextricably intertwined. He was a crusader but also an entrepreneur, drawing together human and material resources, whose privileged position allowed him considerable scope for independent action.[10]

It is important to remember, however, that Henry was not operating in a vacuum. His enterprises received legitimation via the king of Portugal in a series of papal bulls, which provided an important legal mandate. The bull *Dum diversas,* issued in 1452, authorized the conquest and subjugation of the enemies of Christ and other unbelievers and the transfer of their property to the throne of Portugal. The bull *Romano Pontifex*, issued in 1455, specifically acclaimed Henry's deeds up to that time, affirmed the Portuguese monopoly of conquest and discovery (as well as the benefits of commerce flowing therefrom), and gave impetus to his goal of circumnavigating Africa to seek a way to the Indies. In the following year, the bull *Inter caetera* granted Henry, as master of the Order of Christ, spiritual jurisdiction over the conquered territories from Cape Bojador to the Indies.[11]

Henry's enterprise thus took shape and changed as it proceeded. The bulls of the 1450s, which conferred a seal of approval on actions already accomplished, show that it was only late in Henry's life (he died in 1460) that the broader vision of permanent expansion emerged with any clarity.[12] Henry was many things: a crusader, a merchant, a medieval prince, and even a nationalist in the context of his time.

Ceuta and the Way Around Africa

From Lagos, Henry embarked in 1415 on the conquest of Ceuta, a North African stronghold of the Moors east of the Straits of Gibraltar. His mission was fraught with many unanticipated but far-reaching consequences. The successful campaign fulfilled the crusading dream of two centuries, carrying the struggle against Islam to enemy territory and pushing back the Muslim tide. Such an enterprise might well have other rewards, and embedded in this holy and high-minded cause was the prospect of commercial profit. From the North African coast, trade routes penetrated the interior to the south, bringing out gold. The gold trade, crossing the Sahara from sources deep in central North Africa and terminating at various points on the northwest African coast, was a powerful attraction in the fourteenth and fifteenth centuries, drawing the explorers seeking new outlets along the western Mediterranean coast and out into the Atlantic.[13] By using Ceuta as a base from which other strategic and commercial points could be taken, the Portuguese hoped to tap the wealth of the interior of Africa. Therefore, the Ceuta expedition brought together the two motives so closely entwined in later Portuguese and European enterprise abroad: cultural expansion and commercial profit.

European colonization began in the eastern Mediterranean with the Crusades at the end of the eleventh century and was carried forward by the western Mediterranean conquests of Aragon in the thirteenth and fourteenth centuries.[14] These enterprises led, in turn, to the northwest rim of Africa and the quest for the gold trade. The threshold between the closed world of the Mediterranean and the virtually limitless Atlantic thus was reached by the fourteenth century. The reconquest of Iberia, especially of Andalusia and the Algarve, established the means to cross the ocean and ultimately propelled the Europeans into the Atlantic.[15] If a continuity thus existed between the expansion of Europe in the Mediterranean and in the Atlantic, along the northwest rim of Africa, the Atlantic prospect was a new departure of almost incalculable consequences in terms of the people involved and the forces that drew them forward.[16]

In this respect at least, Ceuta was the beginning of European expansion overseas, the first expedition of permanent conquest launched from a Portuguese Atlantic port, beyond the confines of the old Mediterranean world. Yet if the path that led to Ceuta had been followed subsequently, the ultimate shape of that expansion might have been very different. Henry may have foreseen a conquest of North Africa, driving toward the eastern Mediterranean heartland of Islam. But the possession of Ceuta did not bear fruit in the expected commercial opportunities, and moreover, Henry's attempt to take Tangier in 1437 failed. Though it was not immediately apparent, his inability to follow the conquest of Ceuta with other similar conquests in the next few years deflected the Portuguese enterprise in a fundamentally different direction over the long run.[17] Thereafter, he began to probe the West African coast, at first perhaps to find some other point of access to the African interior. Already, in 1434, Henry's captain Gil Eanes doubled Cape Bojador. Gradually, a new and bolder design emerged, born out of the failure of the earlier one. It is likely the old plan would have been played out in the more limited, traditional world of the Mediterranean periphery, but this new plan was conceived on a far grander scale and was far more ambitious.[18]

It is questionable whether, during Henry's lifetime, the Portuguese had yet conceived any coordinated plan of discovery and conquest. Too many uncertainties existed at first, both in the nature of the goals and in the means to achieve them. The knowledge required had still to be gathered and brought into a coherent form. Technological developments, the instruments of expansion—including not only nautical improvements in shipbuilding and design but also navigational aids and devices—were still being refined.

By the last decades of the fifteenth century, however, technical competence and geographical and political knowledge had converged to make possible a clearer vision. It was nothing less than to outflank, by the circumnavigation of Africa, the Islamic political and commercial power in the Middle East. The plan had two inseparable goals: first, to tap the known wealth of Asia in commodities commanding a high value in Europe but then monopolized by the Mediterranean trading powers and, second, to attack the power of Islam from behind with the help of an anticipated alliance with a Christian kingdom believed to exist somewhere in the region of East Africa or South Asia. With these goals in mind, Vasco da Gama sailed for India in 1497, following the route that Henry had first opened. Barely twenty-five years later, Portuguese merchants would make the first European landfall on the South China coast, and within fifty years, they would reach Japan. If the conquest of Ceuta, then, was an act of finite proportions and limited consequences, the way around Africa opened possibilities that were potentially almost limitless. What brought da Gama to this new threshold?

It has been suggested that Portugal was impelled seaward by its geography and its maritime tradition.[19] Yet, though Portugal was the westernmost country of Europe and Cabo São Vicente was the end of the world, Portugal's geography initially did not favor maritime activity. Because Portugal had few suitable harbors or natural outlets from the interior, life there was not at first oriented primarily to the sea.[20] Along the southern coast, which remained largely under Muslim control until the thirteenth century, fishing was sufficiently well developed to encourage maritime exploration and trade with other Muslim countries in the eleventh and twelfth centuries. But in the north, under the expanding Portuguese kingdom, fishing as a livelihood developed slowly and relatively late, in small fishing villages, and was of peripheral importance in the economy until perhaps the late thirteenth century.[21] Combining the maritime experience of the Muslim south and the Portuguese north, the small seafaring population developed and perfected sailing and navigational skills, gradually becoming more daring in its voyages, and ultimately provided a reservoir of practical knowledge for more ambitious endeavors.[22]

More important in the economy at first were the inland valleys of the mountainous north, where cattle, sheep, and goats were raised, and the coastal littoral and plains of the south, where cereals such as wheat, millet, barley, and rye prevailed. The topography of the colder, landlocked north preserved a more isolated and introverted society, unlike the more open, maritime south, but it was from the north that the impetus for unification and expansion arose. The seafaring tradition and commercial experience of the coastal regions were to provide, nevertheless, the means for expansion that followed national unification.

Portugal's eccentric location on the European continent could be considered a potential liability to development. But its intermediate situation on the Atlantic rim between northern and southern Europe, at the entrance to the Mediterranean, made it a natural stopping place for fleets of crusading armies sailing for Palestine, as well as for the expanding coastal trade between the Italian trading states and northern markets. Thus, by the thirteenth century, the commercial expansion of Europe stimulated the economic and political development of Portugal. Throughout the 1200s, the commercial importance of Portuguese ports—notably Lisbon, Porto, and Lagos—grew as they were drawn into the maritime trading network embracing Italy and Flanders, England, Brittany, and Normandy.[23] Portuguese merchants took an increasingly active part in the trade, along with Italian merchants who settled in Portuguese ports and provided a wealth of experience in commercial practice.[24]

A community of Portuguese settlers had appeared in Flanders as early as the end of the twelfth century. By the close of the next century, that community had acquired tangible organization under the auspices of the Portuguese king, leading to the establishment in the fourteenth century of a permanent representative (*feitor,* or factor) at Bruges, with quasi-official and quasi-commercial authority.[25] Proceeding hand in hand with this development was the growth in shipbuilding, which received royal patronage in 1377, and the enactment of a maritime insurance law in 1380.[26] The Portuguese were soon second only to the Italians in maritime enterprise.

Advances in the technologies of shipbuilding and navigation aided the Portuguese expansion. Learning from and sometimes directly guided by the Italians, the Portuguese pioneered in nautical technology. The traditional fighting ship of the Mediterranean, the galley—a long, narrow, rowed vessel—was fast but not suitable for heavy cargoes or rough seas. Round ships with square-rigged sails, such as the Portuguese *nau* (which were only twice as long as they were wide), were slow but capacious and seaworthy. Both kinds of ships were employed in the expedition against Ceuta. A smaller version of the nau, the *barcha* of less than 30 tons, was more maneuverable and could sail in high seas and adverse weather; it was used in the initial exploration of the African coast.[27]

From these ships, the Portuguese developed, evidently under the influence of Arab practice, the *caravel,* which became the workhorse of Portuguese expeditions until it was succeeded by the larger carracks and galleons of the fully established Carreira da India. The caravel was a hybrid vessel, narrower—about three times as long as it was wide—and rigged with lateen sails that were more easily managed and permitted the ship to sail close to the wind. These were the ships that carried Vasco da Gama to India. As the reach of the expeditions lengthened and the need for cargo capacity for trade increased, the caravels evolved to incorporate three or four masts carrying a combination of both square-rigged and lateen sails and a larger hull on which artillery could be mounted without making the ship unstable.[28]

The optimal size of the *Nau da Carreira da India* proved to be between 300 and 450 tons. In the late sixteenth century, to increase the trade volume, ships commonly reached 800 to 1,000 tons, but these vessels proved dangerously unseaworthy and as often as not failed to survive the voyage.[29]

The expansion of maritime trade throughout the continent contributed to the rapid spread of the black death in the mid-fourteenth century. The plague arrived in Lisbon by sea in 1348, and it devastated Portugal's cities. It is estimated to have killed one-third of the population of Europe, and its impact on Portugal was probably much the same. The sudden and drastic reduction in the urban population created a labor shortage and drove up wages, which drew people from the countryside to the cities. Among the long-term consequences of this migration were the creation of a poorer class in the cities and riots and rebellions brought on by the social dislocation, which was to find an outlet in the overseas adventures and voyages of discovery in the next century.[30]

Beginning in the twelfth century, the process of national unification and consolidation in Portugal had created, by the end of the fourteenth century, the first independent, territorially unified state in Europe. Afonso Henriques (1112–1185) of the House of Burgundy had carved out a feudal state based on the northern castle towns of Braga and Guimarães. By midcentury, the king of Leon and Castile had tacitly acknowledged the legitimacy of the monarchy, and in 1179, after a protracted diplomatic campaign, the pope finally recognized Portugal as a kingdom under Afonso Henriques.

The formation of the new state was inseparable from the reconquest of Portugal from the Moors. Invading the south in a daring campaign, Afonso Henriques won a clear, if not definitive, victory over the Moors at Ourique in 1139—it was only a raid, and his army withdrew. But pushing south again and taking advantage of the presence of northern crusading armies on their way to Palestine during the Second Crusade, Afonso besieged and took Lisbon in 1147. Still, for the time being, a strong continental orientation continued to shape the kingdom. Not until the middle of the next century, with the conquest of the Algarve under Afonso III (r. 1245–1279), did the reconquest of Portugal draw to its completion.

The threat of Muslim counterattack was not ended for another hundred years. In 1340, Castile and Portugal joined forces to defeat a resurgent invasion attempt by the Moors at Salado, in Andalusia. Not long thereafter, the extinction of the male line of the Burgundian dynasty threatened to cause the Portuguese throne to revert to the kingdom of Castile. To prevent this,

João I (r. 1383–1433), of the House of Avis, defeated the armies of Castile at Aljubarrota in 1385 and brought about the final consolidation of Portuguese independence under the Avis dynasty. João now sought to channel the energies of the new state outward and, at the same time, to repair the social and economic crisis of the fourteenth century through commercial enterprise and expansion.[31]

Thus, in the three centuries since the reign of Afonso Henriques, a gradual reorientation had occurred, from a continental, feudal struggle for independence to an extroverted, maritime outlook linked to the fortunes of a newly centralized monarchical state. The prolonged war against the Moors as both internal and external enemies had built up a momentum of conquest. The accumulated energy was now redirected and released seaward in a new kind of crusade that was partly religious, partly political, and partly commercial.[32]

Nanyang

When Prince Henry sent out his first expeditions, the cliffs of Cabo São Vicente marked a clear and abrupt termination, the edge of a world sharply drawn. The only familiar trade routes went north, hugging the coast, to England, France, and the Low Countries, or east past Gibraltar through the Mediterranean. To the west and the south lay unknown seas. The Azores and the Canary Islands, far beyond the horizon, were only distant outposts. Beyond lay the still uncharted coast of Africa, a continent whose shape and extent remained a mystery, and the undiscovered continents of the Americas. No commercial and cultural intercourse linked those on the edge of this world with other peoples. To sail beyond this boundary was to commit oneself to a momentous journey, the destination of which was unknown. A certain resolution was required to step beyond the edge of this world.

The South China coast, by contrast, forms no such sharp line of discontinuity. Land gives way to sea in easy and indistinct stages. Where the land, crosscut by the confusing channels of the Pearl River delta, ends and islands begin is a matter of uncertainty. Ships and boats traveling the coastal waterways could spend their entire journeys comfortably in sight of land on all quarters.[33] Those who ventured beyond this fringe of coastal islands and passageways would travel well-established routes to lands and peoples with which communications had been routine for centuries. Chinese may have traveled the South China Sea and the Indian Ocean as early as the Han dynasty in the second or third century A.D. By the eighth century, maritime trade with India and the Middle East was flourishing at Canton, and in the tenth century, Chinese merchants were participating in the Indian Ocean trade.[34]

Geography was important. The Chinese coast, unlike the hard line of Portugal's Atlantic coast, was soft and enveloping. It demanded no irrevocable separation from the land for those who set forth from its shores. The true barrier there was of a different kind—a less tangible but nonetheless formidable cultural frontier.

In 1405, while the youthful Henry was still only dreaming of the expedition to Ceuta, another expedition set out from South China under the command of Grand Eunuch Zheng He, an admiral serving the Ming court. Judging by the expedition's design as well as its results, Zheng He's purpose seems to have been to extend over the maritime regions to the south and southwest the Chinese hegemony that had lapsed during the previous centuries. This area, which the Chinese knew as Nanyang, "The Southern Seas," included the island and mainland portions of Southeast Asia. It ended at Malacca, on the eastern edge of the Indian Ocean, but Zheng He was to sail beyond that point and on through the Indian Ocean to the west.

Even by today's standards, the expedition was planned and executed on an immense scale. The fleet that sailed in 1405 comprised 62 large ships, including huge oceangoing junks up to 400 feet long constructed with four decks and watertight compartments, plus 255 smaller vessels. The expedition's ships carried as many as 28,000 men. Zheng He sailed through Nanyang, overawing the states of the region, and continued across the Indian Ocean to Ceylon and Calicut. On the return voyage, he decisively defeated a notorious pirate fleet that had been preying on ships passing through the Strait of Malacca and returned home with its chief, who was to be executed at Nanking.[35] No preliminary voyages of exploration and reconnaissance were required to open the way for the expedition. It followed routes known and used for centuries, to countries that formerly had intercourse with China.

Hardly had the fleet returned in 1407 than a series of subsequent expeditions were launched, seven in all, some of which were as large as the first. Sailing in 1413 and returning in 1415, the year Henry captured Ceuta, Zheng's fourth voyage reached Hormuz on the Persian Gulf. Detachments of the fifth and sixth voyages reached the East African coast. The seventh expedition, from 1431 to 1433, was as large and ambitious as the previous ones, and it, too, sailed as far as Hormuz.[36] The next year, Gil Eanes, sailing from Lagos on his fifteenth attempt, doubled Cape Bojador a few hundred miles down the West African coast from the Strait of Gibraltar.

Zheng He's voyages were a powerful extension of the Chinese tributary order over the states of Nanyang. The crews returned with strange and wonderful things to delight the Ming court—zebras, ostriches, lions, a giraffe—and, far more valuable than all of these to the court, expressions of submission from distant rulers. Yet, strangely, the voyages ended as abruptly as they had begun and were never resumed. They remain a curious anomaly but a tantalizing suggestion, nevertheless, that the Chinese would have been capable, if they had possessed the will, of great feats of seafaring and maritime expansion.

Nearly a century passed before Vasco da Gama and his successors, sailing from the opposite end of the earth, crossed the same seas and visited many of the same ports with ships and numbers of men that paled by comparison with the Chinese efforts. The Portuguese established a permanent presence in Asia and opened the door to irreversible European expansion that would last more than four centuries. They returned with new knowledge and cargoes of commodities that altered the commercial and political balance between European nations, influenced European art and architecture, and ultimately transformed Europe's outlook on the world. The Ming expeditions had no such enduring consequences. Indeed, the trail that they left in the vast historical corpus of China was hardly commensurate with their ambitious conception and execution. They inspired no epic paean such as Luis Vaz de Camões wrote about the deeds of Vasco da Gama nor any sense of world-encompassing destiny such as the Portuguese have continued to feel even long after the demise of their empire. Confucian officials, on the whole, condemned or ignored the voyages.[37]

Why, then, did Zheng He launch his voyages in the first place? And why did they end so suddenly, with so little to show for such magnificent effort?[38] The answer—and the key to the very different influences that Portugal and China would have on the world—lies not only in the very different personalities of Prince Henry and Zheng He but also in the differing outlooks of these men as expressions of their respective national characters.[39]

The Yongle emperor had ascended the throne in 1403, only two years before the first expedition sailed. The third Ming emperor, he was an energetic ruler, determined to reassert Chinese hegemony over the surrounding regions.[40] The tributary system of suzerain-vassal relations that had previously governed intercourse with other countries had fallen into disarray following the collapse of the Tang dynasty in the tenth century; it had been displaced through the Song period from the eleventh through the thirteenth centuries by the rise of powerful central Asian nomadic nations that successively reversed the role until the final conquest of China by the Mongols in 1279. Now the Ming, under its founder, Zhu Yuanzhang, the Hongwu emperor, had restored native Chinese rule to China.

While the Yongle emperor dispatched Zheng He's fleets to Nanyang, he was also organizing massive military expeditions into Mongolia, with the objective of overwhelming the Mongols and crushing any resurgence of their power.[41] He personally commanded the first campaign, which kept him away from the capital for more than a year. To be closer to the inner Asian frontier and shorten his lines of communication with his forces there, he moved the capital from Nanking, on the lower Yangzi River, permanently to Peking, near the Great Wall. For the Ming, as for every dynasty since the first unification of China, inner Asia was the critical frontier. It was all the more understandable that the Ming emperors, who had only recently thrown off the Mongol occupation, were preoccupied with that region.

Zheng He had risen to a position of trust in the service of Zhu Di, the fourth son of Zhu Yuanzhang, who was to become the Yongle emperor. He had been recruited from a Muslim family of southwest China at the age of ten, then castrated and placed in imperial service as a eunuch. At age twenty, he joined Zhu Di and later participated in Zhu Di's campaigns against the Mongols. When Zhu Di rebelled against his nephew, the second Ming emperor, following Zhu Yuanzhang's death in 1398, Zheng supplied critical support for his master's successful bid for the throne.[42] Although the second emperor presumably died in the rebellion, rumors persisted that he or his heirs had escaped. In the improbable event that the second emperor was at large somewhere in the south where he might stir up trouble in the future, Zhu Di sent his trusted eunuch to search Nanyang for the fugitive. This, at least, has been suggested as one motive for the voyages.[43] It was precisely for such personal service in the interest of the autocrat's enhanced power that eunuchs fell under a pall of suspicion among the regular bureaucratic ranks. Even if such a personal motivation were put aside, however, the combination in Zheng of heterodox religious origin and eunuch status made him and his mission, whatever its purpose, anathema to orthodox conservative Confucian officials.

At first sight, many parallels exist between the efforts of Prince Henry and Zheng He. Each was acting for his king, as royal kinsman or imperial servant. Nevertheless, the position of each was, to a degree, institutionally as well as geographically eccentric—Henry as master of the Order of Christ, Zheng as a eunuch commander of military forces. Both operated beyond the direct control of their respective monarchs but pandered to the court's sense of glory with the trophies of exploration. The two men shared certain important personality traits as well: a taste for independent action and an entrepreneurial disposition; curiosity, perhaps; and a powerful personal commitment to their tasks.

More broadly, the expeditions they launched were impelled by similar objectives. For both men, circumnavigation of the continental lands to the south guided the course of their voyages. Both sought allies in distant parts, and the extension of a world order was for both a higher rationale, though their conceptions of their respective worlds were very different. For Henry, it was the supranational Christian kingdom of God represented by the authority of the universal Church that gave legitimacy to his discoveries; for Zheng, it was the extension of the universal Chinese order, *tianxia*, "All Under Heaven," under the Chinese emperor, the Son of Heaven.

Behind both movements lay a common theme: the momentum of national consolidation. Several centuries of instability and conquest by alien invaders had shaped the processes of unification completed by João I of Portugal in

1385 and by the Hongwu emperor of China in 1368. Both rulers created a centralized monarchy indebted in certain critical respects to the culture and institutions of the invaders, as well as to more fundamental social and cultural roots that ran back to models of greater antiquity.

If the Yongle emperor seemed to divide his forces between the landward and seaward frontiers, the Portuguese were afflicted by a somewhat similar divergence of attention between their land battle with the Moors, first in Iberia and subsequently extended to Africa, and their seaborne enterprise of trade and exploration. Yet there were significant differences in this regard. For the Portuguese, the two impulses were harmonized in the dual mission to seek "Christians and spices." To push outward beyond the shores of Europe and reach India was a natural outgrowth of national unification. If this was, at first, also true for the Ming, it soon ceased to be so, for no logical connection with inner Asian strategic interests sustained the Ming court's maritime enterprise. Nanyang was not yet the source of any identifiable challenge to Ming rule, nor could the penetration of the region be expected to forestall resurgent nomad power in central Asia.

With the collapse of Mongol control across central Asia and the unification of China proper under the Ming, China turned increasingly inward. A large agrarian nation with a population approaching 100 million and essentially isolated from surrounding civilizations by vast natural barriers and great distances, China's political and social systems and its worldview continued to develop largely unaffected by exogenous influences. Portugal could hardly have posed a greater contrast. Occupying a peripheral position in European developments, it was a small nation of less than 1.5 million people, seldom isolated from influences emanating from other parts of the continent.[44] Although the Chinese emperor and the entire Confucian bureaucracy abjured commercial affairs and took no direct interest in trade as a national resource, the Portuguese king became the premier merchant of the nation, daily supervising the preparation of fleets and the sale of the goods they brought back.[45] His nobles and officials followed his lead, participating in the business of trade.[46]

The Chinese experiment with maritime expansion ended abruptly with Zheng He's seventh voyage, but the Portuguese effort continued and grew. Under da Gama's successors, the methods, if not the motives, of expansion changed. Francisco de Almeida, the first viceroy of the Indies, established a permanent armed naval presence in the Indian Ocean. And Afonso de Albuquerque, the architect of enduring European power in Asia, founded a string of fortified bases from East Africa to the Strait of Malacca that became the foundation of the Estado da India only a little more than a decade after da Gama reached India and less than a century after Henry conquered Ceuta. It was from Malacca, seized by Albuquerque in 1511, that Portuguese merchant captains reached the frontiers of the Ming on the coast of China a few years later. Ironically, the Ming founded a reasonably stable and self-sufficient political, economic, and social order that endured with little disruption or fundamental alteration in course for five hundred years, until it was overwhelmed in the nineteenth century by the Western assault the Portuguese had set in motion; the Portuguese empire, by contrast, flourished for barely a century before it was displaced by the rising power of the Dutch and English. Yet by the nineteenth century, China became a largely passive and helpless recipient of cultural and economic influences from abroad, while Portugal, though it soon lost its military empire, became an enduring intermediary between Europe and Asia both economically and culturally.[47]

The Empire and the Garden

China and Portugal can be viewed as contrasting cultural archetypes. To treat them so is, of course, to greatly simplify, as the notion of archetype is intended to do, the vast complexities of the two cultures. Nonetheless, cognizant of the distortion inherent in any generalization, I wish to consider them as such here in order to evoke the very different cultural and social mentalities of the two worlds in their encounter at Macau, lying on the border between them.

The cultural archetypes of the two worlds are perhaps expressed most vividly in their most famous literary works of epic mythology and narrative—*Os Lusiadas,* by Camões, and *Hong-lou meng,* by Cao Xueqin. The two works may be understood as distillations of their respective cultures' worldviews.[48] In them, we find juxtaposed mythology, often reinterpreted, and narrative of contemporary history and culture in an allegorical form. In both, the gods intrude in the process of worldly, mortal affairs, sometimes in dreams—guiding the action, interfering at critical points, and then letting events follow their courses. Yet the two portray very different perspectives on the world, one an enclosed, self-contained, introverted, and gardenlike totality, the other an unbounded and extroverted but incomplete empire pursuing an unfulfilled, world-encompassing destiny.

The Lusiads is the epic celebration of the Portuguese race composed by Camões in the course of his travels through Portuguese Asia and back to Lisbon between 1553 and 1570. Camões takes the voyage of Vasco da Gama to India in 1497 as his narrative focus. Inspired by classical Roman models, especially Virgil's *Aeneid,* and borrowing the pantheon of Greco-Roman mythology, he exalts the Portuguese as the embodiment of a heroic legacy. The descendants of the heroes of classical antiquity, surpassing them in deed and daring as the new heroes of Christianity tested in the Crusades and the reconquest of Portugal, the Portuguese are recipients of a world mandate, prophesied for them by the gods. It was their destiny to establish a new world order:

> *Fortresses, cities and high walls,*
> *You shall behold built by them, my child;*
> *The cruel and warlike Turks*
> *You shall see ever defeated by them;*
> *The kings of India, free and secure,*
> *You shall see by their mighty King subjected;*
> *And at last masters of all, they*
> *Shall give to the Earth better laws.*[49]

The factual narrative of da Gama's voyage is interlaced with fantastic encounters with adversities and enemies that da Gama and his mariners had to confront and overcome by bravery or cunning. These challenges were raised both by those among the gods who were jealous enemies of the Portuguese and by the actual earthly enemies of the Portuguese—the Muslims and their allies. In the course of meeting these challenges, the Portuguese were constantly tested and forced to prove their valor and the righteousness of their cause. At the threshold of the Indian Ocean on his passage around Africa, da Gama encountered the Cape of Storms, personified as the dreadful giant Adamastor:

> *Since you have come to see the hidden mysteries*
> *Of nature and the watery element,*
> *To none in all humanity permitted*
> *Whether of noble or immortal merit,*
> *Hear the punishment that I have prepared*
> *For your inordinate audacity,*
> *Over all the vast sea and on the land*
> *That you will subjugate by cruel war.*[50]

As Mary Helms notes, the heroes of each succeeding age believed they had surpassed the achievements of those of earlier times. The travelers and explorers of the Age of Discovery surpassed those of earlier ages in both the nobility of their motives and the genius of their means (especially the art of navigation). The travelers of medieval times ventured into regions characterized by an aura of immortality associated with the original paradise believed to be located there and with the notion of apocalyptic destiny:

Now it was the travelers and their kings and princes who sought immortality as "second creators" of distant worlds which for them were newly established and newly regarded not only with fear and fantasy, but also with the confident superiority of men, who, now God-like as much as God-fearing, having conquered the ocean with their bravery, skills, and intelligence, believed they could conquer whatever else they encountered.[51]

The logic of Portugal's struggle for national unification and independence involved the Portuguese people in an ever widening centrifugal movement of discovery, conquest, and subjugation. The heroic Portuguese world of the fifteenth and sixteenth centuries—from João I to Manuel I and João III— was portrayed as a stage in a historical continuum from classical antiquity to world empire, broken by no clear boundary or resting place. It was a potentially unbounded world.

The conflicts and tension engendered by a social system in a state of flux were carried outward to a world replete with dangers and disorder to be overcome and surmounted, an arena for adventurers and heroes. The Portuguese world, extending beyond the cramped confines of the nation, was consequently confronted by the challenge of surrounding moral disorder. The Portuguese were the instruments of a teleological imperative of evangelical expansion and conversion to Christian law and faith, designed to set the world in order.[52]

Very different was the world depicted in *Hong-lou meng*. The novel, as much a mixture of fantasy and verisimilitude in its own way as *The Lusiads*, is a sweeping, complex description of life within a great gentry family of late seventeenth- and early eighteenth-century China. Cao Xueqin, the original author, was the descendant of just such a powerful and influential family, which served as the loosely autobiographical model and inspiration for his work.[53] The story centers on the younger members of the Jia family and the ramified and often morally confused relations between them.

Baoyu, the hero of the novel, is a boy when the story begins. During the several years that pass as the narrative progresses, he is involved with various young female relatives, friends, and servants within the extended family, which is depicted as a virtual society within a society, administered by its own elaborate administrative bureaucracy. The foreground of the novel is the young people's comfortable and often effete life, passed within the confines of the immense garden that occupies an important part of the twin family compounds. In the background is the official world beyond the walls, in which Baoyu is expected to eventually take his place. The novel begins, however, in the supramundane world of the gods:

> Long ago, when the goddess Nu-wa was repairing the sky, she melted down a great quantity of rock and, on the Incredible Crags of the Great Fable Mountains, moulded the amalgam into thirty-six thousand, five hundred and one large building blocks, each measuring seventy-two feet by a hundred and forty-four feet square. She used thirty-six thousand five hundred of these blocks in the course of her building operations, leaving a single odd block unused, which lay, all on its own, at the foot of Greensickness Peak in the aforementioned mountains.[54]

This leftover block, transformed into a pendant-size stone with magical powers, lay unused until it was picked up by a passing Buddhist monk and a Taoist priest. Many ages later, the stone is discovered again by another

Taoist, who finds on it the lengthy story of its experiences in the mundane world of men, where it had hung on the neck of Baoyu since his birth. Having read the story on the stone, the Taoist

> could see that its main theme was love; that it consisted quite simply of a true record of real events; and that it was entirely free from any tendency to deprave and corrupt. He therefore copied it all out from beginning to end and took it back with him to look for a publisher.[55]

The events of Baoyu's story pass almost entirely within the boundaries of the Jia family compound and its refined garden. Yet the family is a world unto itself. Indeed, the Chinese family, which, in its simple form, is the basic cellular unit of society, is, in its extended form in *Hong-lou meng*, a microcosm of society as a whole. Even the hierarchical bureaucratic organization of the state, with its reliance on record keeping, is replicated within the family.

> Wang Xing's wife approached and said she wanted a tally authorizing the purchase of silk cord to be made into carriage trimmings for the funeral. She handed Xi-feng a slip of paper on which the order was written. It specified the number of network trimmings that would be required for two large sedans, four small sedans, and four carriages, and the number of pounds of silk cord that would be required for that amount of network. Xi-feng made Sunshine read it out to her, and having satisfied herself that the figures were correct, told him to enter them in his book and to issue Wang Xing's wife with one of the Rong-guo tallies, whereupon the latter hurried off to complete her mission.[56]

Conversely, the ideal Confucian state was a family-like unit, reflecting the same moral obligations and relationships. And just as kinship ties and tensions create conflicts within the family, so can they disrupt the larger society.[57]

Completing the self-contained totality of the world modeled in the novel, the elaborate family garden, in turn, presents a microcosm of the natural world, just as the family is the microcosm of the human world. Chinese gentry-literati gardens were conceived to represent, in a controlled setting, all of the fundamental aesthetics of nature in a balanced harmony: water, mountains, and vegetation. The Jia family garden goes beyond this to include even exemplary agricultural activities carried on by members of the household. The social world and the natural world are thus paired in harmonious association.

Within the Jia family compound, as within the Confucian state, a closed hierarchical order prevails, its stability secured by the routine performance of ceremony and ritual. The moral confusion and ritual violations prevailing among Baoyu and his companions become the source of the fatal corrosion of the family, as of the larger social order.

The Garden's society was now larger and livelier than it had ever been before. With Li Wan as its doyenne it numbered—if you counted Xi-feng as an honorary member—thirteen people: Li Wan, Ying-chun, Tan-chun, Xi-chun, Bao-chai, Dai-yu, Xiang-yun, Li Wen, Li Qi, Bao-qin, Xing Xiu-yan, Bao-yu and Xi-feng. Apart from the two young married women, the rest were all fifteen, sixteen, or seventeen years old. Most of them were in fact born the same year, several in the same month, and a couple on the same day. Not only Grandmother Jia and Lady Wang and the servants, even the young people themselves had difficulty in remembering who was senior to whom, and soon gave up trying, and abandoned any attempt at observing the usual formalities of address.[58]

Disruptive events arising from outside but attributable ultimately to lapses in the moral order of the family are conveyed inward by a centripetal attraction.[59] The world beyond the confines of his closed garden is threatening to Baoyu, a source of constant confusion regarding the distinction between the real and the unreal, between truth and falsehood. No such uncertainty afflicted Camões's heroes.

The Chinese world was a closed, organic totality, possessing an inherent moral order governed by ritual. The traditional tribute system of relations with states beyond the borders attempted to project the hierarchical moral order of the center over the periphery and, by ceremonial performance, focus attention inward. Whereas the Portuguese world was characterized by heroic continuity, the Chinese world was characterized by hierarchical continuity.

An analogue of the cultural world described by *Hong-lou meng* may be found in the Chinese garden. The garden was a contained world, complete and self-sufficient within its walls, where natural and artificial elements were juxtaposed in an aesthetic (and moral) balance. The architectural components of the garden exhibited a stylistic refinement and elaboration that frequently elevated superficial decorative flamboyance over substance and simplicity.[60] By the Ming and Qing era, the process could be carried, as it was in the seventeenth century, to a point at which form was confused with substance.

> He led them inside the building. Its interior turned out to be all corridors and alcoves and galleries, so that properly speaking it could hardly have been said to have *rooms* at all. The partition walls which made these divisions were of wooden panelling exquisitely carved in a wide variety of motifs: bats in clouds, the "three friends of winter"—pine, plum and bamboo, little figures in landscapes, birds and flowers, scrollwork, antique bronze shapes, "good luck" and "long life" characters, and many others. The carvings, all of them the work of master craftsmen, were beautiful with inlays of gold, mother-o'-pearl and semiprecious stones. In addition to being panelled, the partitions were pierced by numerous apertures, some round, some square, some sunflower-shaped, some shaped like a fleur-de-lis, some cusped, some fan-shaped ... The *trompe-l'oeil* effect of these ingenious partitions had been further enhanced by inserting false

Chinese garden (Zhuo Zheng Yuan), Suzhou

windows and doors in them, the former covered in various pastel shades of gauze, the latter hung with richly patterned damask portières. The main walls were pierced with window-like perforations in the shape of zithers, swords, vases, and other objects of virtù.[61]

This effect was true as much for ritual performance as it was for architecture and aesthetics.

> For a highly stylized government such as ours, form was substance. The sovereign's readiness to subject himself to his assigned role marked the extent of his prior commitment to a state of make-believe, which alone could inspire others and make them sincere and honest. It was a gratifying experience to see the emperor putting his heart and soul behind ceremonial proceedings, sometimes even enlivening them with an extra effort and a personal touch.[62]

The seventeenth century was the great age of decorative art, and although the Qing achieved an empire of unprecedented size and stability, the tendency toward superficial elaboration and involution reflected a cultural effeteness that is all too well exhibited in the character of Baoyu and his companions.

In opposition to China's enclosed garden world, the Portuguese world of the sixteenth century was an expansive yet incomplete and unfulfilled cultural empire. It was a world shaped by a process of continual evolution, not involution. The decorative flamboyance of the Manueline period of the early sixteenth century bears only a superficial resemblance to the style of seventeenth-century China. Sinuous columns, twisted like ropes, serpentine figures, armillary spheres, sailors' knots, and doorways like entrances to undersea grottoes identify Manueline architecture as the "style of maritime discovery."[63] Nothing better exemplifies this age than the Jerónimos monastery, built on the bank of the Tejo River at Belém, on the spot where da Gama set out in 1497.[64] This, the most original architectural style of the Portuguese—carried forward in the passionate construction of churches and monasteries

Doorway, University of Coimbra

paid for by the wealth derived from the discoveries of the fifteenth and early sixteenth centuries—conveys a restless enthusiasm for materialism and exotic eclecticism.

The undisciplined extravagance of the Age of Discovery lasted less than a century. It was cut short by its own excess, by military disaster and setbacks in Asia, and by union with the Spanish crown in 1580.[65] Yet the style of maritime discovery had an enduring influence on the Portuguese mentality as well as on the remnants of the Portuguese empire in Asia.

The Chinese were content to explore the world within the confines of their own garden-world, by compressing the chaotic world within a bounded space, seemingly disordered but actually tamed and controlled in a harmoniously ordered hierarchy.[66] If discordant elements remained, they were merely part of an agreeably contained dynamic that lent excitement to the experience without requiring individuals to venture beyond the enclosed garden-world. Writing on gardens in the seventeenth century, Ji Cheng observed, "If one can find stillness in the midst of the city toil, why should one forgo such an easily accessible spot and seek a more distant one?"[67] The Portuguese spirit was very different. Although the Chinese found no impetus to venture out in the world, the Portuguese sought to impose order on a disordered world by exerting force beyond their borders.

Perspectives on the world are culturally constructed. They derive their features from social conditions, political imperatives, and the cumulative historical experiences of peoples. Perceptions of the "other," thus, are shaped not only by the mentality of the individual observer but also by the need to assimilate the vision of the foreign world in a form congruent with the order of the observer's domestic world.

> The greatest intellectual challenge (and greatest human conceit) lies in combining the two—in seeking to interpret and embed social continuity and harmony at home within the "natural" or cosmological order and in seeking to interpret the nature and significance of the universe within the perspectives of the social order at home.[68]

Where worlds each possessing different perspectives of the other meet, the result is not a static product but a continuing process of mutual adjustment. It is rarely symmetrical and evenly balanced.

سلام سلام سلام

More than geography separated the Pearl River estuary on the South China coast from Belém on the Tejo River. These places were points in two very different worlds, more different from each other in their respective historical origins and cultures than climate, latitude, or any other geographical accident could explain. These two worlds were each, in their own particular

ways, self-possessed, internally coherent cultural mentalities. Their encounter on the South China coast in the mid-sixteenth century began a process
that would be sustained for more than four hundred years, although each experienced fundamental changes over that period. The small promontory of
Macau became, uniquely, the scene of this encounter, an encounter that continues to this day.

The Portuguese extended the boundaries of their own world until they
encountered those of China. At the point beyond which the Chinese world
was not easily penetrable and their own culture could no longer expand,
missionaries took over from the ships' captains, and an enterprise of a different kind began. But on this margin of interaction, the edges of the two
worlds touched: Cultures met and sometimes mingled.

two

Boundaries
On the Periphery

Beyond Laowanshan, the sky and water mingle in an expanse so vast that even with a compass its limits cannot be paced; they are reached only by the legs of the Great Sea Turtle or the Wings of the Roc. Every year in the fifth or sixth month the southwest monsoon begins. Then the foreign ships, driven before it, arrive in haste.[1]

Except for the abundance of small fishing craft and perhaps some larger trading vessels, nothing would immediately reveal to travelers sailing the South China coast in the region of the West River delta that they had reached the edge of a great and populous empire. It was this very landfall, after all, that Christopher Columbus, seeking a new route to China, believed he had found in the primitive islands of the Caribbean. The coastline here is mountainous, and the land is fragmented into many islands lying offshore, obscuring from the observer its shape. In the tropical climate of this latitude, the humidity often causes a low haze to form, flattening the view and blurring the distinctions between one island and another and the passages between them. The peaks of the islands and the mainland are largely granite, barren and rocky at their higher elevations, but the lower slopes of the hills near the shore are covered with a lush, dense growth of vines, banyan trees, and broad-leaved plants growing among the rocks. The soil formed from the disintegration of the decomposed granite is poor and dry, and level areas suitable for cultivation are few.[2] In the inland regions of the West River delta north and south of the provincial capital of Canton, intensive cultivation of the valleys and hillsides supports a dense population, living in large towns and many villages. But along the coast, the population is thin and the villages are few and poor.

The numerous branching channels of the West River estuary—and of the Pearl River, which is the name given to one of its main lower channels south of Canton—further disrupt and fragment the coastline. For many miles, channels of the river divide and join again, separating masses of land into islands that are still technically part of the mainland. The silt carried down by the river is deposited in sand bars and tidal flats, constantly changing the course of the channels and the shape of the coast and filling areas between channels that once were open water.

Where the constant volume of freshwater from the river reaches the sea, laden with the fertile effluent washed out of the interior, fish in abundant varieties flourish, in a hierarchy of aquatic life—from the shrimp and crustacea of the intermediate tidal zones to larger fish inhabiting the deeper waters off the outer islands. Fishing is the principal livelihood for the coastal inhabitants of the area. They troll with nets dragged from the sterns of small junks and sampans inshore or with larger nets suspended from booms on the sides of large junks around the offshore islands,[3] catching several species of *garoupa*, sole, and rockfish. Small brown "mud fish" (*niyu*) that scurry around on the mudflats with stout leglike fins—also known as *sanmianbai* (literally, "hundreds on three sides") because of their large numbers—are also netted by fishermen paddling across the mud on boards.

Seafaring was an ancient tradition among the peoples of the South China coast. Its origins lay in the early settlement of this area as far back as the fourth century B.C., if not even earlier among aboriginal inhabitants of South China. By the Tang dynasty in the seventh century, a maritime tradition was well established. The specialized nautical technologies of ship construction and navigation were thus continuously practiced and refined over many centuries. Small coastal fishing craft were well adapted to fishing the channels and passages among the islands close to shore; seagoing junks, larger and more capacious versions of the smaller boats, embarked on long-distance trading voyages from Canton to the major ports of southern China and to Borneo, the Celebes, Java, Sumatra, Manila, Singapore, Malacca, and Japan.[4] The maritime culture figured prominently in the popular local cults of protective deities among the fishermen and merchants of the area. Their temples and shrines along the rocks of the shoreline provided some of the principal cultural landmarks of the region.[5]

On the tidal flats along the shores and between the islands, oyster beds provided a livelihood for more sedentary inhabitants. Oysters are cultivated on posts set in clusters or rows in the mud of the tidal zone, covered at high tide but exposed at low tide. The most valuable product from oysters is, of course, pearls, but the shells, after being ground up, are used as a construction material in walls and for plaster.[6]

Harvesting of salt, evaporated from seawater in salt pans along the shore either by a natural solar process or by leaching (or, more rarely, by boiling brine), was another coastal activity that provided a livelihood for the local population. Salt was used by local fishermen in the salting and preservation of fish, and the salt production industry was regulated by the government through a monopoly granted to salt merchants, who carried the salt inland over considerable distances in special boats.[7]

By the time the Europeans arrived, a great number of boats and ships of many varieties sailed these channels. In the outer estuaries and among the islands, numerous small fishing boats predominated, but up the channels of the inner passages, above the "gates" at Modaomen and Humen, the variety and number of boats increased, and the closer one got to Canton, the more crowded was the river. In addition to great seagoing junks,

> long tiers of salt junks lined the shore of the island of Honam; these brought cargoes from Teenpak and places on the coast south-westward of Macao. . . . The number of cargo boats from the interior, or passenger boats, floating residences and up-country craft, with government cruisers and flower boats, was prodigious. To these must be added sampans, ferry boats plying to and from Honam, and quantities of barbers' boats, vendors of every description of food, of clothes, of toys, and what would be called household requirements if in shops on shore; besides boats of fortune-tellers and of theatrical performers.[8]

Where the river delta joined the sea, two great systems of transportation met. From the tributaries and portages deep within the interior of South China, barges and riverboats floated down the river, carrying products and people to the coastal cities and their markets. Tea from central China and the lower Yangzi valley; raw silk and finished silk, grown and spun in the farms of the interior and woven in the district towns of the Canton region; zinc, lead, gold, and other minerals mined in the hills and mountains to the west; porcelain from the great factories in Guangdong and farther north at Jingdezhen in Jiangxi; musk and pearls from Guangdong, all were collected here, along with the miscellaneous commodities and curios whose vendors were seeking to find a niche in the market.

On the Canton delta and along the southern coast, this riverborne commercial network met another, more vast maritime trading pattern governed by the periodic monsoons of the South China Sea and the Indian Ocean. In the early spring, as the axis of the earth tilts the Northern Hemisphere toward the sun, the huge continental landmass of central Asia begins to warm. The heated air, which is lighter and rising, creates a low-pressure region toward which the still cooler, denser air of the sea, slower to warm, flows. Thus begin the southerly monsoons, which blow up the Indian Ocean toward the land and eastward and northward along the China coast. By May, the southwest monsoon, driving up the estuaries of the West and Pearl Rivers, is a strong, steady wind, giving a person standing there the sensation of being on the bow of a ship moving rapidly across the water. In the fall, the process is reversed as the landmass cools more rapidly than the warmer ocean when the higher latitudes are tilted away from the sun. Then the denser, colder air of the north flows down across the continent, bringing cool weather and prevailing northerly winds down the South China Sea by early November.

Availing themselves of these periodic changes in the winds, the crews of coasting vessels and oceangoing trading ships would sail north and east up the South China Sea to arrive at the ports on the southern coast of China in the spring and summer, any time between March and August; they would depart for the south and Southeast Asian ports in the winter months between late October and February or March.[9] Roughly coinciding with the monsoons, semiannual trade fairs were held in Canton in January and June.

Laowanshan, a group of tiny, uninhabited, mountainous islands about ten miles out to sea to the southeast, might be the first landfall for a ship arriving at the Pearl River estuary with the southwest monsoon. If the ship was sailing to Canton, it would make a course due north to reach Humen ("Tiger Gate"), where the Pearl River widens into a bay. Midway between these places, the ship would pass the promontory at Majiao Shi ("Horse-Dragon Rocks" or "Horse-Horn Rocks"), the horn of a small peninsula known as Aomen on the west side of the bay, the rocky hills of the peninsula and the islands beyond it barely visible through the haze lingering along the coast. The anchorage it provided offered an inviting and sensible stopping place if the passage beyond Humen was closed or permission to proceed to Canton had not been obtained from the Chinese authorities.

Thirty miles due east, on the east side of the bay, rose the two-thousand-foot peak of Lantao Island, the highest mountain in this part of the South China coast. Its gray silhouette could be seen on the horizon on a clear day from the opposite side of the bay.

Farther out toward the sea, more than fifty miles to the southwest, is Shangchuan Island. During the Ming, the foreigners had first traded at Shangchuan and later at Langbohao before moving to the more convenient location of the Pearl River estuary.

Aomen

Forty miles southeast of Xiangshan city, on the extreme southeastern edge of the district of Xiangshan, a hill called Qianshan ("Front Hill") faced the narrow isthmus of the small peninsula where Majiao Shi jutted into the Pearl River estuary.[10]

The hill occupied a strategic position commanding the approach to the peninsula and the harbor it enclosed. Since 1621, during the late Ming, a well-defended military stronghold surrounded by an earth wall five hundred feet in circumference and eight feet high was located here, near the base of the hill. In 1730, the Qianshan stronghold was raised to the status of headquarters of the county assistant magistrate (*xiancheng*), and after 1744, it was strengthened as a military post of the provincial coast defense forces.

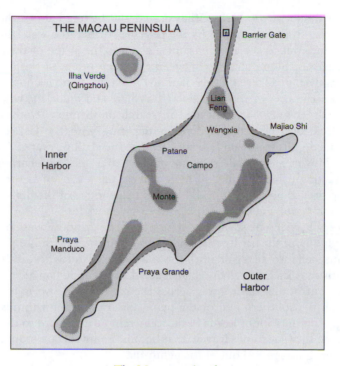

The Macau peninsula

Not far beyond the south gate of this stronghold was a long, narrow sandbar, deposited by a short branching of the river that flows past on its west side, forming the isthmus stretching out from Qianshan on the north to the hills of the peninsula on the south and connecting it to the mainland. To a Chinese visitor viewing this scene from the perspective of Qianshan, the peninsula, with its hills, looked like the bud of a lotus flower and the sandbar was like the flower's stem. So the bar was called "Lotus Flower Stem," and the hill rising where it joined the peninsula was named "Lotus Peak" (Lian feng).

Were it not for the sandbar, the place would still be an island, not so different from the many other small islands dotting this coastal region—steep mounds of ancient rocks, sometimes capped by craggy peaks, with narrow yellow sand beaches and coves separated by abrupt shores of fallen boulders. In the shade trees and brush overhanging the water, several varieties of small birds made their home: the yellow-brown, thrushlike *hwa-mei*, whose melodious song made it a prize captive in Chinese gardens; the tiny, green-and-yellow white-eye, another popular cage bird; the black-and-white great tit, also known for its variety of calls; and the more common brown-and-gray tree sparrow. The white wagtail and the slate-gray blue rock thrush were frequent winter visitors. Dragonflies darted and hovered above the tops of the flowering trees. Silt carried by the river has turned the water brown for some distance out to sea and constantly changes the shape of the shoreline where it passes, filling in areas between the steep peaks of the islands and creating alluvial marshes and tidal flats. At low tide, some islands were connected to each other or to the mainland by bars and mudflats, where white egrets or larger gray herons waded in search of shrimp. Overhead, large, dusky black kites circled and dived, competing with the fast, skimming black-headed gulls for small fish surfacing in the shallow waters.[11] The bar of Lotus Flower Stem made this one of the better sheltered harbors in the area, attracting fishing boats and merchant vessels—as well as the local pirates who preyed on them. Nor did it escape the notice of the first European traders looking for a convenient place to carry on trade.

In 1574, a barrier gate surmounted by a small guardhouse was constructed at the midpoint of the bar by the local Chinese authorities. Subsequently, the guardhouse fell into disrepair, until about a century later when, in 1673, District Magistrate Shen Langhan reconstructed it and added an adjacent office to better control the traffic going across the bar to the growing foreign settlement on the southern end of the peninsula. Facing the isthmus and the barrier gate, at the foot of Lotus Peak, was a temple dedicated to the goddess of seafarers, the Queen of Heaven, that became an important stopping point for travelers going in and out of the peninsula.

On the eastern side of the peninsula, the waves rolling in from the wide Pearl River estuary broke over the outcroppings of Majiao Shi. Not far from this point, just south of the ridge of Lotus Peak, was the site of Wangxia village, the oldest settlement on the peninsula. When the office of the assistant district magistrate was moved south from Qianshan to be more convenient, given the increasing affairs of the peninsula, it was located in Wangxia village.

Spreading south of the village was a low, flat area of paddies cultivated by the villagers. These fields were bounded on the east by a long ridge running down the eastern side of the upper peninsula from the horn of Majiao Shi, but to the west, they extended to the shoreline where a creek that drained them emptied into the bay. To the southwest, the fields ended at another ridge, green with vegetation and scored by rocks and ravines, extending across the peninsula and dividing it, north and south, into halves. To the north and west of this ridge was the sheltered bay enclosed by the peninsula, and beyond it lay the much higher ridge of the larger island on the west; to its southeast, on the outer side of the peninsula, was a more open bay facing out to the nearby islands and the sea. Both bays provided protected anchorages. Because the semicircular shorelines of the two bays north and south of the central ridge seemed to reflect each other like mirrors, the local people had named the place Haojing ("Mirrored Waters"), but it was also known simply as Ao (literally, "a bay").[12] The name Haojing Ao, "Mirrored-Waters Bay," appeared first in the *Ming shi*, written in the second half of the seven-

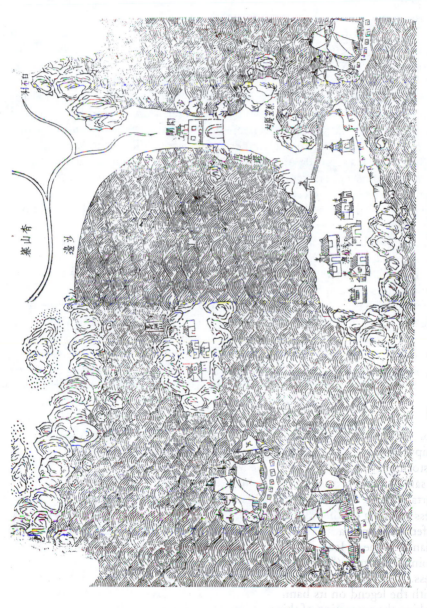

Macau in the eighteenth century (illustration from *Xiangshan xian zhi,* 1750)

teenth century, but other names, reflecting the perspectives of the persons using them, were also common.[13]

South of the central ridge dividing the peninsula was another low area spanning the breadth of the peninsula from the long, sweeping, curved beach of the outer bay to the shoreline on the inner side. From there, the two shores converged on either side of a ridge extending from north to south to a rocky point at the tip of the peninsula. Adding interest for observers of this entire scene was a solitary, small, round island, called Qingzhou ("Green Island"), in the inner bay, in line between Qianshan to the north and the peninsula's central peak to the south. Although it was steep, with great protruding granite boulders, that island was covered with a luxuriant growth of contorted trees and vines that reflected darkly from the water and appeared more cool and dense than the harsher, more barren hills of the peninsula.

South of the peninsula of Ao, four ridges rose from the sea, separated by narrow channels intersecting at their center to form a passage in the shape of a cross, like the Chinese word for the numeral ten (*shizi*). In the lexicon of the people of the coastal region, a navigable passage between islands or bodies of land is called *men* ("door" or "gate"). Thus, this passage and the anchorage it provided was called Shizi Men ("Passage Like the Word Ten" or "Cross-shaped Gate"), and perhaps for this reason, the entire place—the peninsula and its two mirrored bays, as well as the islands to its south and the passage between them—came by convention to be called Aomen ("The Gate of the Bays"). But it was also claimed that the name Aomen came from the resemblance of the hills facing each other on the peninsula to a gateway.

Apart from Wangxia village near the base of the peninsula and some scattered farm settlements nearby, Aomen was only very thinly populated in the sixteenth century. Some of the rocky points and coves there and on the islands along the coast harbored isolated small temples and shrines dedicated and maintained by the local fishermen who frequented the bays. One such temple overlooked Majiao Shi on the eastern shore. On the far southwestern point, where the rocks are particularly steep, a similar temple was built by a shipwrecked merchant from Fujian, grateful for having found safety there in a storm. In the Wanli reign of the Ming (1573–1621), his oceangoing junk, it is said, had encountered a typhoon and was driven toward shore and almost certain disaster on the rocks. When all seemed lost, he suddenly saw a goddess standing on the hillside. Guided by her vision, he and his ship reached safety, and in gratitude, the merchant subsequently dedicated a temple to Tian Fei, the "Heavenly Maiden." The place came to be called Niangma Point, Niangma ("Maiden Mother") being the Fujian name for the goddess.[14] In front of the temple is an image of a ship carved on a large boulder, with the legend on its banner—"Auspiciously Cross the Great River"—invoking the protection of this goddess of mariners.

Niangma, whose most widely recognized name is Mazu ("Mother Ancestor"), is also more formally known as Tianhou ("the Heavenly Maiden") and

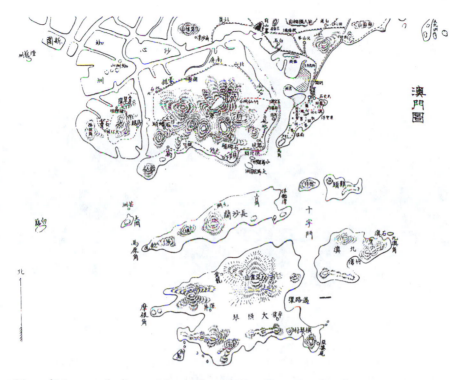

Map of Macau and adjacent islands (from *Xiangshan xian zhi xubian*, 1920)

colloquially simply as Ama ("Mother"). It is popularly believed that when the Portuguese first arrived here, they inquired about the name of the place from the inhabitants they met and were told it was called Amagau or Amakau in the local dialect (the "Bay of Ama," or Amajiao, "Ama Point"), from the prominent location of the temple on the point overlooking the bay, the most readily identifiable landmark for the Portuguese mariners who anchored there.[15] The word *Amakau*, it is said, became corrupted to *Macau* (or *Macao*, which is still prevalent mainly in non-Portuguese writings), the common Western name for Aomen, as it is still known to the Chinese.[16] Of course, since the Portuguese adopted the name before the temple was supposed to have been constructed in the Wanli reign, a shrine or temple to Ama must have already occupied the site for some time before the Portuguese arrived. To confuse matters even further, an alternative explanation of the name Macau claims that it derived from another prominent landfall noted by the Portuguese, the point at Majiao Shi, rendered Makau Seak in the local dialect.[17]

The rest of the peninsula was mostly rocks and precipitous slopes falling to stony shores. Where the shoreline twisted around the hills in an uneven line, there were short, narrow beaches separated by outcroppings. This was a

Ama temple (engraving, ca. 1835)

favorite place for pirates to lie in wait; from these sheltered bays, they could raid the shipping in the Pearl River estuary to the east.

Across the narrow inner harbor enclosed by Niangma Point, a ridge rising higher than the hills of the peninsula blocked the western horizon. Skirting this to the southwest was a passage leading to another bay that formed the main estuary of the West River, from which the Pearl River branched off near the city of Canton. Where the channel opened into this bay there was a small island called Modaojue ("Knife Grinding Point") guarding its entrance, which gave its name, Modaomen, or "Knife Grinding Gate," to this passage. Although less direct than the Pearl River route through Humen and seldom used by foreign traders in the early years, this alternative route up the river from Aomen, known as the inner passage, offered a sort of backdoor approach to Canton. There, along the narrow channels of the interior and away from the harsh coastline, the scene softened; the low banks were lined with orange and lemon trees, peach trees and lychee trees, paddies, and small towns and villages.[18] Numerous small coastal defense forts guarded strategic points along the channels.[19] But in spite of the protection these forts were supposed to offer, the brazen activities of pirates in the area also made that a hazardous route.[20]

The hiatus following the end of the monsoon every year, when the trading fairs were finished and the ships had departed, was known by the foreign traders as the "dead season." The climate of Canton and the other upriver delta ports, lying low on the river and sheltered by the coastal hills from the sea breezes, could become oppressively hot and humid, particularly when the monsoon season had passed. But on the hilly coastal promontories like Aomen, the temperatures were often several degrees cooler, and even when the strong monsoons were not blowing, refreshing sea breezes provided a pleasant respite from the humidity and heat of the interior.[21]

The exposed position of the coast was not always an advantage, however. From as early as July to October and sometimes November, typhoons (*taifeng*, "great wind")—vast cyclonic storms generated by the heating of the ocean surface of the South China Sea and the Southern Pacific in late summer—regularly moved north and west, sometimes striking the coast with great violence. The typhoons presented a mortal danger to ships at sea that were unlucky enough to be caught in them, and they also could cause extensive damage onshore. Moreover, they disrupted the regularity of the monsoon trade winds for days. Particularly severe typhoons hit the Aomen region in 1809, when the barometric pressure fell to 28.30 inches of mercury, and in August 1832, when it fell to 28.10 or lower. On August 5, 1835, after several days of very hot weather with northerly winds, an even more violent storm hit as the mercury dropped to 28.05. Damage was extensive at Aomen and along the coast for some miles inland.[22]

On the night of September 22, 1874, and continuing through the next day, the greatest typhoon in memory passed over the peninsula. Warnings of the awesome storm arrived at sunset. The horizontal rays of the setting sun, refracted from an eerie veil of clouds, suffused the surrounding sea and air with an intense, ruddy light. Suddenly it seemed as if the mouth of an enormous furnace had opened, gorging from its throat a fierce, metallic light that pierced the ragged clouds. Darkness fell quickly as the storm intensified. By 3 A.M., the barometer had dropped precipitously to a low of 27.79. The strength of the wind was not recorded, but the rising sea, driven by its force, swept the entire low-lying area of the peninsula, greatly aggravating the destruction; fires broke out, burning uncontrollably and contributing to the enormous loss of life and property.[23] Many houses and public buildings of the city were totally destroyed; more than 700 large ships and fishing boats and as many as 1,000 small craft were lost completely. The *Príncipe D. Carlos*, a 150-ton armed schooner of the Portuguese navy, was sunk at sea 12 miles from the port; the 80-ton gunboat *Camões* ran aground and was damaged beyond repair 4 miles to the west. Heavy pieces of artillery were dislodged and transported great distances by the force of the waves. The number of individuals killed was put at several hundred.[24]

Xiangshan

The mountainous region on the western shore of the Pearl River bay, from Humen on the north to Aomen on the south, divided from the rest of the mainland by the main channel of the West River and including the islands immediately offshore, constituted a roughly defined but coherent geographical entity. To the north were the interior delta and the valleys of the river; farther to the west was the more homogeneous region of the mountainous southern coast of Guangdong. The boundaries of this area were largely formed by bodies of water: the coast of the South China Sea on the south, the broad bay of the Pearl on the east, and river channels on the west and north. Mountains and water, the classical ingredients of Chinese landscape, thus characterized the geography of the region known as Xiangshan ("Fragrant Hills").

Although the mountains, particularly in the central portion of the region, limited the availability of arable land, there were broad valleys in the center and the west and low-lying areas in the north where the serpentine channels of the delta formed a network of waterways. The mountainsides were too rugged and dry and the population was too sparse for the area to be effectively exploited for agriculture, but people in hundreds of small villages cul-

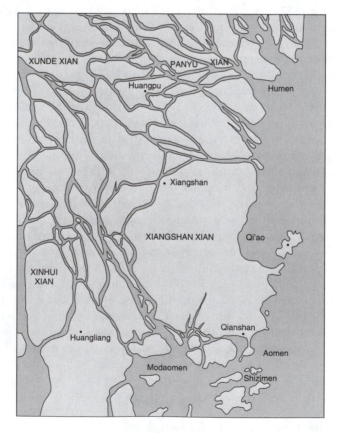

Xiangshan District

tivated rice in the lowlands and supplemented their livelihood with fishing in the river channels. Offshore fishing by the people of the coastal villages and peripheral involvement in the commerce of the Canton region supplied additional dimensions to the economy and society of the area. If it was not one of the richest districts in the Chinese empire, neither was it among the poorest. Its economic diversity and moderate population, as well as the absence of the extremes of natural adversity that affected more northern and less well-watered regions, provided the area with a measure of security.

The villages were tight clusters of houses separated by narrow lanes. The gray houses were made of masonry, usually bricks. The end walls projected from the front walls in ridges to form recesses; the pitched roofs were constructed of tiles. The better houses were usually two stories, and it was common to paint the area below the eaves with murals and bas-relief friezes with decorative themes or figures from stories and myths, as peasants so often did and still do in other parts of China.[25]

Near the center of the district, on the banks of a channel of the river known as the Qi Jiang, was the principal town and district capital of Xiangshan. Though an important focus for the administration and society of the district, Xiangshan was by no means as important a place as the more interior towns and cities of the Canton delta. But it was, in a way, a typical district town, a commercial and administrative center. A tall, red pagoda, standing atop a hill on the east bank of the river near the center of town, marked Xiangshan's location from a distance for boats along the river. On the banks of the river in the town were boats of various kinds—small fishing craft, sampans bringing in local produce, larger freight barges, and "flower boats" on which guests dined and were entertained by "singsong girls."

Xiangshan was made an administrative district (*xian*) in 1162, during the Southern Song dynasty. From that time on, it was subordinate to Guangzhou prefecture (*fu*), the center of which was the prefectural and provincial capital of Canton (also called Guangzhou in Chinese), about forty miles to the northwest. By the late Ming and early Qing, there were some fifteen hundred districts or counties, the lowest integrated units in the empire. Each xian was headed by a magistrate (*zhixian*); as the primary official responsible for the order, peace, and well-being of the local population, the zhixian was colloquially known as the "father-and-mother official." Even if the magistrate occupied almost the lowest level of a vast bureaucratic hierarchy extending downward from the Son of Heaven to his subjects, he was still an awesome figure: Not only did he command considerable power delegated from the emperor, but, as a "scholar," he was a member of a political and social elite that was separated from the common people by its shared literati culture and the explicit symbols of legitimacy and achievement. The magistrate's *yamen*, his official residence and office, was always a walled compound in the heart of the district city, which a commoner would approach and enter only with great trepidation.

In the larger administrative framework of the empire, the remote location of Xiangshan, peripheral even in relation to Canton within Guangdong Province, would have made the district a rather undesirable posting for a magistrate, especially one with ambition for an official career. There would be few other people of his kind—educated retired officials or local gentry—with whom he could associate. Assignment there, for all but the least ambitious, would have been regarded as almost a sentence of exile. Perhaps it is not surprising, therefore, to find that incumbent magistrates did not last long and generally did not possess the highest credentials of their class. During the 276 years of the Ming (1368–1644), 67 incumbents held the post of

Map of southern Xiangshan District, including Aomen (from *Xiangshan xian zhi xubian*, 1920)

Xiangshan magistrate. Only 17 of them (25 percent) held the highest official academic rank, the metropolitan degree (*jinshi*); 25 (37 percent) held the inferior provincial degree (*juren*); and another 25 held lesser degrees or their degree status was not listed. The average term in office was a little over 4 years. In the first century of the Qing, the 102 years from 1646 to 1748, 28 persons occupied the office of magistrate. A mere 4 (14 percent) of these held jinshi degrees, 8 (29 percent) held juren degrees, and the rest (16) held lower degrees or their degree status was not listed. In that period, the average term had fallen to 3.6 years.[26] That Xiangshan attracted fewer individuals with higher degrees in the later years suggests that the district had declined as a worthy assignment for the better scholar-officials.

Outside of each district city, the district was divided for administrative purposes into townships (*xiang*) and villages (*cun*). Depending on the size and complexity of a district's affairs, the magistrate was assisted by a number of regular subordinate officers, as well as a less formal staff of clerks and secretaries—sometimes numbering in the hundreds for large and important districts. The regular subordinate officers were assigned responsibility over specific areas or portions of a district. The magistrate in Xiangshan had one assistant magistrate (*xiancheng*), four deputy magistrates (*xunjian*), and one district police warden (*dianshi*). After 1731, when he was stationed at Qianshan, the assistant magistrate was responsible for two townships, including 56 villages. One deputy magistrate, stationed at Xiangshan, was responsible for 1 township and 8 villages; the second, at Huangpu in the delta region of the north of the district, oversaw 2 townships and 11 villages; the third, at Huangliang in the southwest portion of the district separated from the rest by the channel of Modaomen, had 1 township embracing 161 villages; and the fourth, stationed at Qi'ao on the eastern bay shore of the district, was responsible for 3 townships including 28 villages. The warden, also located at Xiangshan, was responsible for an additional 3 townships, including 165 villages.[27] Altogether, Xiangshan District was divided into 16 townships and 429 small villages. Although Xiangshan was in no way an unusual district as such districts went in the larger administrative framework of the late Ming— neither especially large nor small, prosperous nor poor, politically prominent nor obscure—the affairs of more than 400 villages were enough to keep any district administration preoccupied with the basic functions of collecting taxes and maintaining law and order.

The Aomen peninsula was of little consequence to Xiangshan before the middle of the sixteenth century. That soon changed after the Portuguese settled there and the town and its trade began to grow. There were two dimensions to the commercial activity. On the one hand, Aomen almost immediately became a source of revenue for the district and the province, ultimately contributing to the prosperity of the hinterland. On the other hand, trade would, in the long run, have an effect on the commercial structure of the

South China region. But not every trade commodity that the Portuguese might deem desirable was regarded as such by the Chinese.

From the beginning, it appears, the Xiangshan local authorities collected an annual rent of 500 *taels* from the Portuguese. Although the precise origin of this fee is unclear, it became a regular obligation of the settlement. In addition, annual customs duties amounted to 20,000 taels.[28] Customs charges were derived from anchorage fees based on measurements of the length and beam of the ship and whether it was laden or not.[29] Trade was carried on through the semiannual trade fairs at Canton beginning in 1578. But as the scope and size of the trade increased, this mechanism was not sufficient to control it. A little more than one hundred years later, by 1688, as the Manchus were consolidating their hold on South China following the Rebellion of the Three Feudatories, the Chinese established a branch customs office—the "hoppo" (a colloquial abbreviation for *Yuehai guanbu*, the customs administration of the Guangdong coast)—at Macau. Henceforth, this office collected customs duties on shipments arriving and departing from Macau as well as tonnage dues on shipping.[30] All ships were required to stop at Macau to pay customs duties. Cargoes were measured and recorded and then placed in warehouses pending trade with Chinese merchants. When the goods exited Macau, the customs duties were collected.[31]

The size of the trade and the official revenue derived from it inevitably influenced the local officials charged with controlling that trade and collecting the duties. To the extent that they benefited personally from the opportunities it afforded for irregular levies and fees, they developed a vested interest in its undisturbed continuation.[32]

More disturbing were the political and legal ramifications of the expanding settlement at Aomen. From the beginning, the foreign presence there caused concern among Chinese officials and engendered problems with which they were forced to deal, however inadequately or unsuccessfully. Soon after their arrival on the South China coast in 1513, the Portuguese got off on the wrong foot with the Chinese, and friction between them, arising from the aggressive behavior of the Portuguese, caused endemic bitterness between them. The first Portuguese fleet arrived in 1517 under the command of Fernão Peres de Andrade. Contacts with the Chinese began well enough, and before he departed, Andrade managed to convince the Chinese to accept an embassy under Thomé Pires to negotiate commercial relations at Canton. Unfortunately, Fernão's brother, Simão de Andrade, who arrived with another fleet in 1518, behaved in a high-handed manner. He constructed a fort on an island and executed one of his crew for misdemeanors, violations of sovereignty that greatly displeased the Chinese. Rumors began to circulate that the Portuguese were kidnapping local children and eating them, which actually may have reflected Portuguese attempts to take Chinese slaves.[33] When Simão assaulted a Chinese official who protested these acts, the Chinese retaliated by attacking him and driving the Portuguese away. Other clashes followed in the next few years. In the meantime, the envoy Thomé Pires, who had remained at Canton, managed to get to Peking in 1520. But because of the aggressive behavior of the Portuguese, he was sent back to Canton and seems to have died in prison there.[34] Chinese resentment at what was perceived as foreign arrogance persisted following the settlement of Macau.

> The Portuguese were unimpeded at sea. . . . They conducted commerce at Hao-jing, and built houses and walls, arrogantly occupying the coast like an [inde-pendent] state. Their unscrupulous officials aggressively behaved like a foreign government. . . . People of other nations avoided them in fear, so that they ex-clusively occupied the place.[35]

As the settlement grew, the Portuguese expanded to the surrounding areas of the peninsula. In 1606, the Jesuits built a large monastery on Green Island. The Chinese sources described it as sixty to seventy feet high, with a secret and capacious interior, unlike anything that had been seen in China. District Magistrate Zhang Dayu ineffectually demanded that the Jesuits dismantle the structure. In 1621, however, the *Daotai* (circuit intendant), Feng Cung-long, forced them to destroy the walls, but by the next century, the Jesuits had permanently occupied the island.[36]

By the late nineteenth century, the Portuguese had begun to occupy the land between the old city wall, bisecting the peninsula along the ridge line occupied by the Monte fort, and the barrier gate on the isthmus. The Chinese drew a definite distinction between this area, which was public agricul-tural land, and the peninsula south of the wall, which was leased to the Por-tuguese. Besides Wangxia village, which controlled 400 *mou* of cultivated land (about 55 acres) paying annual grain taxes to Xiangshan of 30 taels of silver, there were six other, smaller settlements within this area occupied by people of various classes who paid no taxes. In 1887, Governor-General Zhang Zhidong complained that the Portuguese had installed street lamps in Wangxia and levied fees to maintain them. They had also affixed registration plaques to the houses and attempted to collect land rents from the residents.[37]

Officials were increasingly preoccupied with problems of controlling the foreign presence in Macau, especially the foreigners' constant going and coming and access to the settlement by those who were deemed undesirable. Piracy was an endemic problem along the coast during the Ming, and soon it became implicated with the Portuguese presence in Macau. "Japanese pi-rates" (*wokou*) had appeared in the early Ming, but their depredations reached their zenith at the end of the sixteenth century. The wokou were ac-tually a combination of Japanese and Chinese seafarers operating in the East China Sea between Japan and the South China coast. Their activities were fostered by two things—the Ming attitude toward legitimate trade during this period, which was at best ambivalent and at worst hostile, and the political instability in Japan attendant on the gradual disintegration of the Ashikaga shogunate and the ensuing century of civil war (*sengoku jidai*) ushered in by the Onin War (1467–1477). By the 1550s and 1560s, when the wokou spread southward to the coastal region of Fujian and Guangdong Provinces and launched plundering expeditions into the interior of the Yangzi delta area, the Ming became increasingly alarmed and was forced to take more energetic measures to suppress the piracy.[38] It was just at this time that the Portuguese were settling Macau.

As early as 1563, this situation had begun to concern the local authorities, who believed the Portuguese were harboring the pirates. The pirates could be controlled by force, but the Portuguese presented a more insidious difficulty. In that year, Governor-General Zhang Mingwang argued that endeavoring to control and confine the Portuguese in their settlement was preferable to attempting to expel them to some other place where they might be less tractable.[39] Perhaps his opinion reflected a concern for the hidden benefits of the foreign trade enjoyed by local officials.

In any case, a gradual reorientation of the district administration to the existence of Macau had become evident by the early eighteenth century. In 1731, the assistant magistrate's office was moved to the Qianshan military post, far from the district capital but close to the source of the ever more complex affairs arising from the settlement. Now termed the Aomen assistant magistrate, this official was exclusively responsible for dealing with the growing population of Chinese and foreigners there.[40] As the Chinese moved to Macau to work as servants for the foreigners, the problems of maintaining law and order and adjudicating legal disputes led to the development of more regular procedures. In 1743, a Portuguese named Anselmo mortally wounded a Chinese servant. The Chinese protested attempts to protect the foreigner, with the result that it was decided that henceforth in cases of offenses involving Chinese and foreigners, the persons charged would be turned over to Chinese authorities for disposition.[41] Macau was now occupying an increasingly important place in the administration of Xiangshan.

The Hinterland

The economic influence of Macau gradually spread beyond the coastal district of which it was a part, to affect not only the rest of Guangdong Province but also the neighboring provinces of Guangxi and Fujian. Opportunities afforded by the trade quickly attracted merchants from Guangdong and Fujian, for whom Macau was easily accessible by sea along the well-established local trading routes. Foreign merchants also used Macau as a base for their trade with the Fujian coast.[42] Moreover, customs revenue from the trade became an important factor beyond the immediate uses of the local provincial authorities. A levy on the trade became a component of imperial revenue in the form of tribute, and customs duties provided a critical supplement to the regular provincial taxes that were used for the administration and military expenditures of Guangdong and Guangxi. (These areas were linked under the authority of the governor-general of the Two Guang.)[43]

Well before Macau was founded by the Portuguese, Lin Fu, the military governor of Guangdong, had noted, with some foresight, the beneficial effects of foreign trade on the prosperity of the region's population:

> The common people rely on commerce for their livelihood. Every *qian* worth of commodities derived from the development of trade is relied upon by them for food. . . . Strengthening the state and enriching the people are mutually dependent. For this reason the people's benefit is indeed a benefit, and not to encourage it would be a very great calamity for the people.[44]

Writing later, probably in the early seventeenth century when trade was already flourishing, the maritime geographer Zhang Xie predicted that any attempt to interfere with the trade at Macau would have serious consequences for the coastal population:

> Along the seacoast the land is largely infertile salt land, where farmers have no possibility of a harvest and look upon the sea as an obstacle. Long ago it became the custom for the wealthy families to go abroad for commodities to ship home for the use of the poor, and to provide ample grain for themselves. To abruptly proclaim martial law and prohibit going to sea would cut off their livelihood. Because this class is proud and strong and will not submit willingly to poverty and distress, the outbreak of uncontrolled disorder would arise [from this policy].[45]

Macau's critical role in the trade network between Japan, South China, Southeast Asia, and India, which flourished from the 1550s until the system's collapse in the 1640s, made the city one of the wealthiest and most prosperous trading bases in Portuguese Asia. Through Macau, silk was exported to Japan, where it was sold for silver. (Silver commanded a substantially higher price in China than in Japan.) The silver was, in turn, used to purchase exports in Macau and Canton for sale in Southeast Asia, India, and Europe. Thus, the importation of silver bullion to China through the intermediate role of Macau contributed to the expansion of the late Ming economy, especially in the coastal regions of the south and southeast.[46] Moreover, the greatly expanded export of silk to Japan via Macau at the same time stimulated the economic prosperity of the silk industry in the nearby district of Shunde (Shuntak).[47]

Hence, over a century or more, an economic interdependence of sorts between Macau, Xiangshan, and the much wider region of South China (including Guangdong, Guangxi, and Fujian) emerged. Indeed, the abrupt decline in Macau's commercial activity in the 1640s—brought about by the closing of Japan, the restoration in Portugal, and the Dutch offensive against Portuguese possessions in Asia—precipitated a fiscal crisis and a sharp decline in the previously inflated Chinese economy, which may have contributed to the fall of the Ming in 1644.[48] If so, nothing more clearly testifies to the role Macau had assumed in the economy of the region. However much the interdependence between the city and the coastal periphery might have fluctuated subsequently with the rise and fall in the fortunes of trade and political relations, it would never entirely disappear.

By the nineteenth century, Macau was becoming increasingly integrated with the life and economy of the entire delta region. In 1887, Zhang Zhidong, governor-general of Guangdong and Guangxi, reported on the expanding commercial activity with Macau and its attendant problems:

> Both good and bad people from Guangdong have moved to Macau in large numbers. Merchants from the districts of Nanhai, Panyu, Xiangshan, and Shunde, exceeding tens of thousands, come and go between Macau and the province. They frequently set up livelihoods and establish businesses in both places, unrestrained by the borders, which causes excessive lawlessness among the people. Their endless traffic is like the weaving of cloth.[49]

Communication was another aspect of this increasing interdependence. Letters and parcels relating to the commercial activity of the region could be dispatched between Macau and other towns and cities of the delta, including Canton, Foshan (Fatshan), and Xiangshan, by couriers employed by privately owned post offices, according to regularly established schedules and postage rates. Postage between Canton and Macau, a distance of ninety miles, for instance, was about forty cash (*qian*, a Chinese coin).[50] Although Macau's commercial importance was eclipsed by the emergence of Hong Kong and the treaty ports after midcentury and although its economy languished until its slow recovery in the late twentieth century, its unique cultural identity persisted.

As the political and economic focus of Xiangshan and the Guangdong hinterland shifted southward toward Macau in the eighteenth century, a broader orientation to the coastal periphery and the West was also emerging. With the growing importance of silk manufacture and later of tea exports and the illegal opium trade, the economy of the region was becoming interdependent with the global economic structure, increasingly dominated by the Western powers. This reorientation had important demographic consequences that linked Macau more closely with the coastal periphery.

In the nineteenth century—driven by mounting poverty and social and political instability in South China engendered by the population growth since the eighteenth century and attracted by economic opportunities—the Chinese of Xiangshan and other neighboring districts of the delta region began to emigrate in increasing numbers to Western colonial possessions in

Southeast Asia, including the Philippines, Annam, Cochin China, Borneo, Malaya, Singapore, and Indonesia, as well as to Hawaii and the western United States, Canada, and South Africa. Many of those emigrants never returned to their homeland, and Chinese from those districts came to predominate among the permanent overseas Chinese communities of Southeast Asia and the United States.

Overseas Chinese populations totaled over eighteen million by 1969, 96 percent of whom were distributed in Asian countries.[51] The great majority of Chinese emigrants originated from the coastal districts of the Canton delta of Guangdong, eastern Guangdong, and southern Fujian as far north as Amoy. Although most of them came from the villages and rural areas of these regions and represented the lowest social stratum, in their adopted homes abroad they overwhelmingly moved into the intermediate commercial ranks of petty merchants, entrepreneurs, shopkeepers, and artisans after initial employment as laborers at the bottom of the social scale.[52] Perhaps because the number of Chinese emigrants was greatly augmented throughout the nineteenth century by contract labor recruitment, which drew mainly from the male population, there was a paucity of women among the emigrants at least until the early twentieth century.[53] This condition fostered intermarriage among Chinese and indigenous peoples, especially in Southeast Asian countries, but Chinese emigrants nonetheless retained a strong orientation toward their native places, even after many years of residence abroad; this attitude was instilled by deep ancestral bonds and Confucian values stressing filial piety and family and clan obligations. Consequently, they kept their Chinese cultural identity, including language, education, and religious observances, and many looked forward to returning home with their savings and settling down with newfound status and wealth. At least they hoped to be buried with their ancestors in their ancestral village.

Some continued to remit a portion of their earnings to their families who remained behind, contributing from a distance to the economic vitality of the region. Remittances thus became another significant economic link between emigrants and their native homes. In the 1880s, more than $1 million was being remitted annually to the Canton region by San Francisco Chinese.[54] By the 1930s, annual remittances from overseas Chinese communities had risen to a value of $80 to $100 million, and they resumed at a level close to $50 million after the end of World War II and the establishment of the People's Republic.[55] The ambiguous status of Macau and Hong Kong made both places important conduits for communication between overseas emigrants and their relatives at home and for the transmission of remittances. Hong Kong, with better banking facilities and financial institutions, was the route by which 95 percent of all remittances were transmitted back to China. Direct access was easier through Macau, however, than through Hong Kong.[56]

Still other individuals, among the more prosperous groups, eventually did return with their new wealth to reestablish their lives in their old villages and towns. Returning emigrants were anxious to convert their new wealth to social prestige in their communities. And nothing could better evoke the admiration and respect of one's neighbors and secure recognition of one's new status as a successful emigrant than to build a large and impressive house. These foreign-style houses (*yanglou*), exhibiting a mixture of indigenous and modernistic Western architecture, were typically three stories tall and featured richly decorated parlors and living rooms, perhaps a yard in front and a garden in the rear, and a third floor roof garden with potted flowering plants and caged birds.[57] Today, substantial, multistoried houses with imposing facades elaborately decorated around the roofs and eaves are everywhere evident in the villages of rural Xiangshan, standing out from the more modest houses of the neighbors who remained behind. Even to the present, emigrants are returning to build yet more modern houses and contribute to the prosperity of the region.

After the Communist revolution in 1949, large numbers of overseas Chinese returned to China in the 1950s and 1960s, although they were regarded with some suspicion by the Communist government as ideologically corrupted petite bourgeoisie influenced by Western bourgeois thought and capitalist society.[58] Up to 1959, 80 percent of these emigrants returned to Guangdong. The anti-Chinese riots and persecutions in Indonesia in 1959 drove large numbers back to their homeland. Many of them were settled in state-owned overseas Chinese farms between the years 1950 and 1964. A considerable proportion of these farms were concentrated in the Canton delta region from which many of the emigrants had come.[59] Previously isolated culturally and politically as sojourners in their adopted homes abroad, they were again isolated and controlled while living among their compatriots in their native land.

Another, less fortunate side of the wave of voluntary emigration in the nineteenth century was the coolie traffic that supplied cheap contract labor for colonial enterprises, particularly in Cuba and Peru. Coolies sometimes escaped their harsh lot to become part of the permanently settled population of these areas.[60] But many more were compelled by their contracts and the masters who had purchased them to work as virtual slaves.

As Macau's economic importance in the China trade declined precipitously with the opening of the treaty ports and the growth of Hong Kong following the Opium Wars (1839–1842 and 1856–1860), the fiscal loss was partially compensated for by the development of the export of human labor.[61] During the middle decades of the nineteenth century, Macau became the infamous center of the coolie traffic, in spite of efforts to mitigate its worst abuses or to eliminate it altogether. Macau's ambiguous international status, as well as its peculiar internal conditions, contributed to the city's rise

Yanglou, Xiangshan District

as the center of coolie trade. A serious riot by local residents of Amoy in 1852 succeeded in discouraging the trade at that port, where it had briefly flourished.[62] Although the trade shifted subsequently to Hong Kong, strong British legal action there between 1852 and 1857 drove the traffic to Macau, where conditions were less hostile to its growth. Macau already possessed extensive trading connections with the Southeast Asian ports that were the initial destinations of many contract laborers. Moreover, an extensive underworld controlling drugs, slavery, and prostitution flourished in Macau, providing a ready-made vehicle for brokers and illegal activities. Finally, Portuguese officials tacitly encouraged and colluded in the practice, and, in fact, a number of Portuguese merchants were leaders in the coolie trade.[63] From the 1850s to the 1870s, the coolie traffic through Macau assumed the proportions of a virtual slave trade, as abusive and inhuman as the African slave trade across the Atlantic.[64]

In Macau, an elaborate structure was created to handle the export of contract laborers. Chinese from the villages throughout the delta were often duped or coerced by various means to sign contracts from which they could not escape.[65] Edward Fuller, a traveler visiting Macau in 1866 at the peak of the coolie trade, described the practice at that time:

> A planter in need of men in S America, or Cuba, sends an agent here to "hire" five hundred Chinamen. This agent employs compradores (Chinese) to go into the interior after his men. Mr. W this evening gave me an instance of how they get them. One of these well paid compradores entered the hut of a poor wretched coolie a few days since, gave his children a few cash, and told him he was a foolish fellow for lieing idle—that if he would come with him to town, he would insure him 4$ (good wages here) per month. The poor devil swallowed hook and line at a gulp and that night found himself on board a coolie ship, bound for Havana. . . . The Capt, when he gets his "freight" on board, gives them 8$ each in money, and two suits of clothes—more than they (half of them) ever had before in the world. While this is fresh in their minds the Harbor Master comes off, and (it is said) asks each if he is willing to go. The poor wretches, bewildered with the "advance" and having not the most remote idea of what they are acceding to, generally say yes, upon which the ship receives her papers—sets sail—and coolie is a slave for life—unless he dies on the voyage, which is about the same. Contracts have been entered into for delivery—this year—of twenty five thousand coolies![66]

Local native brokers held coolies in houses called "barracoons," pending their export across the Pacific by those who had purchased their contracts, on ships in which the conditions were almost as bad as in the Atlantic slave ships. In an approximately six-month period from late 1866 to early 1867, for example, as many as fifty such ships exported 13,500 laborers.[67]

Barracoons—there were 5 in Macau in 1856, 300 by 1872—were little more than prisons in which coolies were beaten and tortured if they did not assure foreign buyers they had signed voluntary contracts.[68] Those who survived the barracoons faced the grim prospect of a long sea voyage, imprisoned below deck by iron gratings under deplorable conditions. Many died en route. Of the 740 coolies transported in two ships from Macau to Peru in 1850, 247 died before reaching their destination.[69] One of the most notorious events involved the Peruvian coolie ship *Don Juan*, which caught fire at sea on May 6, 1871, two days out of Macau, with 665 coolies on board. The captain and crew abandoned ship, leaving the coolies to perish. Only 50 survived.[70] Another incident, which helped to focus attention on the abusive trade, was the *Maria Luz* affair. After leaving Macau on May 28, 1872, with 225 coolies aboard, the ship was forced off course to Yokohama. One coolie escaped to a nearby British ship, where he related the conditions on board the *Maria Luz*. The British captain refused to return him, and the adjudication of the dispute created a scandal over the traffic.[71]

During the approximately four decades that the coolie traffic flourished, the average price per head was about $50, including shipping costs. Prices of coolies at the point of sale in Cuba or Peru ranged from $120 to as much as $1,000.[72] Between 1845 and 1873, of a total of 322,593 Chinese contract laborers exported from China ports, 143,472 were exported through Macau alone.[73] Only in 1873 did Portugal succeed in suppressing the traffic. The disastrous effect this action had on the Macau economy was testimony to how important the trade had become to the city in this period of decline.[74]

As Xiangshan and the delta hinterland gradually became more politically and economically oriented toward the presence of Macau and long before returning emigrants in the nineteenth century brought back with them to their old villages elements of Western culture that they had absorbed abroad, Macau inevitably exerted other kinds of influence on the cultural complexion of the region. New foods imported by the Portuguese or grown by them in neighboring areas initially for their own use, including such vegetables as green beans, lettuce, watercress, and chilies, and fruits such as pineapples, guavas, and papayas, were incorporated into the domestic economy of the local population.[75]

The first contacts between Chinese and foreigners were restricted largely to commercial transactions, mainly at the semiannual Canton trade fairs, and to the employment of limited numbers of Chinese as menial servants. There was very little social interaction between foreign settlers and the local population of Xiangshan, and Chinese merchants normally did not travel to Macau for business. But there were exceptions, and those Chinese who did manage to make regular visits could not help but be fascinated by the exotic Western culture they found there. Some observers left detailed descriptions of what they saw.[76]

In the sixteenth century, intermarriage between the Portuguese and Chinese was unusual, and most of the women who entered the city to become the wives of Europeans had arrived from other areas of Asia, including Japan, Indonesia, Malaya, and India.[77] Language was a significant barrier to extensive interaction between Chinese and foreign residents, but for those who were able to overcome this obstacle, Macau presented attractive opportunities for economic advancement, and intermarriage between the Portuguese and Chinese families of Xiangshan became more common in time.[78]

The evolution of a creole dialect, a mixture of Portuguese and Chinese with other words from Malay—peculiar to Macau—must have facilitated communication among the Europeans, their servants, and the resident commercial population of Chinese merchants and shopkeepers. Later, as Britain became established as the dominant trading power in Canton and English became the preferred language of commercial and social interaction, this would no longer be the case.[79] But in the meantime, practical language handbooks and lexicons issued by Chinese publishers in Canton reflected the interest of at least some Chinese in surmounting the social and cultural barrier. One such book, the *Aomen fanyu zaze quantao* ("A Complete Collection of the Miscellaneous Words Used in the Foreign Language of Macau"), listed the pronunciation of 1,200 foreign words in categories including food, furniture, social relations, natural objects, buying and selling, and weights.[80]

The aggressive evangelism of Macau's Jesuits and members of other Christian orders also had an effect on the surrounding areas. By the seventeenth century, Chinese observers, complaining of the surreptitious spread of the Catholic religion, reported that crosses could be seen hanging on doors of houses in the towns and villages of Xiangshan and Shunde Districts.[81] But such instances were nevertheless socially limited and isolated.

和   和   和

As the city grew on the remote Aomen promontory of the South China coast, it became increasingly implicated in the life of the region that surrounded it. And the region itself also became implicated in the life of the city. In one sense, gradations of interaction extended outward (or inward?) from the growing settlement to the rest of the peninsula, to the district of Xiangshan to which it was attached, to the larger South China hinterland. But a frontier between cultures is never a smooth continuum; if it were, it would cease to be a challenge, for discontinuities are as important as continuities, and they create opportunities as well as barriers.

Boundaries, particularly cultural boundaries, are more than lines sharply drawn on a map. They hold symbolic meanings for the worlds they separate, defining the limits of each while remaining porous to influences from either side. "Boundaries can make the *edge* as important as the *center*. Whereas zones, particularly of the concentric variety, can give a sense of graduated change from the center out toward the periphery, boundaries or thresholds mark the point *within* which proper life is expected to exist, and separate it more definitively from that which lies without."[82]

Thus, boundaries, like thresholds, face two ways; they not only confine and divide but also offer opportunities to cross over: They are doorways between different worlds.

However much the influence of Macau pervaded the region surrounding it, affecting economic and political life, a cultural boundary remained. Where the two worlds met on the edge of the West River delta, they became interdependent in certain ways but they always remained distinct, and mutual accommodation was confined within narrow limits. And yet Macau itself did not belong purely to either world—it existed simultaneously on the cultural periphery of both, like a threshold joining two very different rooms.

three

Memories
The Architecture of History

Sometimes different cities follow one another on the same site and under the same name, born and dying without knowing one another, without communication among themselves. At times even the names of the inhabitants remain the same, and their voices' accent, and also the features of the faces; but the gods who live beneath names and above places have gone off without a word and outsiders have settled in their place. It is pointless to ask whether the new ones are better or worse than the old, since there is no connection between them.[1]

In the quiet refuge of the Old Protestant Cemetery, the sounds of singing birds in the Camões Garden nearby float through the fragrant frangipani trees. There, crowded under the trees inside high, peeling, gray-and-white walls, stones tell the story of another time and another city. Some relate a life tragically cut short:

To the Memory of Captain William Huddart, Commander of the York East Indiaman who after a long and painful Illness which he bore with the utmost fortitude departed this Life in Macau Roads on his passage to England March 29th 1787 Aged 24 years.

Other lives barely touched Macau:

To the memory of Samuel Smith seaman who died by a fall from aloft on board the U.S. Plymouth Macao roads August 26, 1849. This monument is erected by his messmates.

And some who are buried there left their mark on the city—like Robert Morrison, the first Protestant missionary to China, who published a dictionary of the Chinese language—or witnessed the passing of an age—like

George Chinnery, English expatriate painter, who made it his home and sketched its daily life.[2]

Macau is a city of memories—memories of many cities in different times, preserved in its architecture of monuments and stones, in its buildings and walls, in the lines of its streets, and in its gardens and shrines and temples. Its personality as a city changed as its purpose and its people changed. The present city of Macau is thus a composite of many cities, some still existing in substance, others persisting only in memory. Some of these cities of the past remain only in remnants, squeezed and surrounded by the present city. But many of the vestiges of past Macaus have faded entirely, demolished as the living city of Macau grew. Some of the cities have blended so well that they have become virtually indistinguishable from each other and have become one city. Others exist side by side with one another but hardly touch, like parallel cities.

The City of Sojourners and Settlers

Macau's first city was rooted in the commercial orientation of the first Portuguese pioneers and traders. Trade—or the hope for it—brought the

Gravestone, Protestant cemetery in Macau

Portuguese to the China coast. The first to arrive came aboard hired Chinese merchant junks from Malacca, the great entrepôt of trade on the eastern rim of the Indian Ocean captured by Afonso de Albuquerque in 1511.[3] Malacca was the terminus of Chinese trade to the west, and it was there that the Portuguese first encountered the Chinese.

Sailing in May 1513 under the orders of the Portuguese captain of Malacca, Ruy de Buto Patalim, in a junk from Pegu and accompanied by five other junks, Jorge Alvares and two other Portuguese made the first European landfall on the China coast. They erected a *padrão* (a stone monument laying claim to a discovery) from the king of Portugal where they landed on Lintin Island in the Pearl River estuary.[4] Based on information received in Malacca, they expected to find a lucrative trade. Patalim had reported that

> from China come amber, pearls, all kinds of satins and damasks and porcelains, brocades and such things. The rulers of China are tyrants, and they sell in great quantities. Their land is the largest known in these parts. They take from Malacca pepper, and many other kinds of spices that may be found, and grain and gold, and many other things. They know how to trade; from them can be obtained nothing except at the proper value.[5]

The results of several subsequent expeditions bore out these high expectations, although those expeditions were marred somewhat by conflicts with the Chinese authorities.

In China, they tried several locations, including Langbohau (Lampakau) and Shangchuan Island (St. John's) west of Macau, before settling on the barren little peninsula at Macau, which seemed to offer the most convenient access to the Pearl River estuary and the port of Canton.[6] In 1553, their request to rent land there to dry and store their goods was granted by Wang Bo, the provincial assistant commissioner for maritime affairs (*haidao fushi*).[7] By 1557, the town had become formally established, but even before that, a considerable number of foreigners had begun to settle there.

The first city of Macau was hardly a city at all. Rather, it was a temporary settlement clinging to the shore and the security of the hillsides. Its earliest structures were built of ephemeral materials—straw and wood, or "mat-sheds," as chroniclers are fond of calling these first buildings. It was not long, however, before the Portuguese imported wood, tiles, and other building materials, and the settlement began to seem more permanent—much to the chagrin of the Chinese. Larger and more ambitious buildings were going up, their "high-ridged roofs and overhanging rafters crowding together like the teeth of a comb."[8] There were no permanent fortifications at Macau until the early years of the seventeenth century. In the meantime, the town was protected with ships' artillery, crude bulwarks, and artillery batteries mounted on the strategic points.[9]

When the Portuguese first settled the peninsula in the 1550s, it was probably almost deserted. The few Chinese who lived there were clustered in the village of Wangxia, near the base of the peninsula on the north. A few others, mostly fishermen, may have lived in what became the village of Patane on the shore just west of Monte hill, on the small bay on the northeast point of the peninsula, and near the extreme southern tip around the Ama temple. The Portuguese seldom mingled with the Chinese during this period.[10]

If it was the last fortified outpost on the trade route around the world from Lisbon, Macau was not, at first, the endpoint of that trade. For the first century of the city's existence, that position was occupied by Japan. Macau's importance and its prosperity depended on an intricate trading system of which it was only one segment. At the western end of this system was Goa, from which the administration of Portuguese Asia emanated. At the extreme eastern end was Japan. In between were Malacca and Macau. Periodically, perhaps once every two or three years, the Japan voyage set out from Goa. The ships carried cotton cloth from India, especially in demand in the Indies; glassware; silver, both in coins and in ingots; ivory, to be exchanged for other merchandise in China; Spanish velvet and scarlet cloth, to be sold to the Portuguese residents of Macau; and olives, capers, olive oil, and wines of various qualities, all consumed in Macau; and other European wares. At Malacca, the crews traded some of their commodities, including cotton, for pepper, spices, and aromatic woods more suitable for China and Japan. At Macau, the ships would remain for several months, as the crews traded their commodities destined for China at the semiannual trade fairs at Canton and waited for the favorable southwest monsoon, before sailing on to Nagasaki. From Macau, they carried white silk, fine red silk, finished polychrome and embroidered silks, cotton thread, and buckram; white lead, tin, and mercury; porcelain; musk, China root, licorice, and white and black sugar. In Japan, they sold these goods, especially their silks, at great profit for silver bullion, as well as copper, swords, laquerware, and painted screens. On the return leg of the voyage, the process was repeated in reverse. Silver commanded a much higher price in China than in Japan and was used to purchase merchandise for the westward voyage to Goa, some ultimately destined for Europe—white silk, silk damasks and taffetas, and colored, unwoven silk; gold, mercury, and wrought and unwrought brass; fine gold chains and brass bracelets; earthenware and porcelain; musk, China root, camphor, vermillion, and sugar; gilded beds, tables, writing desks; hangings, bed curtains, canopies, and short cloaks—as well as to invest in silk for future sale in Japan.[11]

The round-trip, from Goa to Nagasaki and back, might last three years. In exchanging commodities of local value from point to point across the complex Asian maritime trading system, the Portuguese had discovered the lucrative interport trade that their successors, the Dutch and English, were

洋
舶
圖

Foreign ship (drawing from *Aomen jilue*)

to exploit even more effectively. This trade was far more profitable and efficient than the direct European trade in spices that had originally drawn the Portuguese out to the Indies, and it was to be the basis of Macau's great prosperity. Beginning about 1571, the trade between Manila and Macau, which linked Macau indirectly to the trans-Pacific galleon trade with Spanish America as well, added to the city's wealth.[12]

In the long months and years between visits, Macau waited, abiding as if in suspended animation. When the ships appeared, the city came alive again with a rush of excitement and activity. The supreme authority over the city was held not by a resident official but by the *capitão-mor* (captain-major) of the Japan voyage, and problems that had been deferred for months could at last be settled. Long-awaited letters and precious provisions might arrive from Europe. New visitors, fresh faces, would also arrive—some would stay on and perhaps settle permanently—infusing new excitement and life into the culture of the city. But at first, most were sojourners, like the priests and soldiers who followed the merchants.

The Fortified City

Among the first things the Portuguese did in the course of their expansion and settlement across Asia was to build fortresses. They could retreat to these fortresses in case of attack by enemy forces, an ever-present danger considering the often provocative behavior of the Portuguese captains, whose brutality made them many enemies. The Portuguese also mounted artillery on their fortresses to protect their ships and warehouses.

The Portuguese had refined the art of castle building during the long history of their wars of consolidation and separation from Spain and their reconquest of Portugal from the Moors. Fortresses dot the landscape of Portugal. No town is worth the name without its castle; no commanding height or coastal inlet is left undefended. It was only instinctive for the Portuguese to carry this tradition overseas, where, after all, they were projecting the heritage of the reconquest and their destiny of national greatness.

In Macau, the Portuguese builders sited their fortresses at each end of the Praia Grande, the beach where ships loaded and unloaded, and on the commanding hilltops behind it. At the south end of the Praia was the Bom Parto fort, at the north end the São Francisco fort. On the heights behind the Praia was the Monte fortress, and farther to the north, on the highest peak, the Guia fortress, where a lighthouse would be built in the nineteenth century. At the extreme south end of the peninsula, on the point that protects the entrance to the inner harbor on the opposite side of the peninsula, the São Tiago de Barra fort was built.

In a parallel development, the Chinese walled off the peninsula at the isthmus connecting it to the mainland in 1574.[13] The Chinese at first had resisted the construction of the Portuguese fortifications, which were initially oriented, by and large, to defending the peninsula from attacks from the land.[14] Indeed, the Chinese were suspicious of any permanent construction, especially the churches, which appeared to them (not without justification) to be fortresses since the Jesuits had constructed the first fortresses on Monte hill next to São Paulo Church. Later, fortifications were prompted by a growing concern for attacks from the sea, either by well-organized pirates or by the European enemies of the Portuguese.

The construction of walls and fortifications and other buildings that the Chinese took to be fortifications had, on several occasions, been halted or reversed after Chinese objections were made. In 1605, fear of Dutch attack had prompted the beginning of a wall along Monte hill near the Jesuit College in conjunction with the reconstruction of São Paulo Church, but the work was discontinued. When the Jesuits put up a small building on Ilha Verde in the inner harbor, the Chinese suspected them of fortifying the island; they drove out the occupants and burned down the building. Matteo Ricci, the pioneer of the Jesuit mission in China, called it "a little house"; later, the Jesuits returned to the island and erected more imposing buildings, which the Chinese described as a "monastery, sixty to seventy feet high, having a spacious and hidden interior, unlike anything in China."[15] It was particularly the high walls that offended them. In 1621, they succeeded in forcing the Jesuits to dismantle the structure.[16] In the same year, in response to rumors that a Dutch attack was imminent, the Portuguese "dug some trenches, which the Chinese quickly dismantled, fearing lest that fortification was made against themselves; for they have never consented to wall the city, cast artillery, or make other preparations for war."[17] They did manage to persuade the Spanish in Manila to give them six pieces of artillery for defense. But after the Dutch attack actually came in 1622, the Chinese ceased their opposition to the building of fortifications, and a frenzy of ambitious construction ensued through the next decade. It was then that most of the early fortresses and walls assumed the forms that would remain for the next three centuries, until modifications and additions were made in the late 1800s. The fortresses were greatly improved and walls were constructed along the northern and southern sides of the city between the existing hilltop forts. The northern wall ran from the garden surrounding Camões's grotto up to the Monte fort, down the other side and up the hill below the Guia fort, then down to the São Francisco fort on the point at the northern end of the Praia Grande. This wall had two gates, Santo Antonio gate near the garden and São Francisco gate between Monte hill and Guia hill.[18] Only partially closing off the southern end of the city, the other wall descended from the top of Penha hill to the Bom Parto fort at the southern end of the Praia Grande.

Ironically, the forts served little further practical purpose, at least for military defense, after this time and certainly after the instability surrounding the collapse of the Ming and the Qing conquest ended by midcentury. The batteries on the forts were used mainly to salute visiting Chinese and other foreign officials, a ceremony that never failed to please the Chinese.[19] Otherwise, the walls actually did more to serve the Chinese interest in containing and isolating the foreigners and preventing their ingress to China than to serve the Portuguese interest in defense. Together with the barrier gate guarding the isthmus, they became the symbol of the city's isolation on the coastal fringe of the great empire to which it clung and sharply demarcated the separation between the two worlds.

The result was often viewed with a mixture of alarm and contempt by European visitors, who thus betrayed their ethnocentrism as much as any realistic assessment of their position. One visitor observed:

> Beyond the Barrier there appears to be a piece of neutral ground. The distinction between occidentalism and orientalism; between civilisation and barbarism; between the European and the Asiatic is noticeable at once; for the well-made Portuguese road is at once changed for the wretched little foot-path, meandering hither and thither, ragged and uneven, never properly made, unkept and uncared for, running through a perfect necropolis of poorer graves.[20]

View of Macau, including Monte fort (engraving ca. 1835)

But however much Macau might be regarded by Europeans as the triumphant outpost of worldwide European hegemony, for the Chinese it was situated on the remote and undeveloped frontier of their civilized world.

The granite forming the hills of Macau and the nearby islands provided an abundant supply of stone to build the fortresses' foundations. Walls were constructed on these using a material called *chunambo* or *taipa*. A mixture of earth, straw, and lime derived from oyster shells was layered with reinforcing wooden strips and compressed by pounding. The material acquired extraordinary strength and resiliency, such that it was superior to stone walls: Stone would crack and crumble under bombardment, whereas taipa walls would absorb the shots.[21] This material was also used for large public buildings such as churches and for houses. The exterior of the walls was usually finished with a smooth plaster.

Built of such enduring stuff and on sites that were otherwise useless, these fortifications or their later modifications and improvements still remain, albeit in remnants. This early city of the late sixteenth and early seventeenth centuries was actually a fortified commercial trading base. Its population was mostly Portuguese, encompassing as many as 900 soldiers and traders and some Jesuit missionaries. Few, if any, brought their families to such a remote and dangerous place. The work of building, as elsewhere in Portuguese Asia, was done mainly by African slaves, but Southeast Asians—Malays—from Malacca and the Indies came with them, particularly Malaccan women.[22] They were to be the progenitors of the Macanese people of the next century.

The second city of Macau was a city of soldiers. The Portuguese were militant but defensive (for they were very few in number, then and later), and Macau was the last of a string of fortified bases leading all the way from Moçambique on the African coast, across the Arabian Sea and the Indian Ocean, through the Straits of Malacca, and on to Japan.

The City of the Name of God in China

The third city of Macau grew with the settlement of the second, developing between and around the fortresses even as they were being built. The first Jesuits arrived in 1561—and they would prove to be no mean fortress builders themselves. By the end of the century, the great work of the Christian evangelization of Japan was under way, and yet to be opened, the vaster field of China lay before them. Missionaries stopped in Macau on their way to Japan or waited there for the precious permission to enter China. Churches and convents were built, and the Jesuits founded a college to train workers for the Japan field. The establishment of the Santa Casa de Misericordia (the Holy House of Mercy), which ministered to the poor and the sick, was an indication that the population was increasing. Residents no

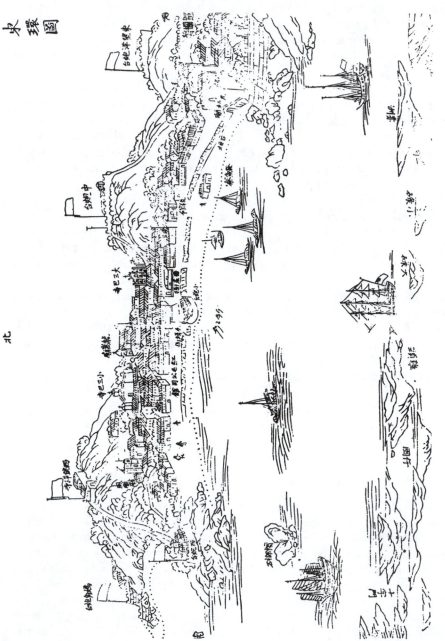

View of Macau from the east (drawing from *Xiangshan xian zhi xinxiu*, 1827)

longer comprised just a few Portuguese and their slaves but also Japanese, Malays, Indians, and a small number of Chinese, in addition to a growing population of mixed Portuguese Asians.

The first Jesuits who would remain in Macau arrived in 1563. At the time, the order had no permanent residence in the city, and the priests lived and worked temporarily in a house provided by a wealthy Portuguese benefactor. Two years later, they built a small "matshed" chapel, but it soon burned down. Local residents helped them build a more substantial residence and chapel, constructed of wood with a tile roof, that served as a hostel for Jesuits passing through on the way to and from Japan.[23] In the next few years, they opened a school next to the residence, presumably to teach the growing number of children from mixed unions of Portuguese and Asians. By 1584, the school enrolled two hundred pupils.

The growth of the Jesuits' activities soon required more extensive facilities. Between 1573 and 1579, larger buildings and a church were constructed of taipa and wood. The residence, with spacious corridors and fifteen rooms, was large enough to house twelve priests. The expanding Jesuit establishment was located between the Monte hill, on which the Jesuits later built the first fortress, and Camões's grotto. It was here that the Oratorio of St. Martin was built in 1580 by Michele Ruggieri, specifically as a center for Chinese converts and a house where he and later Matteo Ricci could study the Chinese language.[24] But at that time, Japan was the more fertile field, and a place was badly needed for training Japanese converts in a European environment.[25] Thus, an even more ambitious college was planned. Money was donated by the people of Macau and appropriated by the *Senado* (Senate) from the revenue of the silk trade with Japan.

The Jesuit College was opened in 1594. Initially, the curriculum comprised theology, philosophy, and rhetoric. Later, Chinese studies as well as Latin, mathematics, and music were added. The college, which grew to become virtually a university, possessed a printing press and a library of 4,200 volumes. Until its destruction in 1835, the school was one of the great centers of learning in East Asia.[26]

Meanwhile, members of the Dominican order arrived in the late 1580s. They built a monastery and a chapel on the low ground at the foot of Monte hill in the 1590s, the predecessor of the more elaborate São Domingos Church erected a few decades later.[27]

In 1601, the Jesuit church again burned down. Macau was now entering its great age of wealth and cultural glory. The city's commercial expansion was echoed not only by evangelical successes in Japan but also by the opening of the promising China field. While missionaries arrived in a steady stream on their way to Japan or China or for training and study in Macau, converts came from the opposite direction—some to work and study at the college, others to travel on to Europe. New, more permanent and substantial buildings reflected the city's prosperity and hopes. A more magnificent church was planned to express the optimism of the evangelical mission.

The cornerstone of the new church of São Paulo was laid in 1602. Its inscription testified that its cost was underwritten by the city of Macau.[28] Indeed, by 1578, the Jesuits had already entered into an agreement with the merchants of Macau whereby they would receive a fixed share of the profits from the Japan trade, thus solving the difficult problem of financing their expanding mission.[29] The church was completed in time for an opening mass on Christmas Eve in 1603. Constructed of taipa and great wooden pillars, with three stone arches and a vaulted roof, the building was more than 60 feet wide and 120 feet long, its walls almost 40 feet high.[30] The arched ceiling was divided into square panels carved in wood, joined by large rose designs of many leaves in deep relief, lavishly gilded and painted in vermillion and blue.[31] On the altar, according to a Chinese description, was "the one they call the Mother of Heaven. Her name is Maria, and she holds an infant called the Lord of Heaven, who is Jesus. She wears curious clothes and a veil made of glass beads; her hair appears life-like."[32]

Construction of the immense stone facade was begun somewhat later than the main building itself and was not completed until the 1630s. It has remained, to this day, the most magnificent relic of that age—the singular monument to the city's glory days and its most enduring symbol. More than any other structure, it reflects, in the Asian embellishments wrought by Chinese and Japanese craftsmen on its Christian themes, the peculiar eclecticism that characterized Macau's culture and society.[33]

A broad flight of stone steps leads up to the front of the church. The facade rises in four tiers supported by ten stone columns of varying types and capped by pediments, above which the central four columns project in the form of obelisks. The first tier (at ground level), largely undecorated, contains the main door to the church in the center and secondary doorways on each side. Above the main entrance is the legend "Mater Dei." The second tier has three openings above the doors, which may have held windows. Between the openings and the ends of the tier are niches holding the statues of four saints of the Jesuit order, including Ignatius Loyola and Francis Xavier in the center positions. The central opening was reported to have once enclosed a female figure representing the Queen of Heaven standing on a globe.[34]

In the central niche of the third tier, above, is a bronze statue of the Virgin Mary surrounded by six angels and, between the columns, the Tree of Life and the Fountain of Life. To the left and right of these, in turn, are depictions of a dragon being trampled by the Virgin and a Portuguese nau in full sail, watched over by the Virgin. Further to the left and right where the tier slopes downward to follow the line of the roof are reclining figures: a skeleton pierced by arrows, with the inscription in Chinese, "He who remembers

Facade of São Paulo Church

death shall be without sin," and the devil shot with an arrow, with the inscription in Chinese, "It is the Devil who entices man to evil."

In the center of the fourth tier, having six pillars, is a statue of Jesus surrounded by panels depicting the instruments of the crucifixion. On either side are angels holding the cross and the scourging pillar. Finally, surmounting the last tier, is the pediment. In its center is a bronze dove with outstretched wings, surrounded by the sun and the moon.[35]

There, on the great church's facade, is the entire narrative of the Christian message brought to Asia by the Jesuits, beginning with the cosmos and the symbol of peace and descending through the crucifixion, the Virgin Mary, and the saints of the Jesuit order, who, along with the Portuguese discoverers and their nau, were the instruments of its transmission.

Probably at about the same time that the São Paulo Church was erected or soon after, the new São Domingos Church was being completed. The design of its facade echoes that of the Jesuit church, though it is much simpler, with eight columns rising through three tiers, capped by a pediment, and finely decorated but without the visual narrative of São Paulo's.

The third city of Macau, then, was a city of priests, missionaries, and scholars, of ideas and expectations, some fulfilled, some disappointed.

The Cosmopolitan City

The early seventeenth century was Macau's golden age. Trade brought wealth to the city, and the city grew. Warehouses, customhouses, and facilities for ships were built—and, of course, religious and government institutions flourished. Since Macau's establishment had resulted largely from the initiative of local Portuguese traders from Malacca rather than from any grand strategic design emanating from Goa or Lisbon, merchants dominated the local affairs of the settlement from the beginning and were to shape its character for the next century or more.[36]

In 1582, prompted by the recent union of the crowns of Spain and Portugal, the principal citizens came together to form an elected governing body, the *Senado da Camara*. They also chose judges, a secretary of the Senado, and a *procurador*, the chief civil officer of the city and representative of its government to the Chinese authorities, who recognized his authority.[37] (The military command of the settlement and of its forts continued to be exercised by the captain-major of the Japan voyage or by a governor after 1623.)[38] The Senado derived its revenue almost entirely from duties levied on trade. It not only governed the trade of Macau but also financed its military defense as well as its various institutions and charitable activities.[39]

The most important of these institutions was the Santa Casa de Misericordia, the Holy House of Mercy. The Santa Casa in Macau was founded in 1569 as a branch of an ecclesiastical institution that was ubiquitous throughout the Portuguese empire overseas. But a close reciprocal relationship always existed between it and the Senado (the latter supported the Santa Casa but sometimes raided its treasury), and the respective buildings of the two stood adjacent to one another at the center of the city.[40]

Now at its zenith, Macau enjoyed a reputation for prosperity and elegance unrivaled in Portuguese Asia.[41] The wealth of the city's inhabitants was reflected in the enthusiastic new architecture. A construction boom was under way, and the growing population of Portuguese and Portuguese Asian traders and merchants built fine residences above the Praia Grande and the inner harbor and against the hills. Houses had two or three stories, with spacious rooms and deep verandas. The dark ground floors, enclosed by heavy masonry arches, were used for storing merchandise and supplies and as living quarters for servants and slaves. The exteriors of the buildings were generally finished in white stucco at first, but the exuberant affluence of their builders was expressed in a profusion of elaborate forms and styles. The Chinese, accustomed to the understated exterior appearances of private and most public buildings, marveled at the variety of shapes: "They are square, round, triangular, hexagonal, octagonal, angular, flower shaped, no two of them identical, rivalling each other in artfulness and elegance."[42] But the population of poor was also growing, and squalid *barrios* undoubtedly huddled against the walls of the city.

If the Monte fort was the symbol of Portugal's militant expansion overseas and if São Paulo Church was the symbol of the ecclesiastical mission in Asia, the Senado was the symbol of the commercial activity that sustained the others. Without commerce, expansion and evangelism would not have been possible. Yet although the architecture of fortresses and churches left its enduring, if forlorn, mark on the city, little trace remains of the early architecture of commerce—the present Santa Casa and Senado buildings are constructions of a very different age in the late nineteenth century.

Macau's commercial prosperity was fragile, depending on a scheme of things that could not last forever. The Portuguese monopoly of the wealth in

View of the Praia Grande from the north (engraving ca. 1835)

Asian trade aroused the envy of other European nations, and by the early seventeenth century, the Dutch and English were chipping away at Portuguese power in the Indies. And in Japan, political changes and the very success of the missionary enterprise portended disaster for the trade. In 1641, the Dutch captured Malacca, breaking the Portuguese chain of trading posts. But the end of the era had actually been sealed three years before when the Portuguese were evicted from Japan. By 1640, Japan's seclusion had become all but complete, and the most important segment of Macau's trade was cut off. In that same year, Portugal, after sixty years of union under the Spanish crown, reasserted its independence. Virtually in one blow, the Japan trade came to an end; Malacca, the commercial entrepôt for the Southeast Asia and India trade, was lost; and the lucrative trade with Manila and through Manila with Spanish America collapsed.[43] In the very midst of Macau's brilliant affluence, the trade that had sustained it now languished:

> Whosoever considers how this city of Macao fell from the peak and summit of its prosperity and ease, will find that it was the turn of Fate's wheel which upset and reversed it; the present poverty being all the greater because whilst it contains so many valuable diamonds, rubies, pearls, seed-pearls, gold, silk and musk, it is as if there were none, since the inhabitants of China care nothing for such precious things but prize only silver, which is today precisely what we lack, after suffering such heavy and grievous losses, so that we are living proof of the fable of Midas, who died of very hunger at a table of golden dishes. Such is happening to us now, for having our tables replete with gold, silks, diamonds, rubies, pearls and seed-pearls, we are dying by inches.[44]

Hard times settled on the city like a cloud. Money was short, the government impoverished, and the population cantankerous and rebellious. In 1647, the governor was assassinated by the mutinous citizens.[45] Plague, spread by the civil war that erupted after the Manchu conquest of the south, carried off seven thousand people in the city.[46] Visits were now less regular and less frequent. The Dutch were everywhere; their warships preyed on Portuguese shipping, making communication with the outside world, on which Macau's affluent life and cosmopolitan culture depended, all the more tenuous. Those who did visit were more likely to stay on and settle down; they were no longer the glamorous captains and soldiers of the former era. Newcomers included wealthy crypto-Jews or recent European Christian converts from Judaism—*christãos-novos*—fleeing the Inquisition to the most distant refuge they could find.[47]

Early in the seventeenth century, affluent Portuguese families and some Portuguese Asians from India were still a minority among a population of several thousand. Matteo Ricci mentioned intermarriage between Portuguese and Chinese merchant families, but intermarriage generally with the Chinese seems to have been uncommon then.[48]

View of the Praia Grande from the south (engraving ca. 1835)

The population of the city was never very stable; although its European component may have fallen abruptly following the catastrophic midcentury changes, refugees from China (fleeing the upheavals attendant on the Manchu conquest of the mainland that was occurring at the same time) temporarily inflated the population.[49] By the end of the seventeenth century, although there were many fewer pure Portuguese families than formerly, there was also a large population of Christian Eurasians and Chinese, estimated to be as many as 20,000, largely female.[50] The population subsequently declined again, falling to perhaps several thousand Portuguese and Portuguese Eurasians (excluding Chinese) by the late eighteenth century, but intermarriage with the Chinese had become commonplace.[51] A native population of Macanese—a mixture of European Portuguese, Portuguese Asians, and Chinese—had emerged.[52] These were the *casados*, married settlers who formed a resident private merchant class that dominated Macau from the later seventeenth century and was responsible for the city's survival.[53]

So as Macau languished through the remaining decades of the seventeenth century and into the next, its complexion changed. In the more sedate and settled routine of tropical life, no longer periodically excited by intrusions from Europe, a new cultural pattern emerged. It was a mixture of elements, native and exotic, that were previously undigested. The crisis of the mid-seventeenth century had a profound effect. For the first time, the people of

Macau became aware of their cultural isolation. The Macanese had begun to acquire a distinct character and identity as a permanent population, some- times strongly and even fiercely expressed.[54] From the early interaction and marriage between Macanese and Indians, Malays, and Japanese, a peculiar Macanese dialect came into use.

The uncompromisingly European and rather neoclassical architectural fashion of the early seventeenth century now gave way to a less ambitious and less pretentious local style. In the sixteenth and early seventeenth cen- turies, mutual influences between Portuguese European and Chinese styles had been slight; they were confined mainly to Oriental influences on the su- perficial decoration of churches, the facade of São Paulo being a case in point. But now, an architectural adaptation to permanent life in the Tropics had emerged. Mutual influences went beyond mere decoration and the use of local construction materials like taipa in the design of buildings. These adaptations were most evident in the houses of the native-born Macanese and the Chinese residents—large, roomy homes built in Chinese style around a spacious central court with airy second floors and tall, shuttered European windows and doors that were shut up at night but opened in the morning to admit cooling breezes. The walls of such houses were constructed of masonry or taipa, and, with rows of wooden columns around the central court, they supported the heavy-beamed, pitched roof. In Chinese fashion, the wall sur- rounding the main entrance was often recessed and the area under the eaves profusely decorated with carvings, painting, or porcelain figures. From the outside, there might be little else of interest about these buildings, unless a veranda or balcony of European design was added. But inside, they were richly decorated in a medley of Chinese and Western features: carved and painted columns and beams, ornate iron railings, patterned board ceilings, shrines, and lanterns.[55]

It became customary to paint the exteriors of private residences and many public buildings in bright shades of yellow, green, pink, and blue. In the humid, tropical climate, these colors soon became faded and stained by mildew and rain. Though the buildings were often freshened with new coats of paint, the constant weathering produced an endless variation of muted pastel shades that lent to the city a look of perpetual somnolence and decay yet—all the more so for these reasons—a gracious and relaxed ambience that perfectly reflected the lethargic condition of its commerce through the cen- turies after the collapse of prosperity in the 1640s.

Yet Macau was still largely European. Indians, Malays, and Japanese all had been absorbed by the resident population. Other Europeans, especially the English after they became permanently established in the Canton trade from 1699, also lived there as distinct and separate groups. The Chinese ele- ment was still subordinate, restricted from permanent settlement as much by Chinese as by Portuguese regulations.[56]

Windows and balconies

Macau's fourth city had evolved from a community of European pioneers, missionaries, and soldiers, looking toward worlds beyond, to a Eurasian city, living for the present but waiting in expectation for the return of its greatness. But, though the English East India Company and other European trading companies located their main headquarters and seasonal residences along the Praia Grande (since they were not permitted by the Chinese to take permanent residence in Canton), it was Canton that had become the focus and concourse of European trade in China by the middle of the eighteenth century.

The Chinese City

Curiously, the increasing Macanese character of Macau tied it ever more strongly to Portugal, in its own special way. Its citizens were proud of their heritage and their autonomy at one and the same time; the city's motto expressed this pride: "The City of the Name of God in China. No Other More Loyal."

Yet, in some ways, Macau could not properly be called a city. It was certainly not a city in the Chinese sense, like Canton or even the district capital of Xiangshan to the north. It did have walls, which usually distinguished any Chinese city that deserved the name, but they were the irregular fortifications of a Portuguese trading base, not walls built according to the regular plan of a Chinese administrative center, the location of a *yamen* (the mandarin's office and seat of government). From the Chinese point of view, Macau fell under the jurisdiction of local authorities, rather far down on the administrative ladder.

Nor could Macau in its early phases be classified, strictly speaking, as a European city. In different respects, it was controlled from outside both politically and militarily, by the Portuguese administration emanating from Goa and by the Chinese provincial administration centered in Canton. And before the emergence of a Macanese community in the eighteenth century, the city's residents identified with their places of origin, to which many of them (like the traders and soldiers, if not the missionaries) expected to return someday. Indeed, perhaps in this respect at least, Macau approximated the classical Oriental city. However, a gradual qualitative change took place through the eighteenth century as a sense of permanent community arose and autonomy developed. Macau came to resemble the European medieval city. The leveling tendencies of immigration contributed to this change.[57]

Though so intimately associated with China, Macau had remained a city *in* China, as its motto proclaimed, but not *of* China. At first, Chinese who worked there came in the morning and left at night. Surreptitiously, more and more stayed, especially as servants, but they did so against regulations set by the Chinese authorities. Since 1570, if not earlier, Chinese Christian converts, as well as the far more numerous Japanese Christians, lived and studied at the Jesuit seminary, and from at least the early seventeenth century, Chinese Christians were serving as official interpreters (*lingua*) for the city administration.[58] But only beyond the walls, in the still largely rural parts of the peninsula around the village of Wangxia, did Chinese life predominate.

Macau's early prosperity and the complex trade that it controlled had pumped up the Chinese economy for a number of years. The importation of silver from Japan and Spanish America and the greatly expanded export of silk could not fail to influence economic development on the mainland, especially in the southern coastal regions.[59] Consequently, the Chinese economy was, in turn, affected by the collapse of the trade system in the 1640s. Already in the advanced stages of a pervasive political crisis, the reigning Ming dynasty, further weakened by a fiscal crisis brought on by the collapse, fell to the invading Manchus in 1644.[60] As the shock wave of the Manchu conquest spread south through the country, the echoes of Macau's own crisis affected the city as well. By its very nature—its geographical separation and its anomalous political situation—Macau was potentially a place of refuge from troubles on the mainland. Now the settlement was overwhelmed by Chinese refugees from the Canton region, temporarily inflating the population to over forty thousand.[61] The influx subsided, but it was to be only the first of numerous movements of Chinese refugees, many of whom would eventually become immigrants.

By the end of the eighteenth century, the separation of Chinese from Macanese began to break down, and Macau was gradually transformed into a more Chinese city. Formally signaling this trend was the granting of permission for permanent Chinese immigration, which began in 1793.[62] Chinese had already begun to settle in the city in significant numbers as brokers, compradors, and interpreters, as well as craftsmen, peddlers, and shopkeepers. Those in the former group at first came largely from Fujian Province on the east central Chinese coast, and those in the latter were mainly natives of Guangdong.[63] From this time on, Chinese from Guangdong and South China became the largest component of the population, which had subsided to perhaps four to five thousand at the end of the eighteenth century.

The influx of Chinese was as much a consequence of long-lasting social and political changes affecting all of China as it was a result of short-term disturbances. Since the late seventeenth century, with the pacification of the Qing empire under the Manchus and the relative domestic peace and prosperity that ensued, the population of China had begun to climb steeply. From perhaps 150 million in the seventeenth century, it tripled to around 450 million by the mid-nineteenth century. At first, rising prosperity and material welfare accommodated this growth, but by the early nineteenth century, severe strains were being felt. Internal migration was triggered by pressure on the land. And with these disrupting movements and the slow disintegration of political control, incidents of social upheaval and protest became more frequent. These problems were the result of a syndrome of bureaucratic corruption and atrophy, fiscal deficiencies, military decline and weakness, and a decrease even in the vigor and competence of the imperial dynasty itself. The expansion of Western commerce through Canton and rising pressures from Western powers, especially Great Britain, for greater access to the China market complicated these problems.

South China particularly was affected by the rising population and its attendant crises, though no region escaped the related effects. In 1793, the year in which Chinese immigration to Macau was first permitted, the White Lotus Rebellion broke out in the north. It took more than ten years to suppress this rebellion, and it would prove to be a harbinger of both greater and lesser disturbances to come. In 1850, the Taiping Rebellion erupted in the volatile social climate of South China west of Canton and went on to engulf most of China. The upheaval generated great movements of people and refugees hoping to escape the troubles. But the prolonged process of disintegration did not stop there. Fifty years later, the accelerating collapse of the imperial order reached its climax with the Revolution of 1911. Its leader, Sun Yat-sen, was a native of Xiangshan, the administrative district to which Macau belonged, and he had spent part of his early career in Macau practicing medicine. Revolutionary upheaval and civil war continued through the early twentieth century, interrupted only by the more catastrophic Japanese invasion of the mainland beginning in 1937. Hong Kong was occupied in 1941; Macau was spared only because it was the possession of a neutral nation.

Macau could not be unaffected by these events. The successive waves they generated washed over the city, which became a place of refuge for Europeans and, above all, for Chinese. By the early nineteenth century, the new Chinese immigrants were clustering around the village of Wangxia and settling in the still mainly rural lowland (*Campo*) between Monte hill and the village of Patane north of Monte. They crowded into the areas behind the waterfront of the inner harbor and along the Praia Manduco below Penha hill, forming new Chinese districts. With their narrow lanes and alleys running in confusing, zigzag patterns and their densely packed houses and shops, these areas contrasted with the more open and spacious character of the older districts laid out in tidy European order.

Population growth brought with it a new set of problems for the settlement. Instances of crime and unrest rose in the overcrowded districts; where fragile, temporary matsheds huddled against the walls of the older buildings, fires became common; and friction between Portuguese and Chinese or other immigrants sometimes turned into serious disturbances. The widening gap between the wealthy entrepreneurs and traders and the destitute refugees looking for another chance—or any chance—to improve their lot, by legal or illegal means, aggravated the conditions.

In December 1838, a band of thieves disguised as policemen broke into the house of a wealthy Chinese merchant from Singapore, claiming they were looking for illegal opium. In reality, they were seeking a large quantity of cash that the merchant, Tsae Tsanglang, was rumored to have received shortly before in a business transaction. Terrified, Tsae hid as the thieves violently ransacked the house, taking whatever of value they found. Finally, fearing that he would be discovered, Tsae leaped from a window, sustaining serious injuries from which he soon died. Many years before, Tsae's father had gone from Fujian to Singapore, where he had built up a successful

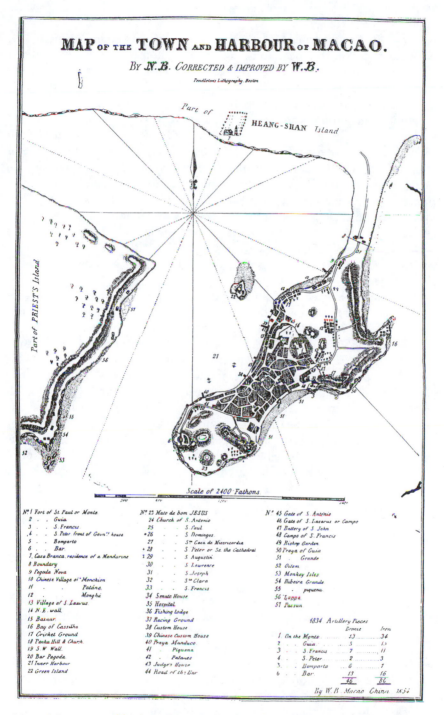

Map of the town and harbor of Macau (from Anders Ljungstedt, *An Historical Sketch of the Portuguese Settlements in China*, 1836)

business. Having inherited his father's estate and improved his business, Tsae had recently come to Macau to be closer to his homeland for the benefit of his children. After he died, authorities questioned some suspects, but the case went unsolved.[64]

One of the strangest cases was the unsolved death of Thomas Beale, a longtime resident of Macau, in 1841. On the evening of December 10, he had set out on his customary walk along the Praia Grande and across the Campo toward the barrier gate. He was last seen on the path near the village of Wangxia, and all efforts to locate him were unavailing. Not until January 13, one month later, did some Portuguese boys report the discovery of a body partly buried in the sand at the north end of the beach at Casilhas Bay, just east of Wangxia. They had first found the body on January 2 and saw it again ten days later, but they did not report it until the next day. An investigation by the Portuguese authorities and the English identified the body as Beale's but found no evidence of violence. Beale was buried the next day in the English cemetery.[65]

The ships had always brought an odd assortment of people to Macau. Besides expatriates like Thomas Beale, there were adventurers, fortune seekers, and rough-and-ready sailors just released from the confinement of weeks or months at sea. Some of them were desperate men for whom Macau was the end of the line. In 1840, a black sailor was shot to death after becoming involved in a disturbance with some Chinese near the Praia Manduco. He had been living in a boardinghouse in the district for some time after being left behind by his ship, the American brig *Duan*. A large, violent man, he had single-handedly overcome the captain and crew in a mutiny and was imprisoned briefly by the governor after the ship arrived at Macau. On the evening of September 9, he was seized by a patrol near Penha hill when he fell into a dispute with some Chinese; he was being escorted to prison when he escaped. After being chased down to the Praia Manduco, where he tried to fend off his pursuers, he was shot by someone in the street.[66]

Minor instances of friction between foreigners, the Chinese residents, and the authorities were not unusual, and confrontations could sometimes take a serious turn. In September 1843, some Portuguese troops responding to a fire outside the Santo Antonio gate were attacked by the people living in the poor sheds that had been built against the wall there. When a soldier was mortally wounded, a guard opened fire on the attackers, killing three Chinese and wounding several others. Macau was then crowded with refugees from the Opium War, which had ended only the year before, and although neither the refugees nor the Portuguese had been directly involved in the conflict, tensions ran high between the Chinese (who felt the sting of humiliating defeat) and the foreign soldiers. Then, on October 1, another Chinese was killed in a disturbance arising from an attempt by a Chinese individual to pick a soldier's pocket, and two days later, a Portuguese soldier was found murdered.[67]

Although such clashes were to become less frequent as many refugees gradually filtered back to their homes on the mainland, the potential for such unrest remained as Macau's growing number of settled Chinese inhabitants adjusted to the city's exotic cultural diversity and played an increasingly significant part in the economic life of the port.

The most serious disturbance began on October 8, 1846, and it would have lasting consequences for Portuguese authority that would not become apparent until much later. The government had passed a resolution to impose a monthly tax on all fishermen and operators of "fast-boats," light Chinese craft used to ferry goods and people between the city and Canton, Hong Kong, and the surrounding islands. When the Chinese forcefully resisted the new tax, some were detained, and in protest against this act, the Chinese merchants closed the markets and shops. The fast-boatmen, determined to have a showdown, began to fire on the customhouse in the inner harbor with a small artillery piece. The Portuguese batteries, aided by armed private English ships placed temporarily under the Portuguese flag, reacted quickly and ruthlessly, destroying all of the fast-boats, killing eight or ten Chinese, and wounding many others. The Chinese began to realize the foolhardiness of the confrontation they had provoked and sought to negotiate. In the interim, Governor Ferreira do Amaral issued an ultimatum proclaiming that all Chinese who wished to leave the settlement might do so and declaring that all the shops and the market would be destroyed in twenty-four hours if they were not promptly opened. The Chinese immediately capitulated, but much rancor remained.[68] Three years later, on August 22, 1849, while riding near the barrier gate, Governor Amaral was assassinated, his head cut off by a band of Chinese who escaped across the barrier into Chinese territory.[69] The estrangement that these incidents fostered between the European and Chinese residents of Macau was perhaps never entirely erased.

So the cultural complexion of Macau changed as the demographic and economic forces pressing on it gradually took their toll. The evolution of the Macau patois, never static, registered the progression of these changing patterns. The infusion of Indian, Malay, and Chinese linguistic elements into Portuguese had produced a peculiar Macanese dialect from the beginning. Now the influence of the Chinese language, as well as Spanish (via Manila) and English, increasingly predominated, corrupting beyond recognition the original pure Portuguese that was still spoken by those newly arriving from Lisbon.[70]

Of course, the people, language, and architecture of the settlement had always exhibited traces of the many cultural influences that passed through Macau. Now, as the city became more Chinese, it became less European in appearance as well.

The architectural styles of the new Chinese districts reflected the prevalent patterns of South China far more than any European or Portuguese tradition. Unlike the immigrants during the slower, earlier growth of the city, the new immigrants came in numbers too large and remained too distinct to be much affected by the European styles of Macau. Houses built by the Chinese were very different from the large, often detached residences of the Eurasian Macanese and Europeans, with their large windows, shutters, balconies, and spacious interiors. The Chinese houses abutted each other and were joined end to end; they often were taller than they were wide and ran back from the lanes in series of dark rooms. The facades of these buildings were generally plain, though they might be decorated under the eaves with murals following the fashion of South China. Often, only the upper story had small windows, and a single doorway in a recess at the center was the only opening on the ground floor. The doorway to domestic residences would have a sliding frame of large, horizontal wooden bars that could be drawn across the opening to prevent entry but still allow fresh air to circulate within. Behind it were solid wooden doors that were closed at night or in cold weather. The defensive character of these buildings was also a reflection of the growing crime in the city.

Although some kind of bazaar or central market probably existed from fairly early times, individual shops did not make their appearance until the Chinese came to settle in large numbers, bringing with them greatly expanded commercial activity, in the early nineteenth century.[71] Shopkeepers tended to gravitate to commercial districts along the waterfronts or to the area around the central market. The design of their shops followed the style of South China also, with upper floors extending over the lower floors to form a covered sidewalk below where goods could be displayed regardless of the weather. The entire front of the shop could often be opened up by removing wooden shutters that were replaced at night. Usually, the proprietor and his family lived above the shop.

The Chinese brought with them their religion and their temples. Only a few of the larger temples date from an earlier time—the Lianfeng temple facing the isthmus below Wangxia hill, the Guan Yin temple in Wangxia village, and, of course, the Ama temple on the Barra point. But as the Chinese population expanded, new temples were constructed: One can discern from their locations where the centers of the Chinese districts were situated. Their size and number reflect the wealth and aspirations of the Chinese commercial class that subscribed to their building and maintenance. At the same time, in every street or subdistrict, small temples and shrines to the city god and the local earth god were built and maintained by the neighborhoods. Temples not only functioned as religious institutions but also served secular purposes. Like their Portuguese Catholic counterparts, the churches, they were centers of charitable activities in the Chinese community, but they were also the social and political focus of their respective districts and neighborhoods.

Portuguese and European influences were waning in other, hardly less tangible ways. The presence of the Jesuits and other Catholic orders had

Houses in Chinese area

been evident in Macau since its founding, visible in their churches, schools, charitable foundations, and seminaries. But the Catholic presence largely depended on circumstances that were essentially external to Macau itself—a favorable religious and political climate in Europe that nurtured the missionary spirit, on the one hand, and the stirring prospect of the realization of the evangelical dream in Asia, on the other. Macau was positioned just at the point where this dream and its practical prospects for success converged. But many of these prospects were shattered by the sectarian bickering during the Rites Controversy among the Catholic orders in the early eighteenth century. The resolution of the controversy at the Jesuits' expense in 1742 fostered Chinese hostility toward the evangelical orders and ultimately led to the withdrawal of those orders from the China field from which they had expected so much. In any case, the religious climate in Europe had also become more hostile, and less than a century later, in 1835, the orders, including the Jesuits, were suppressed in Macau.

No sharp line divided one era from the next. The waning Catholic hope was, after all, almost immediately replaced by the surging Protestant missionary movement. But if any one event put its seal on the changes in this period, it was the burning of São Paulo Church in January 1835.

> At about half past six P.M., on the 29th ultimo, the discharge of cannon from the fort above St. Paul's (Macao), gave the alarm of fire. The signal was quickly answered by guns from other forts, by ringing of church bells, and the beating of drums. The principal authorities, with the troops and many of the inhabitants of Macao, were soon in motion. But, except to those who were near the Church, it was for some moments doubtful what building was on fire;—the state of the atmosphere at the time being such that the smoke could not ascend, but driven by a light breeze from the north-west, it enveloped the whole eastern part of the town. It was not long, however, before the flames, bursting through the roofs, left no doubt about the point from whence they issued. All the apartments which constituted the left wing of the church, which were formerly occupied by priests, but recently by the Portuguese troops, were soon on fire. For a while, some hope was entertained that the main part of the church, the chapel, might be saved. But before eight o'clock, the fire reached the highest part of the building and also the vestry in the rear of the great altar. Dense smoke mixed with flames soon burst from the windows on all sides, and then rising through the roof presented a sight awfully grand. The flames rose very high, and the whole town and Inner Harbor were illuminated. Just at that moment the clock (which was presented to the church by Louis XIV) struck eight and a quarter. Hitherto, efforts had been made to check the progress of the flames; but now, when it was quite evident that they would not extend beyond the buildings of the Church, every one seemed willing to stop and gaze at the scene. . . . The whole is now a heap of ruins.[72]

The church was never rebuilt. Only the stone facade remained, left to stand, like a tombstone, as a memorial to one of the great forces that gave birth to the city.

The permanent Chinese population was now around 30,000 and growing, vastly exceeding the more stable Portuguese and European population of perhaps 5,000.[73]

Parallel Cities

While the flood of immigrants from China was transforming the city almost beyond recognition, another kind of force, with equally momentous consequences, was arriving from the other direction. From about the 1760s, the Western trade at Canton became firmly established under the domination of the British East India Company. The open and legal side of the trade was the export of Chinese tea to the burgeoning market in England, the rest of Europe, and the United States. To offset the ever increasing investment in tea, a variety of commodities were imported, though the only one that commanded a steady sale with the Chinese was Indian cotton. Nevertheless, the value of these commodities was never sufficient to make up for the tea investment since there was nothing that the Chinese consumed in sufficient quantity that they did not already supply themselves. But gradually, by the end of the century, the opium trade from India developed as a solution to the predicament of the tea investment. Opium was prohibited by Chinese edict, but with the connivance of Chinese merchants and officials, the demand for it grew by leaps and bounds and exceeded the value of the tea trade after the early years of the nineteenth century.[74] The opium trade attracted an influx of "country" ships and merchants—those operating exclusively between Canton and India or other Asian ports—especially after 1834, when the East India Company lost its monopoly of the China trade. Yet the entire trade was carried on within a highly restrictive and stereotyped system that prohibited Europeans from establishing permanent residences at Canton and did not permit their families to go up to the "factories" (the trading establishments) there.

Thus, Macau assumed a new importance as the permanent residence of foreign traders of all nationalities between the trading seasons when they went up to Canton and the headquarters of agencies and trading enterprises. Additionally, the Portuguese carried on direct trade, including opium trading, from Macau. Missionaries and other foreigners only peripherally associated with the trade also made Macau their home. For some, it was their final resting place. Most of the non-Portuguese foreigners were Protestants— merchants and missionaries from England, northern Europe, and the United States. Not infrequently, they died there from the rigors of the tropical climate or the hazards of the long sea voyage. Some found a contented life in Macau: Robert Morrison died after a peaceful career in missionary work and scholarship, and George Chinnery, the English expatriate painter, made Macau his home after escaping a troubled life elsewhere. Still others suffered from accidents in the busy Macau harbor. The Portuguese begrudgingly allowed the Protestants to establish a small cemetery next to the East India Company residence.

The influx of the secular, Western international population of traders and expatriates and the minor flood of Protestant missionaries, possessing a new self-confidence in their own missions (both commercial and evangelical), brought influences that were less compromising and adaptive than prior influences. The newcomers regarded the old Portuguese Jesuit presence with thinly disguised contempt, and the priests, in turn, treated the new missionaries with hostility. The two groups warily kept each other at arm's length.[75]

Harriet Low, a young American woman who accompanied her uncle and his wife to Macau in the 1830s, expressed a strong Yankee intolerance for the Catholics and had a hard time accepting even the religious attitudes of her fellow English Protestants; she and those in the social circle in which she moved seemed to have very little to do with the Portuguese.[76] And the new Protestant missionaries and traders harbored a deep-seated suspicion of the Chinese as well, born out of the increasing resistance they encountered both to their rising commercial power and to their evangelical message.

It was not long before there was an increased demand for space in the new Protestant cemetery. The conflict over the narrowly restrictive Canton trading system and the illegal importation of opium came to a head in 1839 when the Chinese stopped the trade and confiscated and destroyed the opium that had been in Western hands. The British, long searching for a way to overthrow the system and open China to wider access for commerce, resorted to war. Macau became a refuge for Europeans caught in the midst of the hostilities, and casualties among the officers and gentlemen of the British forces were buried in the Protestant cemetery.

When the Opium War ended in 1842 with China's defeat, the British victors were determined to acquire a permanent place of their own on the China coast where they would not be dependent on Portuguese goodwill and Chinese restrictions. Hong Kong, an excellent anchorage taken over

The waterfront of the inner harbor of Macau

during the hostilities as a base for British warships, filled the bill and was ceded to the British by the Chinese in the Treaty of Nanking, which settled the war.

Not to be outdone by the British and while the Chinese were prostrate and in no position to resist any longer, the Portuguese demanded autonomous status for Macau. In 1845, the city was declared a free port, and the duties formerly paid to the Chinese were abolished. By the 1880s, following a prolonged series of negotiations, Macau was recognized as a colony under perpetual Portuguese occupation.

Hong Kong, with its deep, well-protected harbor, soon surpassed Macau as a commercial port. In any case, Macau's harbor in the muddy estuary of the Pearl River had been gradually silting up and was no longer suitable for large ships. So Macau, once an active and important place, became a mere backwater.[77]

Though Macau never resumed its former commercial importance, it was now a mature city with a mixed population of Portuguese, Macanese, Chinese, and expatriate Europeans. And as a city of some size and a colony, it required architectural expression in a suitable administrative style. This was the heyday of imperialism, when the assertion of European cultural hegemony was rampant everywhere, and classical revivalism in architecture evoked a new enthusiasm for empire. Ironically, beneath this self-confidence lay a growing sense of insecurity.[78] Thus, Macau, now that its days of glory were past, embarked on the construction of some of its most imposing public and private buildings.[79] The Leal Senado, headquarters of the city government, faced what became the central square of the city; the government palace and the governor's residence, beginning as private residences on the Praia Grande, became the seat of colonial administration. Around the slopes of Penha and Guia hills were the large homes of the city's elite, with wide, shaded verandas and white, columned porches; painted in pastel pinks, greens, blues, and yellows, the houses resembled colorfully decorated cakes with white icing.[80] The styles of these and many other buildings constructed at the time, like the Marine House and the Military Club, were derived wholly from European or Indian models; they owed nothing to Chinese influence.

By the end of the nineteenth century, European and Oriental buildings appeared in a bizarre variety of neoclassical and pseudo-Moorish styles. The cultural eclecticism of an earlier era, exhibited in the Macanese medley in architecture and language, thus gave way to a differentiation between discrete stylistic patterns—Chinese, on one side, and European mixed with Oriental exotic, on the other. Thus, a sort of cultural parallelism emerged; it was particularly evident in the parallel religious institutions of Chinese temples and European churches that evoked such strong impressions among visitors to the city at this time and later.[81]

Zones of distinct architectural styles bear witness to the multiform growth of the city in its mature phase. Extending from the slopes of Penha hill, along the Praia Grande facing the outer harbor as far as Guia hill, and dominating the spine of the peninsula between Penha hill and the Monte fort behind the Praia is the zone of Macanese houses, European public buildings, churches, and schools. There, the buildings are large and often well spaced; there are trees and wide, though irregular, streets, as well as occasional *largos,* or squares. Across the central line running from Penha hill to Monte fort and descending the slopes to the inner harbor on the other side, Western styles give way to Chinese domestic architecture. The buildings there are more closely set or continuous with one another; the streets are narrow, dwindling to tiny lanes and *becos,* or blind alleys. Only along the waterfront of the inner harbor does European influence reassert itself in rows of commercial buildings with arcades, following the pattern of South Chinese cities but embellished with ornate European windows and balconies. This Chinese zone continues into the low commercial district below the slopes on either side of Monte hill toward the inner harbor. A third zone, newer than the other two—described by a more rectilinear pattern of wide streets and avenues planted in rows of trees—lies between Monte and Guia hills on the south and Wangxia on the north. That was the area of the Campo, fields originally separating the walls of the old city from the village of Wangxia. The development there reflects late-nineteenth- and early-twentieth-century European architectural styles and has less of the characteristic Eurasian styles of the older districts.[82] The styles and functions vary greatly, evoking both exotic and indigenous influences: solid row buildings; ornate detached houses with elaborate columns and balustrades, cupolas, and Moorish arches; and early-twentieth-century, bungalow-style residences. Yet it is still true that nowhere in Macau are these zones sharply distinguished from each other; styles interpenetrated, so that every part exhibits surprising variations and distinctive influences brought together in peculiar ways. And here and there, punctuating the city's different zones, are the older monuments—forts and churches—that are reminders of the earlier cities of Macau.

An Anonymous City

Increasingly isolated by the political upheavals of the early twentieth century—revolutions, wars, and invasion—Macau was forced to live by its own wits alone. The cosmopolitan connections that had earlier sustained it, at first through the European colonial trade and later with neocolonial expansion, were broken by the global shifts in the balance of economic and political power brought on by the great anticolonial movements of liberation and world war. Its economy had already suffered devastating blows from the abolition of the coolie trade in 1873 and the destruction wrought

Rua Nova de São Lazaro

by the great typhoon in the following year. Refugees, both European and Chinese, swelled its population and lived by whatever means lay at hand. Now Macau acquired a new, sinister complexion—it became a city of commercialized vice, corruption, and decadence.

Following the establishment of Hong Kong in the mid-nineteenth century, Macau had become a sleepy, pleasant backwater. Its mild climate and its elegant, if somewhat decaying, European houses provided a gracious and comfortable respite for Europeans wearied from the hectic commercial life of Hong Kong and the oppressive climate of Canton.[83] But this image of abandonment had another aspect as well. The relaxed atmosphere of Macau encouraged the growth of vices that were discouraged under the more stern and vigilant administrations of the Chinese and British. It is not clear when gambling first came to the city, but by 1840, it was extensively practiced with the connivance of the authorities, who were paid to ignore it.[84] Gambling was licensed by the government in the 1850s, and organized gambling—though it is unclear in what forms—had grown considerably by 1866, when sixteen gambling houses provided a regular annual revenue to the government of $165,000.[85]

By the 1920s and 1930s, Macau had become one of the world's notorious "cities of sin," where gambling, prostitution, and opium houses flourished. Rows of three-story gambling houses with gaudy signs crowded the narrow streets side by side near the center of town, which acquired an exciting if seedy and decadent atmosphere. The gambling houses, which remained open all night, offered minimal entertainment by singsong girls and doubled as cheap hotels for their patrons by day.[86] In the absence of other significant commercial resources, the administration of the city was sustained by the taxes levied on these activities. Gambling saloons were, at first, entirely devoted to fan-tan, an elementary Chinese game of chance.[87] Horse racing, dog racing, and casinos offering roulette soon expanded the possibilities, and Macau became a gambler's paradise for residents from Hong Kong.[88] Writing about white slavery and prostitution in the Orient, a visitor to the city at this time concluded:

> There is no question that it harbors in its hidden places the riffraff of the world, the drunken ship masters; the flotsam of the sea, the derelicts, and more shameless, beautiful, savage women than any port in the world. It is hell. But to those who whirl in its unending play, it is the one haven where there is never a hand raised or a word said against the play of the beastliest emotions that ever blacken the human heart.[89]

Macau never lost its notoriety as a seedy, disreputable, and sometimes dangerous place, a refuge for the down-and-out and a haven for smugglers, spies, and other malevolent characters.[90]

When World War II ended, the vast colonial tide of European expansion that had risen four and a half centuries earlier with the Portuguese circumnavigation of Africa rapidly receded everywhere. New political and economic forces were reshaping the world in ways more fundamental than any experienced since the Europeans first arrived on the China coast. But Macau, for so long weaned from dependence on world commerce and forced to rely on its own resources, was virtually forgotten. For some years, it lived on as if in a somnolent lethargy after a great trauma. It was sustained by activities no one else wanted or that were prohibited elsewhere—organized gambling, the gold trade,[91] and the manufacture of matches, incense, and fireworks. More casinos were built, and the gambling monopoly, since 1962 under the control of a syndicate known as the Sociedade de Turismo e Diversões de Macau (STDM), supplied approximately half the government's revenue.[92]

Eventually, responding to the newfound economic energy of its neighbor Hong Kong and the rising demand for low-cost labor in the manufacture of consumer goods, Macau began to reawaken. Light industrial products such as textiles and garments, fireworks and matches, fish and other food products, furniture, toys, and plastics became increasingly important as export commodities.[93] Transit trade, mainly with China and Hong Kong, also grew substantially during this time.[94] Above all, tourism became one of the principal economic resources of the territory. Population pressures worked their inexorable effect. By 1960, as immigration from the mainland rose precipitously, the city held perhaps 800 Portuguese and Macanese and almost 161,000 Chinese; by 1965, the population had increased to 250,000, and it continued to grow to over 400,000 in the 1980s. Virtually the entire increase has been Chinese.[95] The influences Macau felt now were those of the modernizing Third World, and with them came the expatriated architectural styles of postwar Europe, the bland uniformity that characterizes every developing city in the world.

As early as the turn of the century, reinforced concrete, the architectural medium of the modern international world, came to Macau, molding styles to its own technological function and obliterating the earlier mutual influences of Chinese and Portuguese architectural traditions.[96] High-rise buildings, which, at first, were rare exceptions contrasting oddly with the old styles, soon sprouted everywhere like aggressive weeds, choking the old city. Mercilessly, the old buildings were abandoned, became decayed, and were destroyed to make room for the new.

Some old houses whose walls are precariously weakened are propped up by huge buttresses of bamboo poles, supported by their stouter neighbors. Others are already empty and gutted, their doors and windows open like the gaping sockets of skulls, their roofs collapsed, their once cool, dark, and quiet interiors now choked with weeds and trash. Next to them and soon to overwhelm them, too, the frantic mixing and pouring of concrete goes on noisily.

Was it always like this, as one city succeeded the other? It had happened before, of course, though on a smaller scale and less ruthlessly. But these new buildings have become anonymous monstrosities, neither truly European nor Chinese, belonging to no particular place or culture, without character of their own. This, the last city of Macau, is an anonymous city, without feeling, pity, or passion.

Macau's architecture is like a prism, refracting the city's past into a colorful spectrum of vivid memories. On the one extreme, representing the distant past, are the old gray-brown fortresses and walls. Next to them on the spectrum, mellower in tone, are the first great churches or their remains. Then come the European commercial and early residential buildings of the eighteenth century, though few of them have survived. The center of the spectrum is occupied by the most characteristic expression of Macau's blend of forms and influences, the Eurasian-Macanese houses. Toward the other end of the spectrum are the Chinese commercial and domestic buildings and the temples of the nineteenth century. The penultimate zone is marked by the raucous variety of architectural forms of the late-nineteenth- and early-twentieth-century European institutional and residential buildings. Last, on the opposite extreme of the spectrum, are the white skyscrapers, standing in such final contrast to the dark fortress walls. Yet, echoing their starkness, these new monstrosities complete the circle—as modern fortresses of money, not of artillery. Even the material used for their construction, reinforced concrete, is, ironically, a modern version of taipa, the rammed earth reinforced by straw, of which the fortresses were built.

Of course, Macau was always about money and the quest for trade. In their own way, the early architectural forms were also monuments to money and its conspicuous consumption. Earlier, that money was derived from maritime trade in tangible luxury commodities; now, it comes from the flow of intangible finance and investment and cheap manufactured goods. The correlative religious mission always coexisted somewhat ambiguously with the materialism of the city, which is now finally triumphant, symbolized by the gaudy casinos that unconsciously echo the lavishly decorated churches of an earlier age.

But cities decay, and memories fade, like the fading spectrum of the rainbow as the hot sun chases away the storm clouds. The prismatic architecture of Macau is deteriorating, its brilliance waning, obliterated by the intense, white light of the impersonal, anonymous high-rise apartments, offices, and hotels. Buildings a hundred years old or less are actually decaying, sinking below the new growth. Structures of much earlier days stand like venerable but petrified trunks of great trees, bearing witness to the climax growth that flourished and perished long ago. In these stones are memories. But stones crumble, and memories fade.

four

⤳

Transitions
Crossing the Threshold

An alien city rimmed by shallow seas
And purple islands, at the world extreme;
A siren land of indolence and ease
Where men live at peace and poets dream.[1]

Turning down the Travessa do Abreu toward the inner harbor from the Rua Padre Antonio, you seem to have entered a dead-end street. Ahead is a blank yellow wall, and the street is deserted. In a few steps, you reach the yellow wall and find a cross-street, the Rua Casa Forte, descending to the left, though it also appears to go nowhere. Facing down the street only a few paces to the right is a high, brick, arched portico; in blue and white tiles above the arch is the name "Patio da Ilusão." Behind it is a narrow courtyard cluttered with castaway building materials and household goods still too useful to throw away, and laundry is drying on bamboo poles. An old woman sits in a decrepit rattan chair under the archway, watching impassively. Which way to go?

You choose the right, toward the patio. There, you discover another hidden street entering from the left; it looks promising. This time, no apparent dead end is visible, and the street, too narrow for traffic, descends out of sight around a gradual bend to the right. The tile street sign in the wall above identifies it as the Rua do Bazarihno—"Little Market Street."

Indeed, just ahead are some people selling vegetables and fish at an impromptu neighborhood street market set up on packing cases beside the doors of the houses. The buildings in this part of town are joined in a continuous facade. The color of the painted walls and the shape of the upper-story windows vary from house to house. On the street level, the doors are the only openings. By the doors are flat, metal mailboxes on which house numbers are crudely painted. Next to them are small wooden or metal plaques bearing the name of the God of Wealth, and just below these are devices to hold a few sticks of incense. These are usually at eye level; down by the threshold are other tablets for the Earth God, also with a place to burn incense, sometimes a pot set in the ground or molded into the masonry.

Curiously, the Chinese name appearing on the sign for Rua do Bazarihno is "Shuishou xijie," "West Sailor Street." This discrepancy between the Portuguese and the Chinese names for streets is common in Macau.

Just beyond the peddlers with their vegetables, two streets enter from the right and the left, not quite meeting at the same point. If you followed the one on the left, Travessa de Maria Lucinda, you would come to the São Laurenço Market on the northern end of the Rua da Praia do Manduco. Unfortunately, there is no record of who Maria Lucinda was or the reason the street was named for her.[2]

On one side of the entrance to the street, low down against the wall of the building, is a small shrine to the local Earth God. Like all such shrines, it is unpretentious, merely a miniature, open altar sheltered by a simple roof, three or four feet high, molded from brick and mortar. Inside is a tablet and place to put incense on the altar. The shrine's presence here suggests that this is the center of a Chinese neighborhood whose residents maintain it and use it on festival days. Now the shrine is partly obscured by the peddlers' stands, and its roof is a convenient spot to rest some empty pots. To the right on the street entrance facing this shrine is another, also quite simple, dedicated to Tai Shan, a Taoist god somewhat less ubiquitous than the Earth God.

A little farther beyond, another street enters from the right. It was once named Travessa do Hospital dos Gatos, but its sign now reads "Rua George Chinnery. Pintor. 1774–1852." The name was changed in 1974 on the bicentennial of Chinnery's birth to honor the English painter, one of the few foreigners so distinguished in Macau.[3] Chinnery lived as an expatriate in a house nearby on the Rua de Inácio Baptista for more than twenty-five years, until his death. The scenes he sketched then are not so different from those encountered today in these same quiet neighborhoods.

The End of the World

For Chinnery, as perhaps for other foreign residents of the city through the years, Macau was a final refuge from accumulated personal problems, including an unhappy marriage. Chinnery was an Irishman who acquired a reputation as an accomplished painter while a young man in London and Dublin. But his restless and undisciplined character drove him to abandon his wife and children in 1802 and go to India, where his family had commercial interests and his brother was a servant in the East India Company.[4] Before sailing for Macau in 1825, he spent two decades at Madras and Calcutta making his living as a painter, doing portraits of the servants of the British East India Company. But his son died prematurely there shortly after joining him in 1822, and Chinnery apparently was under mounting financial pressures.[5]

Chinnery himself made much of his wife's relentless pursuit of him; he described her as "the ugliest woman he ever saw in the whole course of his life." It seems he never tired of regaling his amused visitors with stories of his unfortunate marriage and his efforts to escape from it. Indeed, shortly after arriving in Macau, he moved to Canton, where women were prohibited to go by the Chinese; he stayed in the English factory for fear that his wife might try to join him in Macau but settled permanently in Macau two years later.[6]

Though, in most respects, it was still a European port with many foreign residents and a comfortable life to offer, Macau was as far as one could get from British influence in those days. Chinnery became somewhat of a celebrity in the city, very much involved with the comings and goings in the European community—especially, of course, those of the British, who, by virtue of their major share of the Canton trade at the time, constituted the most consequential group among the foreign residents.[7] There was probably no visitor of note whose acquaintance Chinnery did not make, and he was sought out not only because of his reputation as an accomplished portrait painter but also because he was a local character.[8]

Harriet Low, whose portrait he painted, called him "fascinatingly ugly, and what with a habit he has of distorting his features in a most un-Christian manner, and with his taking snuff, smoking, and snorting, I think, were he not so agreeable, he would be intolerable."[9] The missionaries Robert Morrison and Charles Gutzlaff, both remarkable men in their own ways, also had their portraits done by Chinnery. Even several of the Chinese hong merchants, rich and powerful men who held the monopoly of Western trade at Canton before the Opium War, were painted by Chinnery.

Although he never left the China coast, Chinnery made frequent trips up to Canton during the trading season, along with the rest of the foreign merchant community of Macau, and also to Hong Kong after its cession to the British in 1842.[10] Yet, though he sketched and painted extensively in both places, it was Macau that preoccupied his attention as an artist. During his years of self-imposed exile, he wandered these streets with his sketchbook and easel, recording curious details and landscapes and architectural views or scenes of street life and people. Chinnery worked very much in the late-eighteenth- and early-nineteenth-century British tradition of watercolor landscapes in which he was trained. His style was affected by this background more than by the subjects he recorded as a traveler and expatriate.[11] His watercolors, styled in a realistic and detailed mode, are rather cheerful, light, and sometimes quite whimsical and patronizing. His portraits in oil are bolder and darker but sympathetic. He had a considerable influence on China Trade painting, which was popular among visitors to the China coast during the first half of the nineteenth century.

Macau was fast becoming a backwater in Chinnery's day. Foreign visitors from Canton were charmed by the decayed public buildings, the numerous forts and churches that no longer seemed to serve any function, the deserted gardens, and the odd mixture of the population; some found it all very boring.[12] Chinnery's pictures capture the kind of languid air that was so much at the heart of Macau's appeal. Beyond each end of the Praia Grande and around the Monte fort, there were still open spaces on the hillsides, strewn with large rocks and boulders, where the ruggedness of the peninsula remained largely undisturbed. Yet even then, in the early nineteenth century, Macau was changing, as Chinnery's successive sketches and paintings of the Praia Grande waterfront, a favorite subject of his, reveal.

In some respects, the omissions in his drawings tell as much about Macau's changing character as the details they include. Surely, with such an eye for detail as Chinnery possessed, he would have sketched the complex texture of Chinese culture—including the ubiquitous local shrines and altars, the small temples sandwiched between houses or shops, and the tablets at each door—had they existed in that time. But Chinnery's Macau, though populated even then with a growing number of Chinese residents, was still largely a European city in appearance.

Artists and poets alike found a certain fascination in Macau. But the results, as expressed in their works, depended greatly on their individual temperaments. For Chinnery, at least, there was contentment in the peace and stability of Macau's waning days of glory. It is, indeed, a measure of the rather stolid character of those times that some of his acquaintances regarded him as quite an eccentric.[13]

To be a foreign resident of Macau almost by definition made one an eccentric. Yet some went there for apparently quite ordinary motives. One of Chinnery's contemporaries, Thomas Beale, arrived at Canton from England sometime before 1785 to join the English commercial firm of Shank and Beale, in which his brother was a partner. Beale was then a green young man, only seventeen years old, perhaps looking for adventure while hoping to make his fortune in the lucrative Canton trade. Because foreigners were not permitted to remain in Canton beyond the end of the trading season, sooner or later he must have settled in Macau, as did the other foreign merchants who preferred not to return temporarily to India each year. Whether or not he expected to move on, one year passed into the next, and after many years, he eventually amassed a considerable fortune; this enabled him to live very comfortably in a fine old Portuguese house, which his brother had owned before him, on Beale's Lane. In the adjacent garden, he collected a remarkable aviary, filled with rare birds and plants, that became one of the most notable curiosities of the city. It seems that sometime about 1825, the year that Chinnery arrived in Macau, Beale had withdrawn from the business with the intention of returning to England with his fortune. However, a disastrous business venture he had entered with a Portuguese merchant forced him to change his plans. Two years later, his nephew David died in Macau. Beale remained in the city, his fortune lost and close to poverty, and died there under mysterious circumstances in 1841.[14] For Chinnery, it was a matter of choice to live out his life in Macau, but for Beale, who made it his home for more than fifty years, ultimately there was no escape from circumstances. For both, in different ways, the city was the end of the world, a last resort.

To be drawn to the East, to begin with, was frequently the mark of a restless and volatile personality. Often, it was also, until recently, a sign of either great desperation or determination or a blend of both. Since the first Portuguese explorers broke through to India, the many and varied dangers, anticipated or not, that awaited the traveler there had been the end of some and had daunted many others. So those who went to Macau had passed through a filtering process of sorts (until recently, almost everyone arrived from the direction of India, having already survived such hazards of the journey as storms, shipwreck, pirates, hostile powers, malnutrition, and disease). That passage particularly favored the eccentric and strong over the timid and weak.

Like the painter Chinnery, the poet Manuel Maria Barbosa da Bocage escaped to Macau on the run from India, yet unlike Chinnery, he was a mercurial figure, driven by quite different impetuses. Bocage was born in Setúbal, south of Lisbon, in 1765. He exhibited extraordinary talents and restlessness as a child. His mother, a French woman, died when he was ten, and by his midteens, he had briefly served in the Setúbal infantry before enrolling in the Royal Marine Academy at Lisbon. In the meantime, he became immersed in the bohemian life of the city and began to acquire a reputation as a skillful poet.[15]

In 1786, Bocage left for India with an appointment in the Guardas-Marinhas. But in Goa, his romantic expectations were disappointed—after all, this was nearly a century after the heyday of the Portuguese empire in Asia. In the tropical climate, he fell ill, and he vented his disillusionment in satirical sonnets on Portuguese decadence. A frustrated Bocage deserted from the Damão infantry in 1789 and embarked for Macau, but his ship was wrecked in a typhoon on the South China coast. Impoverished, he recovered for a time in the British East India factory at Canton before finally making his way to Macau in September 1789.

Bocage stayed in Macau less than a year; by late 1790, he was back in Lisbon, where, still impoverished, he resumed his former bohemian existence, writing poetry and earning notoriety among foreigners as an extravagant genius. He died in poverty in 1805.

While in Macau, Bocage had been as prolific as ever, writing elegies in honor of his occasional benefactors and notable Macau personalities.[16] In spite of the brevity of his stay in Macau, his works were well known and earned him the honor of having a street named for him.

Superficially, at least, the Macau that Chinnery settled down in so contentedly in 1825 could hardly have differed much from the place that Bocage had found a generation earlier. But if each man nevertheless responded quite differently to the city, they were traveling in very different worlds. Although Chinnery left the confident, expanding British empire in India for the relative backwater of Portuguese Macau, he still circulated within the dynamic British community of the South China coast at a time when momentous changes were impending. Bocage, by contrast, moved within the more one-dimensional, static vestiges of the Portuguese overseas empire. And yet, Macau was able to encompass both these worlds.

There is a striking similarity between the career of Bocage and the life of Portugal's greatest poet, Luis Vaz de Camões. For Bocage, who apparently sought to emulate Camões, the resemblance was not an unconscious one. Yet more than two centuries separated his era from the age of Camões, when Portuguese expansion in Asia reached its apogee.

It is widely believed that Camões wrote a part of his epic poem, *The Lusiads*, a monument to the Portuguese spirit of discovery and conquest, while sojourning in Macau.[17] If he was ever in Macau—which remains a matter of much debate—no evidence of his passage exists. Perhaps that is hardly surprising; he was supposed to have been there sometime between 1556 and 1559, just as the port was first being settled. The circumstances of the Portuguese acquisition of the territory lie in obscurity, so it is unlikely that any records of those involved survive. Nevertheless, the hill strewn with granite boulders that overlooks the inner harbor of Macau to the north is indelibly associated with Camões's name. There, brooding in a grotto formed by the rocks, he was supposed to have written some chapters of his life's great work.[18]

No doubt he had good reason to brood. Up to that point, his life had been marked by failures and disillusionment. Born about 1524, Camões attended the great university at Coimbra before moving to Lisbon. There, he was soon in trouble at court, perhaps over a youthful love affair.[19] Banished from Lisbon in 1546, he enlisted as a soldier at Ceuta, the Portuguese base in North Africa, where he lost his right eye in battle. Back in Lisbon, he continued to behave impetuously. In a brawl, he wounded a court official and was pardoned from the ensuing prison sentence only on condition of being exiled even farther away in India.

It seems that in Lisbon, Camões had already begun to work on *The Lusiads*, and he may have garnered a reputation as a popular poet in spite of his rash behavior, though the point at which he became inspired to enshrine the

Luis Vaz de Camões (engraving, 1624)

achievements of the Portuguese in a classic epic form is uncertain. That he was a distant relative of Vasco da Gama (who died the year he was born) is probably no coincidence in this emerging conception of his work. The classical education he pursued at Coimbra would have suggested to him parallels with the heroic mythology and epics of the ancient Greeks.

Yet only a half-century after the glorious deeds of the first discoverers, the Portuguese were condemned to efforts to recapture their glory and heroic accomplishments. They had a hard act to follow. The reports of bountiful and fabulous Asia brought back by the earlier voyagers seemed to haunt later emulators, as they did Camões and, much later, Bocage. Thus, "golden" Goa, the brilliant capital of Portuguese Asia, rivaling Lisbon itself as a Portuguese city, was not what the poet expected when he arrived there in 1554. Disillusioned with the corruption that was already sapping the vitality of the Portuguese enterprise, he took out his frustration in satirical poems, as Bocage was later to do. But he continued to work on his epic celebration of da Gama's voyage.

In the meantime, he participated in the military expeditions in which the Portuguese were ceaselessly involved to protect and extend their commercial monopoly. He was sent to the Moluccas, the legendary Spice Islands, and sometime during these travels, he may have passed through Macau, perhaps about 1556, just as it was being founded. By 1559, he was back in Goa after being shipwrecked at the mouth of the Mekong. Following a desultory career in India, he returned in 1570 to Lisbon. There, he completed *The Lusiads* before dying in poverty in 1580.

Macau, then a nearly barren promontory, would not have made much of an impression on Camões, preoccupied as he was with his unpromising and frustrating career in Portuguese India and the life he had left behind. And if he was, in fact, there, he made no mention of the place in *The Lusiads*. The honor he is accorded in Macau today reflects a deep, nostalgic feeling that the city is somehow the unique relic of that great enterprise that Camões celebrated with such passion as much as any personal involvement he may have had with the place. In *The Lusiads*, Camões saw the Portuguese as spiritual heirs to mythological heroes of the classical age, and he cast the deeds of their soldiers, navigators, and kings in that mold. Macau, as the most distant Asian outpost of Portugal's epic enterprise of discovery and expansion, may be seen as the last, lingering symbol of that destiny.

Yet this classical theme sits uneasily in the context of the crusading Christian zeal of the Portuguese, though perhaps it did not seem so uncomfortable to contemporaries inspired by the diverse and sometimes confusing impulses of the Renaissance. That evangelism, sanctioned and encouraged by the Church, lent added dignity to the material and commercial mission of the voyages and expeditions, all the way from North Africa to the China coast and Japan. The commercial motive of the Portuguese, though also seemingly at odds with the grandiose mission Camões ascribed to them, nevertheless lay at the root of their enterprise. The Portuguese kings were also the first merchant entrepreneurs of the land. Macau encompassed these themes as well.

The Threshold to China

Poets, artists, soldiers, and adventurers like Camões merely skirted the periphery of the Chinese world. For most of them, Macau offered only a momentary respite from troubles elsewhere, a resting place in the course of a scattered life; their attention was on the passing moment and was rarely fixed on any enduring purpose. But there were others who saw it as a transition of a different kind, a threshold on another world and merely the beginning of a great mission.

Brooding among the rocks overlooking the China coast, in the grotto that was later to bear his name, Camões had looked backward on a chaotic life and the Portuguese destiny that had thrown him up on these shores. Hardly more than twenty years later, Alessandro Valignano, father visitor of the Society of Jesus to the Indies, surveyed the same forbidding coast from the

Jesuit College on the hill not far from Camões's grotto. He was said to have cried out, "O Rock, when wilt thou open?"[20]

Up to this time, all attempts to enter China had failed. Before Macau was founded, a disappointed Francis Xavier had died on Shangchuan Island west of Macau, waiting for an opportunity that never came. Later, others took up residence in Macau, making converts among the Chinese there but hoping for the opening of the greater mission beyond.[21] One can easily imagine the frustration that they must have felt and that Valignano shared, even more acutely than Xavier, who was not so close. Looking across the harbor from Macau, China's hills were so close that one could see men and women moving about in their daily activities and children playing and hear their voices on a quiet morning, yet they remained remote, separated by a barrier more formidable than any mere wall imposed.

The separation was more than geographic. Under the rule of the Ming, the Chinese had become introverted and increasingly defensive, suspicious of foreigners, and self-contained within their own borders. Chronic depredations and invasions by pirates along the coast, a major military problem for the Ming, had caused the Chinese to withdraw behind the protection of their walls. No wonder that they regarded foreigners with suspicion, especially those strangers inhabiting the outermost periphery of the South China coast.[22]

But in any case, the Jesuits' initial efforts had been concentrated on Japan, where the prospects for converting the whole country seemed so great, and China was, for a time, merely a secondary prospect.[23] Indeed, after arriving in the East from India in 1577, Valignano had spent most of his time in Japan, directing the mission efforts there. He was on his way to Japan when he stopped off at Macau and contemplated China's closed door.

Although preoccupied for the time being with Japan, Valignano was clearly not unmindful of China. The great Xavier himself, after all, pioneer of the Japan field, had come to his end while trying to enter China. Ironically, in fact, it was in Japan that Xavier had first come to appreciate the importance of converting China:

> While Xavier was working among the idol-worshippers of Japan, he observed that whenever they were hard pressed in an argument, they always had recourse to the authority of the Chinese. . . . Whence it happened that they commonly asserted, that if the Christian religion was really the one true religion, it would surely have been known to the intelligent Chinese and also accepted by them.[24]

So Xavier decided to dedicate his energies to winning over the Chinese, a task that he apparently believed would be facilitated by the natural proclivities of the Chinese for receiving the gospel.[25]

In August 1552, at Shangchuan, the barren island off the China coast where the Portuguese had been carrying on their precarious trade with the

Statue of São Francisco Xavier, facade of São Paulo Church

Chinese since 1550, Xavier sought help to enter the empire. It was an unlikely prospect. Shangchuan was actually nothing more than a temporary camp: Because the trading season, dictated by the monsoon winds, lasted from late summer through the fall, only rough shelters were built and the entire place was abandoned by the end of November. Suspicious as always, the Chinese authorities prohibited any permanent settlement there.[26] Anxious not to provoke the officials and disrupt the tenuous trade, Portuguese and Chinese traders were unwilling to assist in Xavier's plan. He persevered nevertheless but found himself virtually deserted as the ships sailed away at the end of the season. The weather had already turned very cold when Xavier, suffering from fever and without any proper shelter or food, died on December 2. He is remembered now in Macau by a shrine in the Church of St. Francis on the island of Coloane.

Xavier failed in his final mission; China remained impenetrable. But his martyrdom served as both a challenge and a beacon to those who followed. When permanent settlement of the Macau peninsula was permitted a few years later, at least the hardships of waiting were made easier. Yet after much waiting and many attempts to enter China over the next several decades, despair and discouragement would also overcome his successors. Contradicting Xavier's sanguine expectations for the conversion of the Chinese, they concluded that one might as well try "to whiten an Ethiopian."[27]

The problem lay as much in Xavier's example as in the antipathy and suspicion the Chinese felt toward foreigners. Xavier possessed a blithe self-confidence and had an utter disregard for cultural barriers, which no doubt awed all those who met him. Although he adopted the most humble manner, he attracted attention wherever he went, especially among the poor, and preached to the people he encountered, sometimes through native speakers or merely by signs. It is said that he had the gift of tongues and could preach in the language of his listeners, but it is clear that he was, at times, forced to use interpreters.[28] The apparent ease with which he communicated with his audiences misled others who attempted to follow in his footsteps, for they took little interest in the culture of people who were to be converted and did not believe it was necessary to learn their languages. But few, if any, among them possessed the remarkable ability of Francis Xavier. Attempting to apply his model to China, even with the relative advantage of the comfort and convenience of Macau that Xavier had not enjoyed, they were sure to encounter disappointment.[29]

Alessandro Valignano sailed for India in March 1574. Was there something in his character—an impulsiveness he shared with the likes of Camões and Xavier, perhaps—that suited him to the arduous mission in the East that would occupy the rest of his life? He seems to have had an exuberant youth and served some time in jail—like Camões—for fighting with a sword.[30] Was it his forceful character that prompted his superiors in the Society of Jesus to appoint him visitor to the Indies in 1573?

In those years and well into the next century, India was a necessary transition point to the East. After the long, grueling voyage following the Carreira da India from Lisbon around Africa and across the Indian Ocean to Goa, new arrivals were exhausted and weak and apt to be suffering from all sorts of maladies brought on by the voyage and the climate. The Carreira, well over 10,000 miles long, took up to eight months to travel. Some never made it.[31] And those who did survive the trip, even if India was their final destination, needed time to recover their health, to feel solid land once again beneath their feet, and to adapt to the new culture. Valignano's two and a half years in India were a prelude to his later work in Japan and China.

Valignano's office gave him immediate authority over all Jesuit missions in the East from India to Japan. In India, he began to formulate the principles of a new mission strategy. Previously, Jesuit missionaries since Xavier had relied on interpreters in preaching to local people, and many preferred to preach to their compatriots instead. Not until Valignano arrived in Macau in October 1577, on his way to inspect the fertile Japan mission, was he confronted with the seemingly impenetrable wall of resistance that had stymied all who had followed Xavier to China. There, more than anywhere else, the failure of the mission strategy was evident.

In Macau for almost a year to await the sailing of the next Japan carrack, Valignano had time to analyze the problem. In contrast to the other Jesuits, who had followed Xavier's example, he was not predisposed to underestimate the character and cultivation of the Chinese. Xavier had appealed to the poor and the lower classes, a tactic that was certain to raise fears of subversion among the official class, but Valignano reasoned that the goodwill of the educated elite was essential to ensure the acceptance of the Christian message in China. If the missionaries were to allay the fears of the officials, he knew, they would have to present themselves as educated persons in ways that the Chinese would respect.[32] But to do this, they would have to learn the language and become familiar with the traditions and learning of the Chinese. Other concessions would also be necessary. Valignano believed that rather than transforming new converts into Europeans, thus alienating them from their own people and provoking fears of cultural subversion, the missionaries themselves must adapt to Chinese ways.[33]

Valignano's experience in Japan soon confirmed his positive assessment of the Chinese character and validated Xavier's enthusiasm for the great prospect of converting China. He had become disillusioned by what he saw as the insincerity of the Japanese converts. The Chinese, by contrast, seemed to him to possess all of the admirable cultural traits the Japanese lacked.[34] But Valignano's new policy did not pass without resistance. Jesuits already in the field were wedded to the old approach and too disillusioned by many failures to have much sympathy for the culture that seemed so impervious to their message. So Valignano sent for a different group of men whose temperament was better suited to the newly defined task.

Michele Ruggieri was the first of these new recruits. Following his arrival in Macau from Goa in 1578, he devoted himself to learning Chinese and cultivating contacts with the Chinese at the semiannual trade fair at Canton. In a separate house called the Oratorio of St. Martin that was constructed on the hill behind the church, Ruggieri had his study and instructed new converts from among the Chinese arriving in Macau.[35]

Yet problems persisted. Many of his colleagues continued to obstruct his efforts. "What is the sense," they grumbled, "of this Father occupying himself with this sort of thing when he could be of service to the other ministries of the Society? It is a waste of time for him to learn the Chinese language and to consecrate himself to a hopeless enterprise."[36] So far had Xavier's dream of converting the Chinese waned in only a few decades that the principal efforts of the priests were now devoted to ministering to the needs of the Portuguese.[37] Macau had rapidly grown into a vigorous trading community, and that community was placing increasing demands on the Jesuits' time and energy. The older, conservative priests found it easier to bend to this pressure than to persist in that apparently "hopeless enterprise," and Ruggieri was obliged to divide his work between the two endeavors.

As his unsympathetic colleagues seemed to recognize, language was Ruggieri's biggest problem. Although he worked diligently at it, mastery of Chinese came slowly and with great difficulty to Ruggieri, inhibited all the more by the constant demands on his time.[38] Passing through Macau with a mission of Japanese Christians on their way to Europe in 1582, Valignano once again confronted the problem. He reorganized the mission, separating the work of the China enterprise from the local mission. He established the Sodality of the Holy Name of Jesus at the Jesuit residence, which was exclusively for Chinese and Japanese converts and under autonomous administration so that the local Jesuit brethren could not interfere in its work. He also brought Matteo Ricci out from India as a reinforcement for Ruggieri.

Ricci evinced a talent for the Chinese language that had eluded Ruggieri. Soon after his arrival in August 1582, he and Ruggieri, who had known each other in Goa, succeeded in penetrating the barrier and set upon the task of establishing a permanent mission in China.[39] Ricci was to become the embodiment of Valignano's policy of adaptation to China. More than any of his forerunners, he was responsible for the development of the mission in China that was eventually to see Jesuit missionaries stationed in many parts of the country and even in the court of Peking itself, where they tutored the emperor in science and mathematics and served as officials in the Imperial Astronomical Bureau.[40]

Even though Ricci spent very little time in Macau, without that city there would have been no China mission and perhaps no Japan mission either.[41] As Macau thrived on the trade, the missionary enterprise prospered in turn; commerce and religion were ultimately linked in the life and culture of the city. In fact, no sooner had Valignano arrived in Macau than he worked out an extremely favorable arrangement for the mission to share in the profits of the silk trade with Japan.[42] Though this activity was viewed uneasily by some and exposed the Jesuits to criticism, it was no more than an extension of the pattern—existing since the beginning of Portuguese expansion—in which zeal for both trade and evangelism were associated. Asked why he had come to India in 1498, Vasco da Gama had replied that he sought "Christians and spices." Those goals were always associated, if distinct, for the Portuguese. And no place exemplified their marriage better than Macau. Whatever the burdens placed on the Jesuits by the Portuguese community that had so frustrated Ruggieri's efforts, Portuguese support for the mission enterprise was, in the end, unstinting. Moreover, the Macau commercial community was a source of regular charity and material support that was frequently recognized and appreciated by Ricci.[43]

But most of all, Macau was a threshold to China. It was a relatively secure place where those who would eventually move on could prepare themselves and study the language and ways of the Chinese. Xavier had had no such advantage. Only later would Valignano contemplate a more autonomous organization of the China mission, as its members spread out through the country and their communication with Macau became more tenuous. But even then, Macau remained the indispensable doorway to China and a source of support and provisions.[44] It was to become a transition between two cultures in another sense, as well.

So bright had the prospects of the China mission become under Ricci's guidance in the early years of the seventeenth century that it seemed to the father visitor that China's promise exceeded even that of Japan. Indeed, he thought it could be the greatest mission of evangelization that Christianity had ever undertaken.[45] Having so far divided his duties almost entirely between Japan and India, with only infrequent visits to Macau, Valignano now looked forward to personally visiting the various mission locations in China and to arranging for them to become more self-sufficient. Once again in Macau in late 1605, he made careful plans for the mission's support. But in the midst of preparing for his visit, he became ill and, in January 1606, died at the age of sixty-nine.[46]

Though Valignano, like Xavier, never visited China, at Macau he had opened the door through which many others later passed. Beginning with Ruggieri and Ricci, a steady stream of aspiring missionaries prepared for China while waiting in Macau for the right opportunity. However, all did not always go smoothly. In 1617, for example, a proscription of Christianity by China led to the expulsion of most priests, which lasted until the ban was withdrawn in 1623. Even though the proscription was not complete, Macau, in the interim, became a place of refuge for the missionaries. In fact, such temporary interdictions in China kept some waiting in Macau for many months before the door would reopen. There, they bided their time and put it to good use preparing for China.

Johann Adam Schall von Bell was one of the new missionaries who found the door closed when he arrived in Macau in July 1619. He had sailed from Lisbon on the *Jesus* in April 1618 with Nicholas Trigault, who had rendered Ricci's journal into Latin, and with twenty-one other priests recruited for the China field by Trigault.[47] The ship was so crowded—it carried 636 passengers—that sickness spread quickly, and more than half the passengers became seriously ill; forty-five died, including five missionaries. The ship arrived in Goa in October 1618, the relative quickness of the voyage compensating, in part, for its misery. But Goa did not detain Schall long; he was needed by the mission in China for which he had been recruited and trained.

Ricci, who was no scientist, had appealed for true scientists to be sent out to meet an insistent demand from the Chinese for competent mathematicians and astronomers to organize the calendar. After his death, requests from his successors became more frequent and urgent. It was to answer this call that Schall and John Terenz Schreck, a talented mathematician and friend of Galileo, had been recruited by Trigault. Schall was born in 1592 of a minor noble family from Cologne. He prepared for the priesthood at the Roman College and entered the Society of Jesus in 1611.[48] Following his recruitment by Trigault, probably in 1615 in Rome, he began an intensive study of mathematics and theology in preparation for his new mission. He continued his studies on board the *Jesus*, as Terenz lectured on mathematics to the other missionaries.[49]

Perhaps Schall's detention in Macau in 1619 was fortuitous because his preparation for the China mission was, at that point, incomplete: He still had to learn Chinese. Waiting for the persecution in China to subside, he studied the language in Macau with Father Vagnoni.[50] Other developments that were to shape his career in China and attach him to the fortunes of the Portuguese in Macau caught up with him there. The Dutch, arriving in Asia only a few years earlier, had begun an aggressive assault on Portugal's presence in Asia wherever they encountered the Portuguese. Attacking Portuguese ships on the high seas along the sensitive trade routes up the South and East China Seas to Japan, they laid plans to seize the Portuguese bases that secured the routes. Macau, where the Portuguese monopolized the China trade, became a prime target. In late June 1622, a large Dutch fleet arrived off the Macau roads.

Although Macau, at that time, was not strongly fortified—the construction of its extensive fortifications was to follow as a consequence of the Dutch attack—the Dutch determined that a direct assault on the city from the harbor would be too risky. Instead, they made a landing on the beach on the northeast end of the peninsula and marched across the fields toward the city from the landward side. Since the Portuguese defenses were undermanned, the Jesuits helped out with cannon fire from the Monte. Caught in a cross fire from the defenders in the fields and on the hills, the Dutch began a disastrous retreat. In the process, most of the landing force was killed or captured, including a Dutch captain taken prisoner by Adam Schall.[51]

With the memory of the Dutch attack fresh in his mind, Schall found himself in Peking less than a year later, in January 1623, after the interdiction

Adam Schall von Bell (engraving from Athanasius Kircher, *China monumentis qua sacris qua profanis, illustrata*, 1672)

against the missionaries was lifted by the Chinese. There, he was immediately absorbed in the purpose for which he had prepared—to put his scientific training in the service of the court as a way of gaining the confidence and acceptance of the Chinese. He had brought with him a number of books on astronomy and mathematics and scientific apparatus. At each opportunity that presented itself, he demonstrated these to visitors. It was not long before he was able to precisely predict a lunar eclipse on October 8, 1623.[52] For the Chinese court, such predictions were viewed as vital tests of the accuracy of the official calendar on which, in turn, the auspices of the dynasty depended. The court believed that the precise observation and prognostication of celestial phenomena demonstrated the cosmic legitimacy of the dynasty; unexpected or unpredicted (or inaccurately predicted) events in the heavens would be taken as omens of imperial decline. The vital task of calendar making was vested in the Imperial Astronomical Bureau.[53] When, partly due to the Jesuit's predictions, a reform of the calendar was ordered in 1629, Terenz and another Jesuit were assigned to the bureau. After Terenz died the next year, in May 1630, Schall was appointed to take his place.[54] Thus began his extraordinary career, which would culminate with his appointment, though a foreigner, as the first director of the Imperial Astronomical Bureau under the Manchus from 1644 to 1655.

Although the scientific enterprise of the Jesuits was intended, as Ricci had foreseen it, to be merely a vehicle for evangelization, it became much more than that. Schall's scientific activities came to occupy much of his time as he satisfied the constant Chinese thirst for translations, new books by the Jesuit fathers, and scientific instruments. A telescope, a celestial globe, an armillary sphere, and a sundial, as well as a growing library of scientific books, all helped to ingratiate the Jesuits with the emperor.[55] In January 1638, Schall predicted eclipses of both the sun and the moon: The superiority of his scientific methods had been clearly demonstrated.

The Chinese were puzzled by the motives of the Jesuit fathers. Why had they come to China?[56] Unlike tribute emissaries, they did not seek commercial advantage or demand political concessions. They behaved (and dressed) like the educated, cultivated Confucian literati; the priests also learned their language and studied their classics of philosophy and history and literature. When the priests spoke of their own religion, they described it in the lexicon of Chinese philosophical and religious concepts.[57] But the Chinese were also fascinated by the Jesuits' new scientific knowledge and their ingenious gadgets and clever maps, and they found the missionaries' mathematical accomplishments invaluable in the construction of the calendar. All of this knowledge the Jesuits freely shared and taught. But some Chinese scholars and officials did suspect that a hidden agenda lay behind the Jesuits' activities.[58]

In the long run, it was not clear whose interest was being served most effectively—that of the Jesuits in evangelization or that of the Chinese in

Jesuit priest (drawing from *Aomen jilue*)

calendrical reform. But whether or not science advanced the evangelical enterprise, it certainly promoted the political influence of Schall and his colleagues. From 1644, with the collapse of the Ming under the Manchu onslaught and the accession of the Qing, Schall occupied a position of influence unprecedented since Marco Polo served under the Mongols in the thirteenth century. In spite of his former assistance to the Ming, Schall was on extraordinarily intimate terms with the Manchus from the beginning. The young Shunzhi emperor called him "Mafa," or "Grandpa," and frequently sought his advice. His protection extended to the entire Christian mission in China.[59] In 1650, Schall was permitted to build a mission compound and church close to the imperial palace; the prospect of the Christian conversion of China seemed closer than ever at this point.

Throughout these times, Macau remained the vital link for both Christianity and science. But it was a tenuous and vulnerable linkage. Schall had witnessed firsthand Macau's vulnerability in 1622. And as the scope and success of the mission expanded in the following years, his appreciation of Macau's importance in that regard must have grown, as well. What would have been the future of the Christian mission and the Jesuits' scientific enterprise in China if the Dutch attack had succeeded? Only through Macau could the mission be resupplied and reinforced with new recruits, and the city itself continued to contribute generously to the evangelical mission.

When a Dutch mission arrived in Peking in 1656, seeking to establish relations with the Qing, Schall, in his position of trust, was asked by the court to act as interpreter. The authorities in Macau urged the Jesuits to orchestrate the failure of the Dutch mission and supplied them with money to secure that result. Acting behind the scenes, by subtle and not so subtle means (including bribery and persuasion), Schall helped to undermine the Dutch.[60]

Several years later, a critical threat to Macau's existence arose from another quarter. The depredations of Zheng Chenggong, better known to Westerners as Koxinga, a pirate-adventurer and protector of the refugee Ming court, were causing great trouble for the Manchus at sea and along the South China coast. In 1660, to remove the resources of the coastal population from Koxinga's control, the court ordered the evacuation of large areas of the coast and prohibited trade and navigation there. The decree included the Portuguese at Macau, and in 1662, its imminent application to the city (which the Qing considered Chinese territory) caused great consternation and prompted efforts to delay or revoke its implementation. For several years thereafter, the fate of Macau hung in the balance. The barrier gate was frequently closed for prolonged periods, preventing food from reaching the city; in addition, trade was stopped, and foreign ships were driven away.[61] Once again, Schall and his Jesuit colleagues used their influence to intervene with the court and get Macau exempted from the policy.[62] But not until 1668 were the evacuation orders revoked, and although the prohibition on maritime trade technically remained in effect, it could then be safely ignored.

In these favorable circumstances and given the position of influence to which Schall and his Jesuit colleagues had risen, it seemed that Valignano's policy, applied and expanded by Ricci and Schall, would gradually come to fruition. But in fact, it was soon to suffer a serious challenge in the attack on the Jesuits in the Imperial Astronomical Bureau by Chinese conservatives, led by Yang Guangxian, the anti-Christian polemicist official.[63] However, the conservatives' success proved to be only temporary and actually served to strengthen the position of Schall's successors (Schall died in 1666). Thus, it is ironic that it was neither the Dutch nor the Chinese who, in the end, destroyed Valignano's dream of the Christian enterprise in China but the Church itself. A controversy was already under way within the Church over the wisdom of the policy of adapting to Chinese culture and the concessions to certain Chinese rites, such as ancestor worship, made by Ricci.[64] The Rites Controversy was finally resolved in 1742 with the papal bull *Ex quo singulari*, prohibiting Christians from taking part in Chinese Confucian ceremonies. That made the approach that brought such success first to Ricci and then to Schall impossible.[65] The prohibition ended the accommodation strategy initiated by Valignano.

Nothing more clearly reveals the cultural gulf between the two different worlds that Macau so tenuously bridged than the tortured history of the Christian evangelization of China that began with the Jesuit fathers. It was as if, while the exchange was going on, the two sides were talking past each other. The fault lay largely with the Jesuits, who, after all, had made the supreme effort to study the Chinese mind. The Jesuits saw their science and technology as a kind of tantalizing lure, an accessory to their true purpose of evangelization. But the Chinese saw that science and technology as a far more important and indivisible whole, a way of looking at the world that was consistent with their own ethical assumptions, at least until the mid-eighteenth century.[66] But who was converting whom? The suspicion of the other orders, the Dominicans and Franciscans, regarding the Jesuits' motives and tactics was, perhaps, not so very wrong after all, if the ultimate goal remained the one set by Xavier—to convert the Chinese.[67]

The effect that the end of the accommodation policy and the proscription of Christianity had on Macau is not easy to measure. Macau's fortunes depended, after all, largely on trade, and the Dutch assault on the Portuguese empire in Asia and the closing of Japan had, in any event, brought an end to the city's glorious prosperity by the mid-seventeenth century, even while Schall's influence was reaching its zenith in Peking. Macau continued, but its importance as a threshold between two worlds diminished. Though, to be fair, it was never clear who was being assimilated, the Jesuits or the Chinese, Macau was no longer a door for either Christianity *or* science.

A Bridge to a New World

The Chinese who went to Macau usually proceeded no farther. Either their ancestors had lived for generations in the few villages already there before the Portuguese arrived or they themselves were drawn by the new opportunities the European presence afforded. They went first as temporary servants and laborers and craftsmen, forbidden by Chinese authorities from taking up permanent residence in the city; later, they went as merchants, attracted by the trade, and became shopkeepers, brokers, hangers-on, and even linguists for the Portuguese traders; later still, they went in periodic but short-lived migrations as refugees fleeing times of trouble in China, swelling the population until many returned to their homes when the troubles subsided.

For these people, Macau was a cul-de-sac on the edge of the Chinese world. Although it was a rather strange place, it was not without precedent on the periphery of this sprawling empire; other Chinese were attracted in similar ways to inner Asian oases settlements, where they mingled with equally exotic caravan traders and Turkic peoples.

A few Chinese, baptized Christian converts of the Jesuits who became lay brothers or were ordained as priests and who sometimes took Portuguese

葛
斯
嘮
廟
僧
圖

Franciscan friar (drawing from *Aomen jilue*)

names, might, indeed, adopt a new and alien culture. Two Chinese natives of Macau, baptized as Sebastiano Fernandez and Emanuele Pereira, presumably received their first instruction in Christianity at the Oratorio of St. Martin. This was near the Jesuit church that became the basis for the Sodality of the Holy Name of Jesus, established by Alessandro Valignano to minister to new converts.[68] After accompanying Father Ricci to Nanking in 1598, these two men were admitted to the order as lay brothers. Ricci thought them more Portuguese than Chinese by that time.[69]

Macau was a lens that refracted the lives and the careers of those who passed through it. Wu Li (1632–1718), a native of Jiangsu Province, was already an accomplished painter and poet before he came into contact with the Jesuits in Jiangsu. After conversion and baptism there as Simon-Xavier about 1680, he went to Macau, where he entered the novitiate of the Society of Jesus in 1682 at the age of fifty. Wu studied for six years in Macau and was ordained in the priesthood in 1688, adopting the Portuguese surname A Cunha.[70]

Wu Li had originally intended to travel to Rome when he left his ancestral home. The preparation in Western ecclesiastical learning and language that he received in Macau might have been expected to reinforce his intention and to further propel him away from his own culture. No doubt his deep immersion in Confucian studies and literati culture prior to his exposure to Christianity militated against such a radical departure from his own tradition. Also, Valignano's policy, implemented a century before, had repudiated the excessive Europeanization of converts. Now, the efforts of ordained Chinese priests and lay brothers were directed back to the evangelical mission in China. So, following his ordination, Wu Li returned to Jiangsu, and from 1695, he worked at the important Jiading Mission, of which he was eventually placed in charge.[71] Since early in the century, Jiading had been a Jesuit center both for the training of new Chinese recruits for the Jesuit order from Macau and for the language and cultural preparation of European priests freshly arrived from Europe.[72] In this sense, it was a kind of extension of the missionary establishment centered on Macau.

For Chinese like Wu Li and other Christian converts, Macau was a significant point of cultural reorientation, even though it did not cause them to break entirely away from the Chinese world. But even if Macau was not yet a stage of departure to a new world beyond China for these people, the world they returned to would never be the same for them again. They were creating a new world within China—part Chinese and part Western, highly circumscribed though it may have been.

For a Chinese with sufficient ability and determination, Macau offered many opportunities. If religious conversion was the key that unlocked the door to many other possibilities, the boundary between them was not always clearly marked—witness the Jesuit fathers' involvement in the Japan trade—and how they were received depended, in part, on the individuals involved. One would not expect a Confucian literatus of Wu Li's caliber to be drawn into Macau's commercial life, but for a clever entrepreneur, the possibilities were almost boundless.

Zheng Zhilong (1604–1661) probably went to Macau in or before 1621 and was employed as a workman or craftsman, for which there was a steady demand. He seems to have quickly worked his way up in status, perhaps working for Chinese merchants and becoming a broker for Portuguese traders. It is said that he acquired the patronage of a wealthy Portuguese, who may have sponsored his instruction as a Christian and who became his godfather.[73] He was baptized Nicholas Gaspard but was more commonly known to Europeans as Nicholas Iquan ("Iquan" was a prevalent expression, meaning "first son").

If, as seems likely, he lived in Macau for several years, he may have witnessed the Dutch attack in 1622 and even crossed paths with Adam Schall. If he was there, the abortive invasion must have deeply impressed him with the power of Western artillery and warships. It is also reported that he visited Manila about this time, probably in connection with his trading activity.[74]

Iquan had come from a poor family of Nanan, near the coast of Fujian Province. No doubt he had arrived at Macau from there aboard a merchant ship. There was little to draw him back to his home, but numerous opportunities radiated from Macau in those years for someone as resourceful as he was. So, in about 1623, he went to Japan, again probably in pursuit of commerce. Iquan's activities during these years are obscure. He had numerous contacts with the Dutch, who were active in trade in Japan, Taiwan, and the East China coast.[75] He served as an interpreter for the Dutch and married a Japanese woman from Hirado, who bore him a son, Zheng Chenggong, in 1624.

The East Asian maritime world—from the Straits of Malacca eastward through island Southeast Asia and northward past the Philippine Islands, the South China coast, and Taiwan, and on to Japan—was a complex region rarely dominated by a single power. There was often little to distinguish between legitimate trade among diverse participants involved in East Asian commerce—the Portuguese in Macau, the Spanish based in Manila, the Dutch from their new base in Java, the Chinese and the Japanese—and the piracy that was endemic in these seas for centuries. The newcomers, the Portuguese and the Dutch, had merely intensified the competition, which, as often as not, was carried on by violent means between hostile powers. The ships of the Macau-Japan trade were constantly in danger from Japanese, Chinese, or Dutch pirates.

It is not surprising, therefore, to find that Iquan soon joined the powerful pirate leader Yan Siqi, who made Taiwan his base, in 1624.[76] When Yan died in 1625, Iquan succeeded him as chief, probably after a struggle with other contenders, and shortly after, he commanded a large fleet that preyed on the East China coast and Dutch and Chinese shipping. By 1627, his force had increased sufficiently for him to capture Amoy, the principal port of Fujian. Iquan's growing power already had made him a serious concern to the Ming, who sought to co-opt him with official position and an opportunity to join the government's side. This policy succeeded in 1628, when Iquan surrendered to the Ming and was made the imperial commander of his forces in defense of the coast against other pirates and the Dutch. During the next two decades, while his power and prestige at the Ming court continued to rise, he seems to have maintained his contacts with the Dutch, though the relationship was punctuated by hostile confrontations, and to have traded with both Macau and Japan from his headquarters at Amoy.[77]

In 1645, as the Ming crumbled under the Manchu invasion, a power struggle ensued in the retreating Ming court. His influence diminished, Iquan perhaps foresaw the imminent collapse of his patrons, and following a crucial victory of the Manchu armies in Fujian, he surrendered to the Qing in late 1646. But his son Zheng Chenggong thereby inherited command of most of his forces and continued to protect the refugee Ming court. Known to Europeans as Koxinga, a corruption of the Chinese title *Guoxingye*, "Lord of the Imperial Surname," which the Ming had bestowed on him, Zheng Chenggong fought the Qing along the East China coast. He eventually established an autonomous regime on Taiwan, whence he continued to attack the Qing until his death in 1662. Iquan, however, was taken by the Manchus to Peking and held for some years; the Manchus hoped this would induce his son to surrender also. When it ultimately became apparent that his usefulness as a hostage was unavailing, Iquan was brought to trial and executed in 1661.

Throughout his life, Zheng Zhilong never completely lost contact with the Western world to which he had been introduced in Macau as a young man. During the late years of his life, while in captivity in Peking, he renewed his association with the Jesuits, first as a patron of their establishment in the capital and finally as a supplicant for their charity after his fortunes and his favor with the Qing court collapsed.[78] In one sense, Iquan's life had come full circle. His bizarre, remarkable career would not have been conceivable had he not first escaped from his own world. Macau was the place and his life there was the experience that allowed him to achieve that initial disconnection. Yet even more than someone like Wu Li, he remained always a part of his original Chinese world. And as much as Wu Li, he was trapped in a career that, nonetheless transformed, was refracted back into China.

For each in his own way, the experience of the West through the lens of Macau was limited for Wu Li and Zheng Zhilong, largely by the ecclesiastical and commercial context of the maritime periphery of which Macau was a part. By the nineteenth century, this context had changed. The more narrow, though nevertheless ambitious, evangelical approach of the Jesuits had passed away with the Rites Controversy in the eighteenth century and was succeeded by the much broader and more radical Protestant assault. Meanwhile, the commercial system of East Asia was in the throes of violent upheaval and transformation. Then, a new kind of experience emerged. Macau now became a bridge to a new world.

The first Protestant missionary to China was Robert Morrison, sent out by the London Missionary Society in 1807. He traveled to China by way of the United States, where he met Secretary of State James Madison and American Protestants interested in the China field. The ongoing connection with the United States would subsequently be a driving force in the Protestant missionary effort in China.

When he landed at Macau on September 4, 1807, Morrison was immediately ordered away by the Portuguese, who were suspicious of this Protestant interloper in what was heretofore an exclusively Catholic field. Thus, he was forced to go to Canton, where he was taken in by the factory of Milner and Bull of New York on the strength of his introductory letter from

Madison. Since the mid-eighteenth century, Canton was the scene of seasonal trading conducted by various European companies in their factories—trading establishments that comprised offices, warehouses, and residences—located along the river outside the city wall.

Immediately, Morrison plunged into the task of learning the language and culture of China. He zealously adopted or imitated everything Chinese—food, the use of chopsticks, dress—and he cultivated the queue for his hairstyle and let his fingernails grow in the fashion of a Chinese scholar.[79] He single-mindedly pursued his Chinese studies in Macau following his return there with the British in 1808—at first, so intensely that he was a virtual recluse. But by early 1809, he had emerged into respectability as an authority in Chinese; on the day of his marriage, he was appointed translator to the British East India Company and henceforth made his permanent residence in Macau.

Morrison's acceptance in Macau did not, however, allay the suspicions of the Portuguese regarding the Protestants' presence there. When Morrison's subsequent collaborator, William Milne, arrived from the United States in 1813, he also was ordered by the governor to leave the territory and had to pursue his language study at Canton.[80] The Portuguese Catholics regarded the Protestant presence as anathema, so much so that even Protestant burial was forbidden. A Protestant who died in Macau would have to be buried in secret outside the walls of the city, where the grave was subject to vandalism by both Portuguese and Chinese, who equally resented the practice. Indeed, it was Morrison who finally succeeded, through his own misfortunes, in correcting that problem. Although his infant son had already been buried in the territory beyond the city walls, when his wife, Mary, died in 1821, the Chinese would not permit her interment in the same place. Faced with this sad perplexity, the East India Company purchased a piece of land near the company residence in the city to be dedicated as a Protestant cemetery. Mary Morrison was the first person buried there, though earlier gravestones were later moved to the new cemetery.[81]

Through his study of the Chinese language and his translations, Morrison contributed significantly to the nineteenth-century revival of scholarship and knowledge about China. It was therefore appropriate that not long after his death at Canton in August 1834, a society was established in his name among the leading foreign residents in China to promote education and Western knowledge.[82] One of the earliest projects the Morrison Education Society supported with money donated by foreign firms and individuals was a small school in Macau for Chinese children run by Mrs. Charles (Karl) Gutzlaff, the English wife of a Prussian Protestant missionary. Started in 1835 under the auspices of the "Ladies' Association for the promotion of female education in India and the East," Mrs. Gutzlaff's school at first enrolled only twelve girls.[83] The $15-per-month subscription from the Morrison

Education Society provided for the pupils' clothing, board, room, and stationery. The children studied English, reading, and writing, as well as geography, history, and the New Testament. They also studied Chinese under the Reverend Gutzlaff and a Chinese teacher.[84]

To an impressionable Chinese child, even one used to seeing foreigners in Macau, Mrs. Gutzlaff was an awesome and initially even a frightening figure. Tall, with blond hair and deep-set clear blue eyes and a strong chin, she possessed a commanding personality. One of the first two Chinese boys to be admitted shortly after the founding of the school in 1835 soon found her, however, to be kindly and motherly.[85] The boy, Rong Hong (Yung Wing, in the local dialect), was also, at seven, the youngest child in the school. He came from the village of Nanping on Lappa Island, not far from the inner harbor. Mrs. Gutzlaff's comprador was also a native of Nanping and a friend and neighbor of Rong Hong's father.

The school encountered great difficulties retaining students, who were often withdrawn by their parents after only a few months so that they would not be too contaminated by Western education. But the little English they learned could be put to good use in the shops and businesses of Macau. Rong remained in Mrs. Gutzlaff's school for several years, probably longer than most pupils, until 1839, about the time the school was disbanded. These were unsettled times. The Opium War was just beginning, and Macau was crowded with Europeans and their Chinese employees who had fled from Canton during the hostilities. Many feared that the Chinese might attempt to attack the city.

Rong returned to his village, and though he was only eleven years old, he helped his family (he had two older brothers and a sister) by working odd jobs, hawking candy, and gleaning fields. When his father died in 1840, his support was all the more important. He had learned a fair amount of English in the school, and now this unusual ability came in handy. He found a job working for a priest in a printing office in Macau, doing simple manual work folding and preparing paper for binding. He was able to send $3 a month home to his mother.[86]

In the meantime, the Morrison Education Society opened its own school in Macau following the demise of Mrs. Gutzlaff's school in 1839. The directors of the society had long been looking for a suitable master for such a school, and they finally found such a person in the Reverend Samuel Brown, a graduate of Yale University who had taught in a school for the deaf and dumb in New York. He arrived in Macau in 1839, and the Morrison School was soon opened, in November 1839, with six boys (from the beginning, unlike Mrs. Gutzlaff's school, it was to be a school exclusively for boys).[87] Although the boys who had been Mrs. Gutzlaff's pupils had scattered when her school was closed, the directors had tried to keep track of them in the hope of bringing them back into the new school. At the same time, the Chinese, confronted now with the need to know more about the strength of the Western powers and requiring interpreters and translators, had also sought out these boys. It was reported that one of them (his name was not divulged) was recruited at Macau in 1839 by agents of Imperial Commissioner Lin Zexu to work as his English interpreter and translator. During his service for Commissioner Lin, who had been sent to Canton in 1839 and charged with the task of ending the opium trade, the boy had supplied Lin with intelligence regarding the English and translated newspaper reports and books. He was well treated, and after Lin's dismissal from office in 1841, though he turned to Chinese studies, the boy continued his English study as well.[88]

Rong was discovered at his job at the printer's by a former friend of Mrs. Gutzlaff who had made his acquaintance at her school. He was subsequently invited to enter the Morrison School, which he did in 1841. At the time, there were only five other boys studying there. Although the curriculum then comprised arithmetic, geography, and reading in English in the mornings and Chinese studies in the afternoons, the purpose was to duplicate as closely as possible the best education provided by a European school.[89] Few concessions were made to the original culture of the pupils, some of whom became so attached to their newly adopted culture that they were extremely loath to be separated from it when their parents, fearing just such alienation, tried to remove them from the school. This problem was aggravated when the Morrison School was moved from Macau to Hong Kong in 1842 following the settlement of the Opium War and the cession of Hong Kong to the British. Although some boys were not permitted by their parents to follow the school to Hong Kong, the new quarters permitted the expansion of the institution to more than twenty pupils in 1844 and to as many as forty by 1845.[90]

In 1846, the Reverend Brown retired as principal of the Morrison School to return to the United States. He proposed to take with him several boys to continue their education in his homeland. As one of the school's earliest and most promising students, Rong Hong was a natural choice. Two other boys, Huang Kuan and Huang Sheng, who had been with the school as long as he, were also selected.

The trajectory of Rong's transition to the West, beginning with his schooldays in Macau and greatly accelerated by his relocation to Hong Kong, now took him completely away from the Chinese world. But he was well prepared for the transition, which carried him from the South China coast to New York in one smooth, almost uneventful voyage; only one year earlier in the Morrison School, he had written a composition entitled "An Imaginary Voyage to New York and up the Hudson."[91] He had, in fact, already taken his biggest step more than ten years before, when his father brought him from Nanping to Macau and introduced him to Mrs. Gutzlaff.

Eight years later, in 1854, Rong Hong returned to China. He and the two other boys had been enrolled in the Monson Academy in Massachusetts.

After graduating in 1850, Rong entered Yale University; he graduated from Yale in 1854, the first Chinese graduate of a U.S. university. His Westernization was complete. As his ship approached Hong Kong, a Chinese pilot came on board. "The Captain wanted me to ask him whether there were any dangerous rocks and shoals nearby. I could not for the life of me recall my Chinese in order to interpret for him."[92] In fact, Rong Hong was forced to immerse himself for several months in the study of written and spoken Chinese to recover the language he had lost or barely known in the first place.

While in the United States, Rong had determined that his goal must be to promote Western education in China. For a number of years after he returned to China, however, he thrashed around, pursuing a variety of leads, unable to find the key to realizing his ambition. He served as a private secretary to Dr. Peter Parker, U.S. commissioner to China at Canton; in succession, he attempted unsuccessfully to enter the legal profession in Hong Kong, he worked for the Imperial Maritime Customs in Shanghai, and he tried his hand at the tea business with some success. The last enterprise led to an expedition to the Taiping rebel capital at Nanking, where he made some recommendations for reform and was offered an official position in the rebel government.[93]

The opportunity Rong dreamed of came at last in 1863 when he was introduced through some friends to Zeng Guofan, the supreme commander of the Qing campaign against the Taiping rebels. Zeng had assembled under the umbrella of his *mufu*, or private secretariat, a corps of talented scholars and experts commanding diverse knowledge that he would put to use in organizing his campaign to defeat the rebellion. In addition to experts in finance, civil administration, military organization, and technology, he sought Chinese who had experience with the West.[94] Rong met Zeng at the latter's headquarters at Anqing on the Yangzi River and was commissioned by him to purchase machinery in the United States for Zeng's new arsenal. For his successful conclusion of this mission, he was rewarded with official rank and decorations. It also provided him with an opportunity to propose his educational schemes to Zeng, who was receptive to the idea of sending Chinese abroad for technical training. Consequently, in 1870, Zeng proposed to the government an educational mission to the United States. The mission departed in 1872 with Rong as co-commissioner.[95]

Altogether, more than one hundred students were sent abroad under the auspices of the Chinese Educational Mission. But from the start, there were problems. Conservative Chinese officials, including Chen Lanbin, the other co-commissioner of the mission, feared the cultural corruption of the students by Western learning and customs. They opposed Rong's policy of encouraging the students' assimilation along the lines that Rong himself had followed. Thus, in 1881, the mission was withdrawn and the students were returned home.[96]

While he directed the Chinese Educational Mission in the United States, Rong concurrently carried out other commissions for the Chinese government. He investigated the Chinese coolie traffic in Peru in 1873, and in 1875, he was appointed joint minister, with Chen Lanbin, to Washington, establishing the first Chinese legation in the United States in 1878. When the Chinese Educational Mission failed in 1881 and Rong was unable to find suitable employment with the government in China, he returned to the United States for more than a decade. In 1895, he was commissioned to negotiate a foreign loan to support Chinese defense in the war with Japan, and he worked on several other projects, mostly without success. He left China for the last time in 1902 to return to the United States for his son's graduation from Yale.[97]

Long before, while a student at Yale himself in 1852, Rong Hong had become a naturalized U.S. citizen. In 1875, he married an American woman, Mary Louisa Kellog, with whom he had two sons. He died in Hartford, where he had been educated and where the Chinese Educational Mission had been located, in 1912.

Although Rong Hong moved far beyond Macau in a career culturally equidistant from both China and the West—like Macau itself, which gave him his impetus outward from China—his life bridged the two worlds. Ultimately perhaps more Western than Chinese, he was, in a sense, a mirror image of Adam Schall, who died equally far from his own culture, both spiritually and geographically, and was, in the end, more Chinese than Western. If Rong and Schall marked the polar ends of a spectrum of cultural metamorphosis, then there were many intermediate positions representing incomplete transitions—positions occupied by men such as Michele Ruggieri or Nicholas Iquan. For all of them, what was required was a place where that cultural metamorphosis, abortive or not, could be mediated.

Rong Hong's generation was almost the last for which Macau could be a threshold between two worlds. Even as Rong's education progressed, Macau was being superseded by Hong Kong and the Western enclaves in the treaty ports that had been established as a consequence of the Opium Wars. Macau had become the backwater that George Chinnery painted, no longer the doorway that Valignano opened.

five

Moments
The Culture of Everyday Life

*So twice five miles of fertile ground
With walls and towers were girdled round:
And there were gardens bright with sinuous rills,
Where blossomed many an incense-bearing tree;
And here were forests ancient as the hills,
Enfolding sunny spots of greenery.*[1]

There are two kinds of moments in Macau: the moment as a pause in the passage of time, oblivious of past or future, and the moment of history. The two moments coexist everywhere yet are seemingly detached from one another.

At the center of the city, in the São Domingos market beside the Leal Senado and across from the Santa Casa de Misericordia, the changeless activity of the business of living goes on with the kind of random intensity of life and decay on a steamy, tropical forest floor. Cars, motorcycles, trucks, bicycles, handcarts, and pedestrians move in every direction, some slowly and seemingly confused, others purposefully on business errands—delivering goods, moving things, repairing utilities, renovating buildings, or tearing them down and starting new ones. In the market is an endless daily turnover of meat, fish, fruit, and vegetables; stalls and peddlers in the surrounding streets offering every kind of cheap clothes, toys, and trinkets; boutiques, stationery shops, pharmacies, and hardware stores selling household goods overflowing onto the sidewalk; and bakeries and cafes tempting the crowds with the morning's pastries. Whole dried fish, their heads covered with white paper hoods, hang by the tail in dry-food stores above burnished canisters of tea and herbs; tiny goldfish swim in clear plastic bags of water hanging on walls; chickens crouch in wire cages; dark orange egg yolks dry in the sun on bamboo trays. There are blind fortune-tellers, scribes who will write a letter for an illiterate customer, and an old man who molds tiny dolls and figures famous in fiction and history from bits of colored dough.

Regularly, every afternoon, immense piles of trash are swept out of the shops and the market, brought down the narrow side streets in carts and bamboo baskets, and loaded into garbage trucks by women wearing bamboo peasant hats and blue aprons marked "Limpeza." This ephemeral routine of collecting the effluent of the day's activities contrasts strangely with the solemn dignity and enduring purpose of the old Portuguese presence in the Leal Senado and the Santa Casa.

Not far away on the Praia Grande skirting the bay and the outer harbor, the monotonous squeaking of the swings under the shade of the banyan trees in the Parque Infintil, like the buzzing of summer insects, joins with the singing of birds and the shouts of children. The children play games with marbles in the twisted ridges and cavities of the exposed banyan roots by the shore. At high tide, little chugging sampans drone methodically, trolling for small fish in the shallow and muddy water, but at low tide, the expanse of mudflats will be exposed. It is there that grand commercial mansions once overlooked the loading of goods carried by great junks and carracks come to trade.[2]

Apart from the impressive buildings—the churches and monasteries on the hills, the fortresses, the Leal Senado and the Santa Casa, the imposing commercial houses along the Praia—daily life in the streets of Macau has long attracted attention from visitors to the city. But in the city's early days, Macau's appearance must have been very different from its later aspect. As early as the mid-seventeenth century, there were Chinese shops catering to the wealthy inhabitants, but goods were more commonly bought from peddlers going from house to house selling clothes, silk, and other wares, often as aggressively as any modern door-to-door salesman.[3] It was probably not until the late eighteenth and early nineteenth centuries, when the Chinese population of the city rose to a significant number, that permanent markets appeared and shops came to line the street of definable commercial quarters. "The smallest spaces are rented to the Chinese, whose shops line the streets in small loft buildings leased for income."[4] George Chinnery's drawings show Chinese food stalls on the streets in the center of town near São Domingos Church; scribes and money changers; barbers and blacksmiths; people huddled together playing games; dogs and cats; women and men carrying things on poles; cattle, goats, and Chinese potbellied pigs. But even in the sketches of Chinnery and Auguste Borget, much of the intense interest of street scenes in later years is absent.

Not until the later nineteenth century, under the governorship of Coelho do Amaral, who substantially redesigned much of the city and extended it northward across the Campo, were distinct and very different residential and commercial quarters created.[5] From then on, the narrow, cobbled streets and lanes, becos, patios, and cul-de-sacs of the older sections south of

Pharmacia Popular

Monte hill contrasted dramatically with the wide, rectilinear boulevards planted with rows of shade trees and flower beds of the new, largely residential sections to the north. Paintings of Macau from as late as the early nineteenth century show few trees, however. Vegetation on the peninsula was scanty and became even more sparse as the population increased—thus the remarkable contrast with the lush Ilha Verde in the inner harbor.

Peoples and Styles

As a place where cultural tides washed together, depositing people and their customs, fashions, and possessions on its shore, Macau was a source of curiosity to people from both sides of the threshold: the way Macau's residents lived, the clothes they wore, their customs and leisure activities, their peculiar behavior and odd preferences, and, of course, the people themselves.[6]

Those who were merely sojourners in the city for longer or shorter times as well as those who passed their entire lives there created a mixed society reflecting the distinct cultures from which they came. But this mixture, in terms of class, gender, ethnicity, and culture, was constantly in flux from the beginning. Until the late eighteenth century, Macau was, in some respects, a bipolar society, composed of the European elite, on the one hand, and their numerous African and Asian slaves, on the other. Such, at least, was the way the Chinese, with considerable justice, tended to view it:

Guangdong is where foreigners from the outer seas congregate. They are both
white and black. Cantonese call them white devils or black devils. The whites'
faces are pink, and their hair is all white. Even the young appear as white as frost
and snow. The blacks' hair is black, and their faces are also black, but lighter
than their hair, like the color of diluted ink. The whites are the masters, the
blacks are slaves.[7]

But in truth Macau's society was far more complex than that.

First were the Europeans, mainly Portuguese in the beginning but including Italians, Spanish, French, Dutch, Germans, and others, especially among
the priests who would follow. Indeed, one could consider the priests a separate class because they lived apart from the secular classes and observed distinctive customs.[8] The Chinese were much impressed by the extravagant appearance of the tall Portuguese, with their pale white faces, their beaklike
noses, their deep-set green eyes, piercing and unblinking like a cat's, and
their abundant, long, curly, "purple-green" hair.[9] The Chinese also took note
of other white Europeans, with red hair and beards—the Dutch.

The Portuguese gentlemen wore wide-brimmed black felt hats or hats
with the brims folded into three corners. These were sometimes adorned
with figures and various motifs and feather plumes. They wore white shirts
with long sleeves ending in elaborately pleated cuffs. Lined trousers extending to the knees and tight stockings were made of patterned weaves. Woolen
coats ending at the waist and capes were decorated with embroidered borders and rows of gold and silver buttons—these were worn regardless of the
weather, and the Chinese thought them very colorful. On their feet, the Portuguese wore black wooden shoes with high heels, fastened with metal buttons.[10] In inside pockets or purses, they kept snuff bottles, self-chiming
watches, and other sundries. They carried swords that, as the Chinese noted,
were so long the ends of the scabbards trailed on the ground, noisily rattling
on the cobblestones. Some also carried canes and leather gloves.[11]

Besides the Portuguese and the other Europeans who lived in the city at
Portuguese sufferance and the priests who were of many nationalities, other
foreigners also made Macau their home, either by choice or by necessity. In
the late sixteenth and early seventeenth centuries, when the Japan trade was
at its height, modest numbers of Japanese went to Macau. Some were connected with the trade; others went for Christian instruction at the Jesuit College or with the priests of the Dominican and Franciscan orders. Later,
Japanese Christians, fleeing the religious persecution that began to exact its
toll in the 1620s and 1630s, also sought refuge in Macau.

At the bottom of the social hierarchy, distinct from the Portuguese and
other Europeans and from the priests, were the black slaves, taken to all
parts of the Portuguese empire from Africa; the servants and slaves from
other regions of Asia, including India, Malacca, and the Indies; and the Chinese slaves and servants, mainly female. Chinese families sold their female

男番圖

Foreign male (drawing from *Aomen jilue*)

children as bonded servants to the Portuguese for terms of thirty to fifty years, after which they were to be freed, and some were sold unconditionally as slaves.[12] The Chinese took little notice of the Asian slaves of the Portuguese, no doubt because slavery itself was not unfamiliar to them, but they were particularly fascinated with the black slaves. The Chinese found them "generally similar to humans" and described their speech as "indistinguishable from the babble of pygmies,"[13] yet they admired them for their character, ability, and strength. Black slaves were probably employed in hazardous jobs around ships and in the water because the Chinese believed they had the ability to dive and swim under water without shutting their eyes and even to "walk on water as if it were level ground."[14] Slaves, both male and female, wore cotton clothes, usually white but sometimes red, purple, or blue, and no shoes.

Because no European women of any class accompanied the early Portuguese settlers to Macau, unions between European men and Asian women, including slaves and servants, were always common.[15] Intermarriage occurred mainly with Japanese, Indian, Malay, and Philippine women at first, with Chinese servants or slaves somewhat later, and with black slaves on occasion.[16] Evidently, it was also not uncommon for households to pair black male slaves with Chinese female servants.[17] The result, over a century or more, was a large and ethnically variegated population of slaves, servants, and household members who were in various stages between servitude and freedom—a population that emerged in the seventeenth and eighteenth centuries as the Macanese. A large proportion of this group seems to have been female. Even as late as the 1830s and 1840s, some estimates suggest, there was a population of approximately 900 Portuguese males, 2,600 females, perhaps 800 slaves, and 300 black soldiers. The Chinese population at that time stood at about 30,000.[18]

The reason for this extraordinary abundance of women is not clear. One explanation is that it was the result of the large number of unwanted female babies sold as bond servants to Portuguese families or abandoned by the Chinese to be cared for by the Santa Casa and other charitable organizations. Because these organizations were unable to cope with so many unwanted children, the young girls were placed in foster families, where they usually became servants, or were abandoned to become prostitutes.[19] It is also possible that male children of mixed unions were more easily sold or sent elsewhere as slaves, leaving a disproportionate number of females behind.

For at least two hundred years, the wives of Portuguese residents and the mistresses of upper-class households were Eurasian women (*mestizhinas*), the daughters from Macanese families and mixed unions, or the women sent out from Goa. Probably in the mid-eighteenth century, European women, mainly Portuguese, began to arrive. One Chinese observer noted the difference in these women: "Those born in their own country have red hair and their eyes are green. Those born in Macau are the same as natives."[20] Still, by the end of the century, there were few European women in Macau, and the expatriate society tended to revolve about them.[21] In the early part of the next century, increasing numbers of non-Portuguese European and American women resided in the city. They accompanied husbands who were engaged in the expanding trade at Canton, and because the Chinese prohibited foreign women from going to that city or staying in the foreign factory area during the trading season, the women resided in Macau throughout the year. Beginning in the 1830s, women also arrived as the wives of Protestant missionaries and sometimes, no doubt, alone. Some of these women are depicted in the portraits by George Chinnery. Mary Morton, the wife of Robert Morrison (the first Protestant missionary in China), died in Macau, and the wife of the Reverend Charles Gutzlaff established a school for Chinese girls and boys in Macau in 1835. Her two nieces went to China to help her in the project.[22]

Harriet Low, niece of an American trader who worked at Canton from 1829 to 1834, was one of the few young, unmarried foreign women in Macau in that period. She immediately became the center of almost desperate attention from the many English and American merchants, most of whom were single. Her presence was consequently in great demand at the numerous balls and parties that helped the expatriate community pass the time, especially in the slack winter months between the trading seasons.

> I danced every time, and got into quite a hobble; for I engaged for four deep about the middle of the evening, and, when it came to the third, could not tell for the life of me whom I had engaged to dance with. Two gentlemen came, both claimed me for that dance, and both were equally urgent. . . . It would not be so if there were many ladies here, but you know they are scarce. There are twenty times as many gentlemen, only a little sprinkling of ladies. I have no rivals, as there is but one other spinster in the place.[23]

During the century of Macau's prosperity, women's dress reflected the affluence of their households in an amalgam of Asian and European fashions. Women displayed costly jewelry in dressing their hair, which was worn on the top of the head, and used richly embroidered, colored silk with gold ornamentation. They wore full-length, wide-sleeved jackets, like kimonos but suggesting Chinese influence. These were brought from Japan or made locally by Chinese.[24]

The Chinese were intrigued by foreign and Eurasian women, with their bizarre appearance, their manners and customs, and their social roles:

女蕃圖

Foreign female (drawing from *Aomen jilue*)

The women are adorned just as in foreign pictures. The color of their hair is the same as natives, but they do not wear the queue. Their hair falls down above their forehead about two inches, in the fashion of unmarried Chinese native girls' hair and it is bound up with painted silk thread [?], which is fashionably referred to as hair coiled like the scorpion's tail. . . . Those with red hair [Portuguese] have naturally curly hair, but those with black hair achieve that effect with curlers. . . . Their bosoms are exposed, not hidden, and they wear their petticoats on the outside.[25]

Young women wore mascara and beauty marks and frequently had pearls and gold bracelets on their wrists. In the summer, they would often carry fans. In contrast to the men, women dressed rather scantily: blouses above the waist and skirts of multicolored satins extending in varying lengths, to the knees, to the shins, or over the feet. They covered their heads with long embroidered shawls when they went out, a custom that came from Goa, but they wore neither stockings nor shoes. Young girls, however, wore "trousers of cloth as thin as the cicada's wing."[26] Macanese women in the eighteenth and nineteenth centuries wore long scarves called *do*, which, like veils, covered their heads and fell nearly to the ground.[27] Although European men's attire closely followed European fashion, women's clothing exhibited many more influences of their countries of origin, including India, Malaya, and Japan. By the nineteenth century, however, dress had come to differentiate the Portuguese and other Europeans (both men and women), who closely followed European fashions, and the Macanese, who dressed more conservatively, predominantly in black.[28]

Portuguese and Macanese women enjoyed much greater freedom than their Chinese counterparts. Not subjected to the custom of foot binding, they naturally were more mobile. And since they were not strictly confined to the home, especially after their child-raising years, they were frequently seen in public. The churches in particular were important social meeting places for older women.[29] The Chinese, perhaps referring only to a custom in Macanese families, reported that marriage was matrilocal—that a man married into his bride's family and lived with them.[30] Within the home, women commanded considerable deference and attention, occupying a place of honor and exercising control over the household—so much so that the Chinese noted they were particularly respected in Macanese society, inheriting their fathers' estates and "transmitting the seals of office."[31] Although the scope of their activities outside the home was nevertheless restricted, one observer commented on the frequency of illicit affairs among women:

While women are very strictly controlled, they delight in pursuing illicit affairs. Their husbands do not dare inquire about them. When the husband happens to return to his country, and the journey is very long, he must ask a friend to live in his house. His friend stays there three or four days at a time. If after several days he does not come back, then the wife seeks him out and upbraids him for his absence. When the husband returns he asks whether his friend was careless or attentive in his visits. If he was attentive, then he is a good friend; if he was careless, then he will no longer have him as his friend. The customs related are all contrary to the teachings of propriety. This is why Heaven separates the Chinese and barbarians.[32]

Although the moral standards of the Chinese and Westerners were perhaps not so divergent, it may be that the difference in the severity of sanctions for moral transgressions shocked the Chinese as much as anything else:

> If a woman has an illicit affair with someone, during religious service she must kneel before a priest and confess, so that the priest may ask the Lord of Heaven to nullify her transgression. What is most important to a woman are her breasts, and only her husband may touch them, the same with Chinese [*Tangren*] intimacy. The priest asks her whether in the past someone has touched her breasts. If she has been touched, then she is warned it may not happen again, and she ought to confess at once. The woman agrees to do so and then withdraws.[33]

The relative freedom of movement enjoyed by foreign women, reported in Chinese accounts, is particularly remarkable in light of the rather severe, traditional Portuguese misogyny that prevailed at home as well as abroad in Portugal's overseas empire. In the home, for example, women were not supposed to appear when a male guest came to dinner, and the seclusion of women presumably extended to appearances in public. This attitude provided the foundation for the Portuguese exaltation of female virginity and chastity, manifested in the celebration of the Virgin Mary, whose cult was especially strong in Macau.[34] But attitude is one thing, and practice is another. Although the social mobility and status ascribed by the Chinese to Portuguese women was, no doubt, an exaggeration, Macanese society was certainly not matriarchal, and women had no direct role in government. Nevertheless, women played an influential role in Macanese society, quite different from their counterparts in Chinese society or, perhaps, in Portuguese society.

Routines of Daily Life

The lifestyle of the upper-class Portuguese and the affluent Macanese was marked by comfort and elegance. The abundance of slaves and servants ensured that little exertion or effort was required of those at the top of the social scale.[35] The primitive circumstances of life in Macau in the first decade or two after its settlement were soon dispelled by the affluence that booming trade brought to the city for almost one hundred years. Limited only by the constraints imposed by the rigors of the tropical climate and confinement to the small peninsula due to Chinese restrictions, as well as the separation from Goa and vastly more distant Lisbon, the residents maintained as much as they could of the life and customs of their homeland and of the Asian upper classes that they encountered.

Following the collapse of the trade after the crisis of the 1640s, life became harder for many. The city's former prosperity waned, if it did not entirely evaporate; poverty set in for many as fortunes were lost; and straitened economic circumstances inevitably affected the entire population. But for Europeans who survived and stayed on, even under diminished opportunities, life in Macau was good. Increasing Chinese immigration, although it put a new strain on the fiscal and charitable institutions of the city, supplied an ever broadening base on which the European survivors could depend for labor, services, and even intermarriage; it also created a foundation for social stability and continuity that the constantly fluctuating population of Europeans and their slaves during the earlier era did not.

For a century or so, life in Macau settled into a relatively stable, less intense routine, as compared to the previous era of burgeoning prosperity. By the end of the eighteenth century, the expanding trade at Canton, led by the English, brought new importance, increased activity, and new cultural influences to the settlement. Observers of Macau in the nineteenth century envied its languid, easy pace of life and the spacious, elegant Portuguese houses, as well as the pleasant climate.

In their comfortable and often sumptuous surroundings, the Portuguese endeavored to preserve European manners while adopting the embellishments of Asian styles and customs. This process was reflected in the routine of daily life, in their food and cuisine, in their amusements and recreations, and in the manners and ceremony with which they surrounded themselves.

The principal meal was taken at midday. In a typical household, a bell was rung to announce the beginning of the meal. A large, rectangular table covered by a plain white tablecloth was set with several dishes and glasses, silverware, and white napkins at each place. Men and women were seated together while a slave brought the food. Curiously, one Chinese account mentions that rose water and flower petals were sprinkled over the heads of the people before the meal commenced and that the family followed a custom of using only the left hand for handling food. Except for the reversal of right and left hands—a detail that was perhaps an error—this reference suggests that Muslim eating customs were observed.[36] An expanded version of the same account, however, refers to the diners' abstention from beef, pork, and shrimp on Fridays and Saturdays, when only vegetables were eaten, but it gives no hint of the Muslim taboo against pork.[37]

When the meal is finished, "they all retire until early evening. Then they rise, light lanterns, and conduct their business."[38] The practice of having a long period of rest in the afternoon following a large meal at midday, reserving the cooler evening for business, was an adaptation to the tropical climate observed throughout Asia by European merchants and their Asian counterparts.[39]

The large residences of the upper class—with their deep, spacious verandas capturing the cooling monsoon breezes and their tall doors and shuttered windows opening into high-ceilinged inner rooms finished in white plaster—were well adapted to the tropical climate and the slow pace of their occupants' lives. Windows were sometimes made of fish scale or thin pearl shell, which admitted a soft, diffuse light into the dimly lit rooms.[40] The large Portuguese houses were richly furnished with curiosities and favored objects of the trade. Brilliantly painted folding screens, lavishly applied with gold leaf, known as *biombu* or *beobu* (*byobu* in Japanese) and imported from Japan, depicted Western and Eastern subjects, stories, natural scenes, animals, trees, and flowers.[41] Gilded lances and weapons were also a favorite decoration, as were hangings, porcelain plates, and tiles.[42] Below the main floor of the typical house and its verandas was the dark, arched ground floor, to which the slaves and servants were relegated and where merchandise and supplies were stored.[43] "Leftover food [was] thrown into a dish like a horse trough for the black male and female slaves to eat as they please."[44]

Since the city was very small, especially before it expanded beyond the old walls in the late nineteenth century, it was not difficult to get around on foot. Nevertheless, the foreigners, particularly in the hot and humid summers, preferred to ride in sedan chairs, emulating the Chinese officials: This mode of conveyance was more appropriate to their wealth and social status, of which they were very conscious. Upper-class women, although they also sometimes went about on foot with their attendants, found sedans a more discreet means of transportation.

There were several varieties of sedans, which, no doubt, reflected the position and social standing of their owners. One was in the shape of a large wooden cabinet, like a small carriage without wheels, which was entered by stepping through an opening covered by a removable hatch at one end. Carried by four bearers, it was used by foreign officials, who were normally accompanied by attendants bearing umbrellas or parasols, weapons, and pennants. A similar sedan, with a door on the side, was used mainly by women. Smaller sedans, carried with poles on the shoulders of two bearers, were lighter but lacked tops and were thus less private. In these, the passenger was carried in a recumbent position. There were two types of this sedan variety: the hard sedan, made of bowed wood and decorated with carvings, and the soft sedan, which was hammocklike and made of knotted rope. The most elegant of all was the Chinese variety of enclosed sedan, made of wood with glass windows and ornamented with pearl shell inlay. These were used mainly by the priests and by Chinese officials.[45]

No doubt, the Portuguese initially used slaves, who were abundant, as sedan bearers. Chinese officials, of course, used Chinese bearers. Later, in the eighteenth century as the number of Chinese servants in the city increased and the slave population decreased in proportion to the foreign population, Chinese servants were employed as sedan bearers. In Canton, foreigners were prohibited from riding in sedan chairs, and the use of Chinese servants as bearers in Macau was outlawed by the Chinese. But the practice was generally ignored by the Chinese authorities, and by the nineteenth century, many foreigners, not only the Portuguese, were using large Chinese sedans carried by Chinese servants.[46]

Sedans gradually disappeared as rickshas, first invented in Japan, spread along the China coast in the late nineteenth and early twentieth centuries. Rickshas, in turn, were displaced by pedicabs, which remained a common mode of transportation in Macau until fairly recently (despite the fact that they could not climb hills, making many areas of the city inaccessible to them). Today, omnibuses and taxicabs predominate.

The modernization of transportation did not have the same effect on Macau that it did on other, larger cities such as Peking. In that flat and extensive city, traditional sedans gave way to rickshas pulled by ricksha men who constituted a significant portion of the population.[47] Macau, by contrast, is comparatively small and easily covered on foot, and it encompasses many steep hills. There, sedans were used to reflect status and ensure privacy, rather than speed, and rickshas added little to these advantages. But rickshas were ubiquitous in Asian cities, symbolizing the joining of abundant native

Closed sedan (drawing from *Aomen jilue*)

硬轎圖

Rigid sedan (drawing from *Aomen jilue*)

軟轎圖

Soft sedan (drawing from *Aomen jilue*)

labor power and Western technological development, and as such, they inevitably came to Macau as well. Thus, sedans, rickshas, pedicabs, and finally automobiles were all reflections of status in Macau—emblems not of liberation from immobility to the newfound freedom of mobility but of social status, importance, and wealth.[48] Prior to the 1960s, when the city still retained much of its sleepy, decadent charm, automobiles were few and limited mainly to taxis, buses, and the occasional private and official car. Since that time, however, the vast increase in automobiles in Macau has actually inhibited mobility and convenience, and traffic has almost reached a point of gridlock.[49]

Much time would pass—months, perhaps—before the arrival of a new group of ships and the return of frenetic activity in Macau—loading and unloading supplies and cargoes, greeting and visiting new arrivals, gathering the news they brought, and arranging the sales and purchases of goods and commodities. In between, the observance of etiquette and an obsession with dress and small matters of style were simple ways to stave off the inevitable boredom.

Guests were entertained in formal gatherings at which tea, fruit, and wine were served, with careful attention to decorum. Tea was served by one of the women of the house, while another added white sugar. Next, a servant led the guests to a large table set in an elaborate style. The mistress of the house and her daughters, if any, were seated next to the guest of honor. The women sliced and served the fruit while a servant passed plates to the seated guests. European wine of different varieties was then served by the host and passed around by the servants.[50] Peter Mundy described a formal banquet served during his visit in 1637:

> Our Dinner was served in plate, very good and savory to my Mynde, only the Manner much Differing From ours, For every Man had a like portion of each sort of Meat broughtt betweene 2 sillver plates, and this often Chaunged, For before a man had Don with the one, there was another service stood ready For him; Allmost the same Decorum in our Drincke, every Man his silver Goblett by his trencher, which were no sooner empty butt there stood those ready thatt Filld them againe with excellent good Portugall wyne.[51]

Even in the mid-twentieth century, teatime remained a favored opportunity for entertainment and socializing in the upper-class home:

> Teatime was a special moment of the day for the ladies. There is no way one can describe the variety of cakes, sweets, and other delicacies offered. It was an exquisite time of abundance. If there was an occasion to celebrate, and this happened often, because people loved to entertain, teatime was the favorite meal, but it was a late tea, when the sun was on its way out towards the horizon, and it was called Cha Gordo (fat tea), where not only sweets were served but also turkeys, roasted chickens, meatballs, and pies, a nonending gastronomic affair, accompanied by hot soups and special spiced teas from the Indies, jasmine tea from China, and, for the more conservative newcomers' taste, English tea.[52]

Staple fresh foods were supplied from the local farms and fishermen of the peninsula and the markets of the neighboring districts; they necessarily depended for their varieties on the existing indigenous economy.[53] Chicken, beef, pork, fish, shrimp, fruits of various kinds, rice, beans, and fresh vegetables were all common components of the residents' diet.[54] Many varieties of fruit grow in the region of South China around Canton, including litchis, citrus of many species, bananas, grapes, figs, and pears, and these items were much appreciated by the Portuguese and visitors alike.[55] But some foods—particularly high-value commodities that were easily transported and foods that were not available locally but were considered essential to a certain style of life—were imported from South and Southeast Asia and even from Portugal. These included spices and herbs—pepper, cloves, curry, and others—olives, olive oil, capers, and European wine.[56] In spite of the great distances over which wine and olive oil had to be carried to reach Macau, their importation was and still is virtually subsidized. Wine was sold at Goa for little more than its price in Lisbon, and by the time it reached Macau, its price had risen only modestly, if at all.[57]

The evolution of the Macanese cuisine was affected partly by the cultural constituents of the population and partly by the availability of specific foods. It reflected the route by which the Portuguese had come—Africa, the southern Middle East, Goa and the Malabar and Coromandel coasts of India, and Malacca—and the places with which Macau carried on trade and communication, especially South China, Malaya, and Indonesia. The result was a varied cuisine that owed its distinctive character to its diverse ethnic and geographical origins.[58]

South Chinese cuisine, not surprisingly, became the dominant influence. With boiled rice as a staple food, water chestnuts and bamboo shoots, sesame oil for cooking and seasoning, and small pastries and candied fruits of various kinds all found their way onto the Macanese menu.[59] The Macanese were fond of breads and pastries of many kinds, cakes spiced with clove, and sweets and candies. Chinese accounts also mentioned the use of betel nut and the practice of smoking tobacco in the form of cigarettes.[60] Although Macanese dishes were more heavily spiced than those of either Portugal or South China, reflecting the Southeast Asian and Indian origins of the Macanese population, the fundamental approach to preparing food remained largely European in its emphasis on substantial proportions of meat in the diet. Thus, as in other aspects of Macau's cultural styles (such as its architecture), the substance was essentially European, and the embellishments came from Asia.

Marvelous Technology

Foreigners brought to Macau the latest technology and mechanical devices of the West, such as clocks, optical devices, astronomical instruments, and firearms. Although Europeans naturally took such things for granted, the Chinese regarded them as marvelous and sometimes dangerous curiosities. Many of the devices, of course, were associated with exploration and conquest. The extent of detail in Chinese descriptions of these technological wonders suggests that the authors were more than casually acquainted with them.

Although some of these technical objects went no further than Macau— merely adding to the general interest of the place as a rather outlandish repository of foreigners, their bizarre customs, and their curious possessions—some made their way into China. The Jesuit missionaries, who mastered astronomical and mathematical expertise as a means of penetrating Chinese resistance to their own presence, made clocks, astronomical and other scientific instruments, maps, and nautical devices an important part of their repertory.

Nothing better symbolized Western technical ingenuity than clocks, which modeled the mechanistic, clockwork regularity of the Western view of the cosmos.

> The clock tower contains a great bell, with strikers in the form of angels standing at the corners of the tower. As the machine turns, chimes are sounded according to the hour, one chime at one A.M. up to twelve chimes at noon, and beginning again with one chime at one P.M. up to twelve chimes at midnight. It revolves day and night without the slightest error. On the front is displayed a round plate with twelve divisions corresponding to the hours the bell strikes, with a figure of a frog that moves to point to each position.[61]

Other kinds of smaller "self-chiming clocks" and watches, as well as music boxes, were also common in the city. There were table clocks, wall clocks, and pocket watches, all of which chimed automatically; music clocks and answering clocks and watches that chimed the hour when a string was pulled; and clocklike instruments displaying the calendar and phases of the moon.[62]

Macau was the central point for the introduction of mechanical contrivances, especially clocks and timepieces, to China, initially through the agency of the Jesuits. Accurate measurement of time was essential to maintaining the official calendar, which specified the important events of the agricultural cycle. The Western mechanical clock displaced the Chinese water clock (the clepsydra), which was less accurate and required regular attendance. But mechanical clocks were prone to break down, and consequently, the Jesuits continued to be employed as mechanics for repairing the European clocks that the Chinese, particularly the court, collected in great numbers.[63]

Complex mechanical musical instruments, such as organs and pianos or harpsichords, were also taken to Macau and understandably garnered much attention from the Chinese since they have always associated music with the harmonious (or disharmonious) functioning of both the natural and the human order.

But what might best be classified as scientific and astronomical instruments were the most important items, and they must have had the greatest impact because they involved discovering new ways of understanding, not simply more refined techniques of measurement. These included telescopes, microscopes and magnifying glasses, and armillary spheres and nautical charts. An observant Chinese visitor was introduced to these remarkable inventions:

> There is a "thousand-li-mirror" [telescope] in which you can see more than thirty li away the small bells on the tip of a pagoda in the minutest detail and every stroke of a character sharply [distinguished]. The moon's center appears like a bowl of water with bits of black paper floating in its surface, covering the background like the wispy clouds in a painting. Light flickers from it like the glow from a transparent paper covered colored lantern.
>
> There is a microscope with which you can see the young—there are three or four—carried on the back of the colored hairy caterpillar, and you can see hair lice, black and as if they were an inch long, [so clear that] they can be counted.[64]

A sense of the excitement inherent in new discoveries is strongly conveyed in this passage. One instrument the author described is difficult to identify. This "thousand-man-mirror" was a complex device of many small mirrors or lenses that multiplied and projected the image of something placed in front of it many times, so that "one person becomes hundreds of thousands of people, [as when you see] in a temple one buddha as if transformed into a hundred thousand bodies." Eyeglasses, small glass hand mirrors, and large vanity wall mirrors were more mundane examples of this kind of curiosity.[65] Although eyeglasses, at least, might be considered an important new technological benefit not previously enjoyed, such devices would become emblems of status for the Chinese who sought to mimic foreign customs as much as practical contributions.

Weapons were yet another dimension of Western technological ingenuity. Firearms were the mainstay of Portugal's conquest of the Indian Ocean and the Indies. But the Portuguese seldom had a reason to use them in China, except against the numerous pirates of the South and East China Seas and against their European enemies, such as the Dutch. Nonetheless, they certainly were well armed everywhere they went. They introduced firearms in large numbers to Japan in the sixteenth century, which significantly affected the great civil war of unification that was then under way; the conclusion of that war ultimately led to the downfall of Portugal's trade with Japan. The Chinese regarded these weapons with considerable misgivings, for good reason. One man's description of what was evidently a pistol reveals a mixture of admiration for its technical ingenuity and fear of its potential:

> As for mechanical weapons called *dimianxiao* [?], the scabbard is concealed in the clothing and protrudes no more than a foot. [This] weapon is so extraordinarily lethal that it is quite dreadful. A small stone the size of a bean held in a cavity is struck from the outside by an iron tooth, [causing] fire to pass into the cavity. It is made entirely of fine iron assembled from more than twenty parts, all fitted together perfectly.[66]

In the long run, the transfer of technology through Macau was, in a sense, abortive: With the possible exception of firearms, the transfer did not lead to a successful native Chinese incorporation and adaptation of the principles of Western technology itself but only to the adoption of its end products in the amusing and ingenious contrivances of the West—mere toys or trivial embellishments to Chinese culture, like the giraffe brought back by Zheng He to the astonished officials of the Ming court.[67]

Chinese accounts of the West, which recorded technological wonders and curiosities of the wider world perhaps not found in Macau, were nonetheless a source of marvels. One, the *Guangyuan zazhi* ("World Miscellany"), described an inflatable naked woman made of leather and silk, carried in a case and taken to bed by travelers. Called a "traveling woman," it was described by the writer as a "particularly obscene device,"[68] and it reinforced the conclusions that the Chinese derived from their observations of the moral behavior of Western women in Macau.

Western books and paintings also interested the Chinese, though not as much as purely technological wonders. Painting was an important medium of illustration and teaching for the first Jesuits in China and Japan. Visual images were capable of conveying powerful spiritual messages, transcending the difficult barrier of language, and the Chinese were already attuned to the rich, visual religious imagery of Buddhism and Chinese popular religion. Some missionaries were skilled artists themselves, and they passed those skills on to their disciples. When Hideyoshi proscribed Christianity in Japan and drove out the Jesuits, many of their converts fled with them to Macau, where they continued their study of Western painting at the Jesuit College attached to São Paulo Church.[69] There, they worked on pious statues of saints and paintings depicting religious themes and events. One of the most famous of these is a large painting, completed in 1640, that shows the martyrdom of twenty-three Jesuit and Franciscan priests and their Japanese converts at Nagasaki in 1597. The crucified martyrs are presented in a highly stylized manner, arranged in a long row straddling the top of a small hill; an inscription below the scene identifies most of the figures.[70]

Chinese and Japanese craftsmen were skilled in stonework and were employed in the construction of São Paulo's immense facade, which consequently reflected both Eastern and European motifs.[71] The interiors of most churches were decorated with Portuguese *talha*, gilded panels elaborately carved from wood in deep relief, with designs of coiled and twisted rope.[72] Such sculptural forms in stone and wood echoed the architecture of Chinese temples, which incorporated deeply carved stone balustrades and columns, as well as altars embellished with richly gilded wooden carvings.

In addition, there were various kinds of secular art in Macau at that time. A large landscape atlas painting of the oceans and seas in São Paulo Church, perhaps more of an exercise in cartography than fine art, was probably executed by Japanese artists working under the supervision of Jesuit priests, and small paintings on leather and glass, fan paintings, and embroidered and woven pictures depicted small scenes, buildings, landscapes, and narratives. The Chinese particularly admired the realism and sense of depth achieved in these paintings.[73]

Slight evidence remains of Portuguese or Macanese religious or secular art after the end of the seventeenth century, when the Chinese and European hostility and the closing of Japan led to the decline of the evangelical mission. But in the early nineteenth century, landscape and portrait painting flourished under the influence of European expatriate artists, among whom George Chinnery was the most famous. Some of these painters were only briefly in Macau, but others, among them Auguste Borget and Harriet Low, lived there for several years, painting the scenes and people of the city. Many artists were influenced by Chinnery, and a few were counted among his pupils, including Guan Qiaochang (Lamqua), who later copied Chinnery's work and painted for the export market in Canton and Hong Kong.[74] Although the influence of Chinnery and his school on Chinese artists was limited to the Westernized coastal periphery of China, their work reflected the sentimental view that Western missionaries, traders, and officials held toward Asian society and their self-confidence about their civilizing mission in the East, as Western power approached its zenith. The earlier artistic movement under Jesuit influence reflected a very different and powerfully optimistic view of the potential of the societies the priests aspired to penetrate and convert. Then, the balance of power between China and Europe was more equal, and the favorable outcome of the enterprise was by no means certain. The secular painting of these later artists, in contrast, was devoid of any explicit religious motive or evangelical theme. These artists were motivated by a conceit that tended to relegate their subjects to the picturesque, where they no longer were capable of posing a threat to Western enterprise. Thus, their paintings reflected the great imbalance of power, now cultural as well as economic and military, in favor of the West. The depiction of Macau by Chinnery and others in the picturesque style of the China Trade painting of the nineteenth century was all the more poignant because the city was even then becoming a quaint backwater abandoned by the onrushing stream of Western expansion, as far removed in spirit as in time from the Macau school of art under the tutelage of the Jesuit painters in the city's heyday in the seventeenth century.

Entertainment and Amusement

The inhabitants of Macau amused themselves as best they could in the small and confined space of the peninsula. In the city's glory days, its commercial wealth permitted extravagant displays of entertainment, such as the great festivals held in 1642 when news of the restoration of the Portuguese crown two years earlier finally reached Macau. But even then, such events were probably uncommon occurrences. Secular public entertainment was, no doubt, limited, but the observance of numerous Christian holidays provided a focus for regular public participation involving all classes of the community. The procession of the holy cross, winding through the streets from the Se Cathedral and marking the nine stations of the cross, was the most solemn of such holy day observances.[75] By the nineteenth century, as the Chinese city grew, numerous popular Chinese religious festivals, paralleling the Christian ones, were celebrated.[76]

The city's principal families availed themselves of almost every auspicious occasion for ostentatious public celebration. Weddings, christenings, the birth of children, and other joyful events gave them the opportunity to stage public entertainments at their own expense.[77] Music was a source of enjoyment at banquets and celebrations, featuring stringed instruments brought from Europe, such as the harp, guitar, violin, and violoncello; harpsichords, flutes, and percussion instruments, including drums, cymbals, and tambourines; and vocal performances featuring boys' choirs.[78] The many varieties of musical entertainment were sponsored by individual households for private and public audiences and by the religious orders. More solemn liturgical music performed in the churches was played on organs, accompanied by choirs and later by military bands.[79] In the late eighteenth century, public concerts were given twice a week, and in the late nineteenth and early twentieth centuries, Portuguese military bands regularly entertained the inhabitants and visitors on Sunday afternoons in the parks.[80]

Theatrical performances were sometimes presented, as they still are today, in public places on temporary stages. These might involve a play acted by children, with dancing, singing, and musical accompaniment on drums, tambourines, and other instruments. The public theaters were paid for by the wealthy houses.[81] Churches also served as theaters, offering performances directed by the priests. Judging by one description by Peter Mundy, these could be remarkably varied and charming:

> [We] were invited ashore by the Padres of San Paulo to see a play to bee acted in Saint Paules Church by the Children of the towne. . . . It was part of the liffe of

their Much renowned Saint Francisco Xavier, in which were Divers pretty passages, viz., A China Daunce by Children in China habitt; a Battaile beetweene the Portugalls and the Dutch in a daunce, where the Dutch were overcome, butt withoutt any reproachful speeche or Disgracefull action to thatt Nation. Another Daunce off broad Crabbes, commonly called Stoole Crabbes, beeing soe Many boies very prettily and wittily Disguised into the said Forme, who all sung and played on Instruments as though they had bin soe many Crabbes.[82]

Mundy explained that performances like these were directed and sponsored by the Jesuits in their capacity as teachers of the town's children. Evidently, they must have been similar to contemporary performances staged by schoolchildren in the West for parents and the community.

In the first century of the city's existence, at least, games of horsemanship and horse races were enjoyed by participants and spectators alike. Most of the horses in Macau were of a small breed, which must have come originally from northern China, but larger breeds were taken by the Portuguese from India or bought in Manila from the Spanish. The games themselves were adapted from Spanish and Portuguese customs. "Tilting at the ring" was a sort of race in which the object was to carry away a ring, while riding at a gallop, by using a lance. The *juego de Alcanzias*, a game originating in Spain, was an elaborately choreographed mock battle using clay balls as missiles, possibly something like a precursor of polo. Contestants and horses were colorfully costumed, and the opposing sides represented Christians and Moors. Riders protected themselves from the balls with leather shields and were attended by costumed slaves, who held their lances and pennants and served them the balls.[83] These events were evidently exciting displays for the spectators, as well as opportunities for the noblemen of the city to show off their skills. By the early nineteenth century, a racecourse had been built near the barrier gate, and horse races were regularly held there. These crowded events attracted the entire spectrum of Macau society, from top to bottom, and, of course, betting was prevalent.[84]

Automobile races, first introduced with the Macau Grand Prix in 1954, can be considered modern successors of such European-derived spectacles. The first grand prix was a gentleman's race for European sports cars, but the race soon attracted international participation. In 1975, the race was put under the jurisdiction of the international motor sports sanctioning organization, the Fédération Internationale de l'Automobile (FIA), and it began to attract large-scale commercial sponsorship. Since 1983, when it became an event for international Formula 3 cars, the Macau Grand Prix has become a stepping-stone to the premier Formula 1 series for world-class champion drivers. The circuit, reminiscent of the grand prix race through the streets of Monaco, begins near the Lisboa Casino, twists along the slopes of Guia hill, and returns along the perimeter of the reservoir and past the outer harbor terminal. Run in the fall of every year since its inception, the race is now an elaborate spectacle spanning several days and encompassing separate races for motorcycles and many varieties of automobiles and racing cars. Spectators and drivers are drawn from all over Asia, as well as from Europe and the United States.

Although the Chinese were traditionally not fond of contests of athletic prowess and competition, such as the formal games of horsemanship played by the Portuguese, they have had an inveterate fascination with games of intellectual skill and cunning and with games of chance. In their leisure, they frequently gathered in twos or small groups at home or in the street to play various forms of chess or games laid out on paper sheets or boards. A large number of George Chinnery's sketches depict Chinese huddled over such games, often observed by several others standing around the players. In the early twentieth century, mah-jongg became the most popular form of private recreational gambling among the Chinese and Macanese.[85]

Organized gambling, which was always patronized mostly by the Chinese, did not appear until the mid-nineteenth century, and it expanded greatly in the early twentieth century, after the decline of Macau's commercial economy in the 1870s and the great influx of Chinese immigrants and refugees in the following decades. In the 1920s, numerous fan-tan saloons provided entertainment to both lower- and upper-class patrons.[86] Other forms of betting, including dog racing, and casinos that offered a wider variety of games (such as roulette, blackjack, and baccarat, in addition to fan-tan) displaced the smaller fan-tan houses in the 1930s and earned for Macau its recent reputation as the Monte Carlo of the East.[87]

In a sense, the contests held during the traditional Chinese Dragon Boat Festival, on the fifth day of the fifth lunar month each year, were exceptions to the normal absence of athletic competition among the Chinese. As in other parts of China where regional districts and communities competed with one another, the festival in Macau culminated in spectacular races between teams of oarsmen from the city and neighboring island communities, each paddling a long, narrow boat with bow and stern carved in the form of a dragon's head and tail while the measured beat of a drummer marked the stroke. Temporary grandstands of bamboo were erected along the shore for the benefit of Chinese and foreign spectators.[88] The festival is still enthusiastically observed in much the same fashion today, but now Portuguese and Macanese, as well as Chinese, compete as teams.

There is no indication that the Dragon Boat races held in Macau were occasions for expressing animosities between local and regional groups or against foreigners, as they were in other Chinese cities. Nor were the celebrations surrounding the races regarded as an opportunity to temporarily run amok in the streets and disrupt city functions.[89] But they were expressions of civic pride, and they reinforced community solidarity through controlled competition between local vocational, professional, and laboring groups.

At times of public celebration and on religious holidays, many of these and other forms of entertainment might be combined in extended festivals.

There were more occasions to rejoice, of course, in Macau's golden era of prosperity than in the later years of decline—public entertainment depended, obviously, on both the mood and the means of the city government and its subjects. With the infusion of diversity in the culture of Macau, secular and religious alike, the celebration of Chinese and Western public holidays would sometimes run together. In the twentieth century, the high point of the year during which several of the numerous festivals arrived in succession was the period from Christmas to Carnival, preceding Lent. In between were the Western New Year and, in late January or early February, the Chinese New Year. Preparations for Christmas began in early December, with the decoration of houses and preparation of special foods—indeed, food was a central component of all these celebrations. No sooner had the numerous social obligations of Christmas subsided than the New Year celebration arrived. Scarcely a month later came the Chinese New Year, again involving much preparation of special foods and social visits lasting three days. Dragon dances were staged, and elaborate fireworks, which were particularly abundant in Macau because they were manufactured there, were featured in both New Year celebrations. Soon afterward was Carnival, likewise a three-day event, with masquerade parties for children and adults.[90]

Unquestionably, the greatest public celebration on record was the three-month-long festival staged on the announcement of the restoration of the crown to Portugal after the sixty-year union (1580–1640) of the crowns of Spain and Portugal. The news arrived in Macau two years later, in June 1642, and from then until September, a brilliant series of demonstrations and displays were held. At the beginning of the festival, the city's officials and citizens took an oath of allegiance to the new king, Dom João IV of the House of Bragança.[91]

Elaborate plans were made for the festival, with major events timed to coincide with the principal holy days of the calendar. Specific streets were designated for particular events, and the city was decorated for a solemn procession of thanksgiving that opened the celebration. A special stage was constructed in front of the Leal Senado for the oath-taking ceremony. This formality was followed by a light theatrical performance by students from the Jesuit schools. Every few days for the next several weeks, there were performances, processions, masquerades, plays, dances, games, bullfights, and parades of the most amazing variety and ingenuity; the participants spared no expense, seemingly competing to outdo each other in the splendor of their costumes. On the night of July 1, the most prominent citizens and officials of the city held a costume parade, complete with floats of musicians:

This began in the courtyard of the Municipality, where everybody assembled on horseback in different forms of fancy dress, accompanied by servants, pages and lackeys dressed in red, blue and other different colours, the horses being caparisoned with costly trappings of silver work. In the Courtyard of the Magistracy, festooned with roses, were placed two ships on wheels, each one containing some of the best instrumental and vocal musicians of the place. Many torches and flambeaux of white wax had been sought out for this occasion, which were not inferior to the best and purest of Portugal, over six hundred in all, these being held burning by the servants. All the richly dressed participants then mounted their horses and formed up in pairs outside the Courtyard of the Municipality, directly facing Saint Augustine's Church, the ships with their band and musicians being drawn by a great concourse of people.[92]

Many of the dignitaries were dressed in colorful Moorish, Turkish, and even Polish costumes.

A week later, more than one hundred young men of the city staged a masquerade procession from São Francisco Church to the Jesuit College near São Paulo Church:

> In front went a masked youth carrying the Royal Standard, and next came a group of dancing peasants and villagers, dressed accordingly. . . . Then followed two ranks of Chinese, representing many senior and junior mandarins of government, identifiable by placards of written Chinese characters. . . . Next came the Japanese with a dance after their manner, a sight worth seeing, they all being natives of Japan and exiled from that Kingdom in past years on account of the faith. . . . These were followed by two rows of Persians wearing resplendent tunics, with coifs on their heads and scimitars at their sides, . . . After these came two ranks of Dutchmen, very well dressed, with the arms and insignia of Holland, in short capes, with breeches after their style, hats, swords and garters and stockings of their fashion, . . . At the end came the Portuguese nation, looking better than any of the others. Outside of the ranks and on both sides thereof was a guard of German Archers, in rear of whom rode a living figure on horseback, who well represented the Royal Majesty, with a sceptre in hand and a crown on his head.[93]

The cosmopolitan diversity of this and similar processions staged during the festival, incorporating national costumes of the many peoples present in Macau, was clearly a thinly disguised political statement. It suggests an attempt to create a symbolic Portuguese cultural hegemony arrayed under the figure of King João IV, whose costumed image the procession honored.

Yet beneath the gaiety and color of this great celebration was a brooding sense of the impending decline that was even then overtaking the city, propelled by the closing of the Japan trade, the aggressive Dutch advance, and the end of the Manila connection through the Spanish. João Marques Moreira ended his fulsome account of the festivities of 1642 with pessimistic foreboding: "We are dying by inches."[94]

For all the color and richness of its masquerade, this great festival bore little resemblance to Carnival in Rio de Janeiro, which was also a mixed Portuguese colonial settlement. Carnival in Rio was an opportunity to mock the fixed social hierarchy and temporarily abandon social distinctions; it was an occasion when one subculture, the slaves and servants, asserted (if in a confusing and sometimes threatening manner) their dominance of the public places of the city.[95] No such uncontrolled intrusion of one culture into the ordered life of the other occurred in the European festivals of Macau, which were sponsored by the religious orders and political elite of the city. Indeed, they were highly orchestrated affairs, and descriptions of these events make it clear that the European choreographers were attempting, in a rather patronizing fashion, to include the stylized elements of other cultures represented in the city.

The orchestrators of festivals and celebrations in Macau (Jesuits fathers, civic leaders, social elites) were trying to encompass and, in doing so, to master the diversity of Macau's populations and their conflicting cultures. But their attempt to reduce this diversity to an intelligible order by symbolically managing it in orchestrated shows always fell short of the movement and energy of Macau's population. Their depictions of cultural groups, reflecting what the orchestrators wanted to see, were at best stereotypes and sometimes gross distortions of the complex cultural texture of Macau; they were defensive structures, like the more concrete fortifications of the city, designed to contain and control the process of interaction.

The Chinese, in particular, celebrated their own festivals, highly developed and deeply rooted in their own history, and they were largely inaccessible to Europeans except as spectators.[96]

Throughout China, temple fairs, often held on the birthday of a cult's patron deity, provided occasions for expressing spontaneity as well as community solidarity. In Macau, the celebration of Mazu's birthday in the third lunar month has remained one of the most popular festivals. Like European festivals, temple fairs offered an opportunity for the population to free itself from conventional social and moral constraints, including the segregation of the sexes and the seclusion of women, that normally could be quite rigid in Chinese society.[97] In some Chinese cities, the Dragon Boat Festival functioned somewhat like Carnival to affirm the popular unity of the underclasses and to assert their control, however briefly, of the streets.[98] In Macau, the Dragon Boat Festival was more accessible to foreigners because it involved feats of competition that were familiar to Europeans used to sporting events and games. But only very recently have European teams competed with Chinese in the races, and such events are now highly organized and municipally sanctioned observances.

For their casual amusement and recreation, the inhabitants of Macau relied on their own resources. These pursuits depended very much on the individuals' means, which were considerable for the well-to-do.[99] The European upper class, at least, delighted in keeping pets—birds, small dogs, monkeys, and mongooses. The tropical climate made birds of several species abundant, available, and easy to keep. Birds and animals seem to have been particularly popular with children. Parrots, parakeets, and cockatoos with scarlet, yellow, white, green, and blue plumage were the most spectacular of such pets. They could be trained to speak both Portuguese and Chinese, and the Chinese people found these birds, which were brought from Hainan and Southeast Asia, quite remarkable and intelligent. One observer noted that "children are fond of keeping them as pets and treat them like brothers."[100] Mynahs and lovebirds (*daogua,* in Chinese) were also common pets.

Macaques are also mentioned in the literature.[101] The name is derived from Portuguese, and it is likely that at least some of these animals were brought from Africa, although they are also indigenous to Southeast and East Asia. Small dogs, too, were favorite pets. According to one Chinese account:

> The foreign dogs [in Macau] are small but fierce. Their fur is like a lion's. They may be worth more than ten silver [ounces?], but they have no other function. The foreigners place great value on them, equal to that of slave children. Nothing is more extraordinary than [these] dogs' care. They are fed all kinds of delicacies. Before feeding they are made to sit and stand.[102]

Dogs, as well as birds, are still popular as pets everywhere in Macau. Indeed, the number of dogs is especially remarkable for such a small place. They seem sometimes to exist almost as a substratum of the population and usually appear to be very well cared for. In cold weather, it is not uncommon to see some of them dressed in children's old sweaters.

Another variety of domesticated animal—the mongoose—was introduced to the Chinese in trade and brought from Siam and not only was amusing to keep as a pet but also had a useful function:

> It is particularly good at catching rats. The foreigners in Aomen are able to tame it. They commonly trade it for Guangdong merchandise. The foreigners value animals but undervalue humans. They regard the mongoose as no different from themselves. The children hold on to them and will not release them, sleeping and waking. Because they prize them, we Chinese also prize them. What sense is there in this?[103]

Trapped on the small peninsula by the barrier gate across the isthmus, through which no Portuguese was allowed to pass, the residents naturally seized opportunities to find leisure on the water and in the surrounding bays and islands. Many had their slaves row them about the nearby channels in small skiffs (*ballões*). Wealthier families owned larger boats called *manchuas,* which were brightly decorated and had carved beaks, single masts carrying square-rigged sails, oars, and covered poop decks. These were adapted from vessels of the Malabar coast of India. Families took them on picnics to nearby islands, where they would erect a tent at an inlet with a creek and stay for several days "camping out."[104] The upper class also sometimes enjoyed hunting expeditions to the surrounding islands or the mainland.[105] Later, the foreign community delighted in taking excursions to Ilha Verde or to Lappa, the large island across from the inner harbor. These were sometimes quite elaborate outings, complete with long hikes, visits to Chinese temples, and elegant picnics. Harriet Low described one such excursion in 1832:

> We had long but very pleasant walk on the Lappa, though rather rough and hilly; but the hills were so green and the scenery so varied that our travellers told us we might fancy ourselves now in the highlands of Scotland and then in the beautiful scenery of Wales. The springs of water on this island are delicious, and a clear stream was running by our side most of the time. . . . No one was sorry, I assure you, on ascending the last hill, to discover in a little valley a table handsomely set for twenty-six people.[106]

Gardens

Gardens were and still are one of the greatest delights of the city's residents and occasional visitors, whether Chinese or European. From very early on, Macau's gardens, both public and private—until recently, they were all private—were, like the churches and fortresses, a primary point of interest in Macau. Many of the early foreign residences had attached walled gardens for the private enjoyment of the owners and their guests.[107]

Not surprisingly, like so much else in Macau, gardens exhibited both Chinese and European influences. The traveler Peter Mundy described private gardens he visited in 1637 that were clearly influenced by Chinese practice:

> Some trees are to bee seene here and there in the Citty and some smalle gardein plottes, butt in their houses Many galleries and tarasses Furnished with Macetas, or Flower potts, made into sundry shapes, wherein were various sorts of smalle trees, plantts, Flowers, etts. Among the rest a smalle tree (common here) growing outt off a Meere rocke or stone, which is putt into a panne or other vessell off water, soe that the water cover the roote and some part of the stocke, and soe it waxeth greater, having seene some off 3 or 4 Foote high. . . . In the said panne they allso putt certaine smalle Fishes as bigge and as long as a Manns little Finger, their scales some of Silver and some off gould coullour shining, boughtt and broughtt from Cantan, Fed with bread, Rice, etts. There they continue a long tyme and breed, running in and outt through holes and concavities of the said rocke, being Artificall.[108]

In one such garden, paths wound through groves of bamboo and luxuriant vegetation, modeled after a traditional garden of South China, but the buildings were of European style. This garden contained an aviary in a small hexagonal arbor. But its principal attraction was a cassowary bird, "as large as a small donkey, with a fleshy horn on its forehead." A Chinese visitor described the scene:

A foreigner takes care of it, and outside the window where it lives is posted a black devil armed with a gun. He stands several yards away, dressed all in black like "Piggy" in the play. His hat is also like "Monkey's" in the play. Across his chest he wears a white leather strap two inches wide, crossing from right to left and used to sling the gun. With his left hand he grasps the stock of the gun, which rests in the leather strap and is held perpendicular in front of his left breast. On the side of the gun is a steel spear [bayonet]. While it [the gun] has two uses, it is very heavy and awkward. The man holding the gun stands motionless, every bit like a wooden statue. When people pass him one eye keeps watch, but he does not turn his neck. Nearby are three or four others, lying on the ground with their hats off, presumably to take turns on guard. These are foreign soldiers. They are well behaved and no officer is present. Outside the front gate is a man dressed in red, like an executioner in a play. His hat is also like "Monkey's," cocked to one side. He guards the gate with a staff.[109]

Since this bird was attended and guarded by so considerable a staff, one wonders whether the owner of this garden, perhaps a wealthy Chinese or Macanese merchant, charged an admission fee to see this curiosity. For Chinese visitors, as well as for some foreigners, Macau must have been something like a fantastic amusement park in which one might encounter the unexpected and the exotic at every turn. The residents themselves and the things they collected, their buildings, and their customs all became part of the show.

Although privately owned and maintained, gardens like that one obviously were well known to both residents and visitors and were not entirely closed to the interested public. Probably the most amazing curiosity of all was the aviary and garden of Thomas Beale, enclosed within high walls and attached to one of the finest old Portuguese houses in the city. Arranged in Chinese fashion, with a vast number of flowers and rare plants growing in pots, it contained several large trees and shrubs—litchi and orange trees and a Bombay mango—a pond, and a small hill. The aviary, made of copper wire, enclosed part of the garden and included many smaller cages; it could be viewed through the house's dining room window.[110]

The gallinaceous birds, pheasants, jungle-cocks, partridges, and pigeons of various sizes and most splendid plumage formed the principal ornaments of the collection in the aviary: the graceful and superb silver pheasant, the splendidly colored golden and medallion pheasants, together with the large and handsome blue crowned pigeon, and other smaller kinds, attracted the admiring gaze of every visitor. Mr. Beale first procured a living specimen of the bar red-tailed pheasant from the interior of China; and the Phasianus Reevesii, or Reeve's pheasant was in his possession several years before it was carried to England by Mr. Reeves. The most distinguishing object of attraction about the house, however, was the bird of paradise, from the Moluccas, whose brilliant plumage held the eye of every beholder; it was kept in a cage by itself, and more than any other of the birds drew visitors to the house. Loris, parrots, cockatoos, minas, magpies, and various Chinese singing birds, each suspended near by its own cage, kept it company in the entrance of the house, each vying with the other in the loudness of its note, and altogether forming a constant vocal concert. A magnificent Indian peacock also attracted its share of attention, and a large cage of canaries, with compartments for the quiet breeding of young birds, sent forth its share of music.[111]

The garden, to which Beale freely admitted friends of friends and casual visitors to Macau, was one of the sights of the city in the 1820s and 1830s. The most famous garden, associated in the minds of European residents with the origin of Macau, is the one associated with Camões's grotto. The grotto itself is nothing more than a natural grouping of immense granite boulders, forming more of a crevice than a cave. Camões was supposed to have enjoyed this spot, which is close to the summit of the hill west of the Monte and commands a view of the surrounding scenery, and it is indelibly associated with his name. A bronze bust of the poet was placed in the crevice between the rocks, with a brief description of the vital facts of his life. Over the years, probably beginning in the late eighteenth century, various improvements to the natural scene, including a masonry balustrade and a small pavilion resting on a raised platform, were made, which have given to the place something of the aura of a shrine.[112] The garden has changed little since Harriet Low described it in 1829:

> We were invited to Mrs. Fearon's [wife of the British East India Company's head], to take tea and walk in the garden. It is the most romantic place, is very extensive, and abounds in serpentine walks. There is a beautiful view of the sea, and immense rocks and trees, and several temples in the garden. In another part there is a cave in the rocks where the celebrated Camoens wrote his "Lusiad." A bust of him stands in the cave. It is a wild and delightful spot.[113]

The extensive garden surrounding the grotto is really more a park than a garden. Since the late eighteenth century, it has been associated with a large private mansion, later to become the Camões Museum. Ownership of the grotto and the garden passed from the Jesuits after their expulsion from Macau in 1762 to the Senado and then to a series of private foreign owners—in particular English merchants of the East India Company in the late eighteenth and early nineteenth centuries, who greatly elaborated on it.[114] It was known then by various names, including Casa Garden and Casa da Horta. Maintained now by the city as a botanical park, the Camões Garden has been planted with many specimens of tropical trees and shrubs from South and Southeast Asia and the China coast and adorned with potted flowers. Public functions and commemorations are held there periodically, the most important being the June celebration of the Day of Camões and the Portuguese living overseas, when the worldwide community of Portuguese culture is commemorated with music and processions by children from each of

Macau's European and Chinese schools. It is rather touching, this mixture of pomp—the military band, the assembled officials in dress uniforms, flags unfurled—with the unpretentious behavior of the contingents of students representing public and private schools and various clubs and organizations, each dressed in his or her distinctive uniform, nervously shepherded by adults anxious to ensure that their groups comport themselves well. After a group of students recite one of Camões's sonnets in unison, the children file by the grotto to lay flowers at the bust of the poet. Then, boxed snacks are distributed to the participants.

There is something both poignant and happy about this celebration of the spirit of the restless adventurer and poet who wrote the great paean to the destiny of Portuguese overseas expansion. If Camões was never, in fact, in Macau, perhaps it really no longer matters. He is very much there in spirit, though it is a spirit much softened and more accommodating than the militant one of *The Lusiads*. But now, there is no tough military posturing, no raucous chauvinism, and little trace of the pretentious colonial mission of that enterprise.

Every day, people of all ages come to the park to enjoy the relative solitude under the huge trees. It is a favorite place for "bird-walking," when men, young and old, bring their pet caged birds to socialize. Bird-walking is a custom practiced among the Chinese almost everywhere (though it seems to be exclusive to the Chinese men in Macau)—keeping songbirds in elaborate cages, often finely carved and appointed with colorful porcelain bowls for food and water. Some of the men have two or three birds in separate cages. In the late afternoon, they gather in several places, setting their cages along low walls or on the grass or hanging them from the branches of shrubs and trees. They fold back the covers of the cages and listen to the birds sing, sometimes contemplatively, sometimes engaging in animated discussions about the relative merits and behavior of the birds. The birds seem to enjoy it, and their songs attract their wild cousins. The birds—the hwa-mei are the best—sing wonderful, lilting melodies of astonishing variety.

It is apparent that bird-walking is as much an opportunity for socializing among residents from different neighborhoods (who might otherwise be unknown to each other) as it is a hobby like raising fish or collecting stamps. For an observer who is attuned to the birds and their appreciative keepers, it is one of the most peaceful and refined of experiences to sit and listen to the melodies of the birds' songs above the chatter of the people, the shouts of children playing, and the noise of the traffic outside the park.

Other habitués of the park, indifferent to the birds, play Chinese chess or checkers or read newspapers for long hours, as children, attended by their mothers or grandmothers, dash along the twisting paths. There, more than in any other location in Macau, the layers of culture seem to harmonize.

The gardens of Macau reflect an intersection of two very different views of the relationship between the urban and natural worlds, between city and

country. Classical Western gardens sought to bring order out of or in to essentially chaotic nature. Versailles's geometric regularity is a case in point.
Refinement of nature's uncontrolled disorder—something to be mastered
and tamed—was the key to these gardens. By contrast, Chinese gardens, especially the literati gardens and, on a larger scale, the imperial gardens,
sought to bring natural rusticity and irregularity into urban regularity. Rural
simplicity was prized over urban artificiality as a source of a priori virtue
and wisdom.[115] Both Chinese and Western gardens might be designed as
conscious repositories of diverse natural wonders and specimens, though a
Chinese garden was never a zoological park in the Western fashion of a zoo.
But Chinese gardens were not meant to be public amusement parks. And
even more so, Chinese gardens were not places where public or official celebrations were held. Macau's gardens, though clearly owing much to the Chinese idea of the garden as a confined place of natural rusticity within the
walls of a city, were also all of these other things.

꙳ ꙳ ꙳

The life of Macau was a cultural kaleidoscope, a jumble of colorful fragments
that were constantly changing. The Europeans and upper-class Eurasians,
adapting to the climate and cultural context and exhibiting the influences
they picked up on the journey through other regions, preserved as much as
they could of the substance and manners of their European origins. Their
lifestyles and customs were accordingly varied and eclectic. Fragments of
culture were not only transported to Macau directly from Europe, largely
unchanged, but also acquired along the way there. To these were added elements brought to Macau from China and other parts of Asia by later visitors
and settlers, so that the cultural complexion of the city was forever changing.

Thus, Macau was a threshold of cultural encounters between two worlds.
Mutual images formed by different peoples across a frontier are reflections
of such cultural encounters. Cultural stereotypes are not only subjective images, varying according to the one who is perceiving the other, they are mu-
table as well, changing over time as the relationship between the people
forming and shaping the perceptions changes. Such stereotypes are often validations of power relationships, so that they vary with the cultural balance of
power—for instance, from conquest or mastery to mutual accommodation.
Moreover, negative stereotypes may be either reflections of cultural defense
against a threat from a different culture or validations of the conquest and
cultural subordination of another group.

Chinese descriptions of foreigners, emphasizing their bizarre features and
outlandish (literally) customs, were as real to the Chinese as corresponding
Western descriptions of the Chinese, equally emphasizing what the respective viewers wished to see and subsuming them under a comprehensive typology. Thus, Chinnery's depictions of the Chinese as stereotypically alien,

rounded, cartoonlike figures in his drawings and paintings reduced them to a comfortable place in the cultural and social environment of Macau. In this respect, indeed, the descriptions of both Westerners and Chinese are essentially "real," for what else can any expression of reality be but the perception of the external world in the eye of the beholder?

There was a perceptible shift in cultural stereotypes that the Chinese and Europeans formed about each other from the sixteenth century to the nineteenth and twentieth centuries. Matteo Ricci, writing in the early seventeenth century, was sometimes critical, but he found much to admire about the Chinese, except in matters of religion and superstition. He saw in the Chinese the virtues of industriousness, vigor, and modesty. He also viewed them as frustratingly oblique in their responses to questions. In a rather mild way, he was critical of their lack of thoroughness, their tendency to settle for something less than perfection and highest quality in their craftsmanship, and their lack of mechanical skill.[116] The latter observations, perhaps not surprisingly, came from the Jesuits, who used their technical mastery of mechanical clocks and astronomical instruments as their means to gaining the favor of the Chinese upper class. But Ricci expressed strong repugnance for what he viewed as Chinese superstition, and he castigated the Chinese for what he believed were failings in moral behavior, such as their penchant for resorting to suicide as an act of spite, for drowning female infants, and for castrating male children to make them eunuchs. Curiously, considering that the Portuguese practiced it so extensively, he also condemned the Chinese for practicing slavery, especially of females.[117]

Protestant observers during the nineteenth century agreed with Ricci's positive assessments in some respects, praising Chinese vitality and industriousness, and also cited the tenacity and sense of humor of the Chinese. However, they tended to find more serious faults in the Chinese character—obliqueness in thought, a disrespect for truth and accuracy, inflexibility and obstinacy, and an absence of nerves.[118] It was not that greater familiarity with China by the later missionaries bred contempt—after all, Ricci acquired an intimate knowledge of the Chinese from the better part of two decades residence in China.

Part of the explanation for the different attitudes may lie in the classes to which each group of critics was exposed; the Jesuits chose to associate with the literati class, but the Protestants preferred to work among the lower classes, with townspeople and villagers. But more important was the changing relationship of power. The Jesuits went to China as equals of the Chinese, initially biding their time in Macau while awaiting the coveted opportunity to enter an empire that was still powerful, rich, and mysterious. The Protestants arrived when China lay prostrate before Western imperial power, weak and subjected everywhere to foreign intimidation and domination. It was easier and more comfortable to blame the character of the

Chinese for their submission rather than to acknowledge European imperialism's responsibility and guilt.

Correspondingly, Chinese stereotypes of Europeans in the eighteenth and nineteenth centuries, before the Opium War had tipped the balance of power, betrayed a condescension and smug superiority, laced, perhaps only slightly, with an anxiety about what might be in store from these formidable people. Chinese observers who reported on the curious foreigners in Macau, though admiring their ingenious technology, derided them for their indulgent character, litigiousness, and inappropriate moral priorities (e.g., valuing their pets more than other humans), and they condemned the foreigners for their moral promiscuity, indecency, and licentiousness and feared their brazen and aggressive behavior. By the late nineteenth century, although xenophobia persisted and grew as a cultural defense, it became increasingly difficult for Chinese admirers of the West to maintain such attitudes. Moving relatively easily in both worlds, Rong Hong revealed no such stereotypes.

Macau mediated this changing cultural encounter. Yet it always remained a cultural enclave, a curious anomaly existing apart from the land to which it was so physically proximate.

But by the mid-twentieth century, the bizarre had become commonplace. Macau was now, with the development of communication and transportation, both more integrated into changing world cultural movements, like many other colonial relics, and more homogenized by the ineluctable process of modernization. And yet, at the same time, the commonplace had become bizarre. What Macau had once shared as an ordinary matter of course with the two worlds whose threshold it straddled became remarkable and anomalous as these worlds, following their own divergent paths, left Macau behind, disconnected from their pasts.

six

∿

Images
Spiritual Topography

This city of indulgence need not fear
The major sins by which the heart is killed,
And governments and men are torn to pieces:
Religious clocks will strike; the childish vices
Will safeguard the low virtues of the child;
And nothing serious can happen here.[1]

One has only to walk down almost any smaller street or lane or turn into a patio or cul-de-sac, particularly in the older sections of Macau, to encounter a small shrine or a miniature temple. It may be no more than a masonry bench built into a wall, perhaps with projecting eaves and a small niche, brightly painted in red and green and yellow. It may hold a small figure or merely a smooth stone or a tablet. Characters above and on each side sometimes identify the object of devotion. A bowl or jar filled with sand and placed in front holds incense sticks; there may be a glass jar for a candle or oil and perhaps a small plate for offerings to the deity—no more. The miniature temples, really nothing more than slightly larger shrines, are hardly big enough for a child to enter, but they enclose a dark, cavelike altar and a kind of platform in front that serves as a table.

Such shrines are sometimes nearly obscured by cast-off junk, building materials, household goods, and whatnot piled around and even on top of them. But in spite of such seeming neglect, they are cared for and used from time to time. Their patrons do not feel that any disrespect is shown by such casual indifference to appearances. So mundane at first sight as to seem almost devoid of any religious meaning, these shrines are nevertheless a manifestation of the underlying religious culture of Macau's Chinese population. They mark the nodes of invisible lines of connection that define the boundaries of the neighborhoods around them, and they create a structure binding the community together.

From the simplest and most naive shrines to the largest and most imposing temples, a complex hierarchy of deities and sects pervades the Chinese half of the city's identity, much as a Catholic hierarchy pervades its other, Christian, identity. In this way, the Chinese city of Macau preserves what many older traditional cities of China once had but have long since lost—a congregation of popular spiritual traditions that enliven the sometimes shabby, monotonous material facade with depth and color. Only in Macau is this dimension more diversified and intensified by the city's peculiar history as a place where numerous cultural influences collected and interacted.

Patrons of Seafarers

The legend of the merchant who dedicated a temple to Mazu, the Queen of Heaven, on the rocky point of Macau after the goddess guided him to safety in a perilous storm testifies to the earliest association of temples with the place that became Macau.[2] The temple was not formally founded until the Wanli reign of the Ming (1573–1621), no earlier than two decades after the Portuguese began to settle Macau. However, a shrine or temple of some kind clearly antedated their arrival and is one of the oldest buildings in the city.[3]

The origin of the cult of Mazu is obscure, and there is much uncertainty about the circumstances of her life as a historical figure. She was a maiden of the Lin family in either Fujian or Zhejiang Province, born in the eighth, tenth, or twelfth century; her father was either a petty official or a Taoist. It is said she died very young, sacrificing her life to save members of her family or others who were seafarers, and was subsequently deified.[4] The cult of Mazu became widely popular among sailors and fishermen and spread throughout the maritime regions of China, but it appealed to other segments of the population as well.[5] Mazu received imperial patronage in the early Ming when honorary tablets were erected to her in 1431 and 1432, and her temple in Fujian was restored by Grand Eunuch Zheng He, who sought her protection for the great maritime expeditions he was then leading to the Indian Ocean.[6]

As time passed, what began as a crude shrine among the rocks at the tip of the peninsula expanded up the hillside behind, which was then still quite wild. Protected by their association with the temple, large banyan trees grew there. Such shrines were not uncommon in the rocky outcroppings of these islands; their patron deities were thought by the local fishermen to ensure abundant catches and provide protection from storms. Under Mazu's benevolence, the fishing off Macau continued to flourish, as it would be expected to do in the fertile effluent of the Pearl River. Carved on the rocks next to the temple are two merchant junks similar to the fishing vessels still found in

Ama temple

that area. "Auspiciously cross the Great River" is inscribed on the boats' flags. Higher up on the rocks, another short inscription simply invokes, "The sea on which no waves rise." As the legend of the temple's origin confirms, shipwreck in violent typhoons and tropical storms was not uncommon. The loss of ships at sea was a frequent hazard for the Portuguese, Dutch, and Chinese merchants sailing the East and South China Seas, and the loss of precious cargoes and supplies brought misfortune to both the European and the Chinese trading communities of Macau.

Inside the temple, a model of a war junk, though its origin and significance is less clear, further testifies to the nautical theme of Mazu's cult, as well as the quasi-official status important temples often acquired. The Tian Hou cult, in particular, received official patronage by the Qing, which thereby hoped to promote stability and quell unrest along the South China coast following the Manchu conquest in the seventeenth century.[7] But Macau was much less under direct Chinese control, particularly in cultural matters. There, the cult was probably largely immune to patronage, and Mazu remained venerated by seafarers of all types who sailed these waters—even the pirates whom Mazu, in the official version of the cult, was supposed to help suppress. Even today, shrines to Mazu are important fixtures in every native junk and fishing vessel.[8]

Mazu is not the only deity who now occupies the temple complex. Another is Guan Yin, the Buddhist "saint" and paragon of compassion, whose presence in a smaller temple high up in the rocks of the hillside exemplifies the eclecticism typical of Chinese popular religion. What makes the Mazu temple fairly remarkable, however, is the number and arrangement of its subordinate shrines and smaller buildings, not its imposing formality. Like many Chinese temples, the Mazu temple was periodically renovated and reconstructed, and as a result, it has changed a great deal in appearance and size, even since the nineteenth century.

Another temple related to Tian Hou, the Queen of Heaven, looks out over a rugged point called Majiao Shi ("Horse-Dragon Rocks") on the northeast spur of the peninsula. Although its age is uncertain, it is no doubt one of Macau's oldest temples. Once a very pretty place frequented by fishermen from a small village nearby, it is now obscured by factory buildings erected on reclaimed land along the shore in front of the temple.

Many temples related to the livelihood of fishing and seafarers were scattered along these islands and shores, but not all were devoted to Mazu. Situated on the western end of Coloane Island, facing the Mazu temple on Macau directly through the Crossroads Passage (Shizimen), is a modest temple dedicated to Tan Gong, a patron god of fishermen. Tan Gong, or "Lord Tan," is classified as an immortal (*xian*), but the legend of his origin asserts that he was the last Song emperor, the youngest of three brothers and only eight years old when he died during the Song retreat in the final phases of the Mongol conquest of Guangdong Province in 1279. Because he was the heroic but tragic champion of a native Chinese dynasty fighting foreign invaders, he came to be venerated by the local population; his cult is limited to the coastal vicinity of Macau and Hong Kong.[9] In his temple, there is another model of an official-looking boat, this one a kind of ceremonial barge constructed on a whale bone, with a dragon's head on its bow and oarsmen and a drummer in traditional Qing-style uniforms. Simple models of such boats, like those used in the annual Dragon Boat Festival races, are found in other temples, as in the Tian Hou temple in the town of Taipa.

It must have been an easy matter for the first Portuguese in Macau to accommodate the cult of Mazu, with which the peninsula seemed so closely

Ship on stone, Ama temple

associated. The cult of the Virgin Mary was already well developed in Portuguese culture, and numerous churches and institutions were dedicated to Mary, especially in Macau, beginning soon after the Portuguese first settled there.[10] Among her many roles, the Virgin was a protectress of seafarers, and the names of an extraordinary number of Portuguese ships invoked the Virgin in one form or another.[11]

"Official" Temples and the Growth of the City

The history of Macau's temples reflects the growth of the settlement on the peninsula. Before the peninsula was occupied by the Portuguese and the settlement expanded with the trade, there were no built-up areas. The earliest temples generally served the practical needs of the few local settlers and fishermen, and almost all were located in rustic settings. The notable exception may be the oldest temple in Macau, the Guan Yin Tang, which was situated in the village of Wangxia (Mongha) on the northern part of the peninsula, bordering the open fields between Wangxia hill and Guia hill. Wangxia village was the only settled area before the Portuguese arrived, and its temple seems to have been established by settlers from Fujian as early as the Yuan dynasty (1279–1368), though it was originally much smaller than it is now.[12]

After successive reconstructions and expansions, especially during the late Ming (1627), it acquired its present imposing size and status as the most important, if not the most interesting or significant, temple in Macau.

The entire temple is enclosed by high, pale green walls. It is entered through a large multiple gate at the front, opening on a spacious courtyard with steps leading up to the main halls. The central building comprises three successive halls with altars, the last and largest one devoted to Guan Yin. The presence of semidetached wings containing administrative offices, residences for caretakers and monks, and meeting rooms reflects the diverse social and cultural functions of a large temple. In the left wing are several halls containing the spirit tablets of deceased parishioners, arranged along the walls in tiers. Some are very elaborate, others more humble, according to the means of the family. Several rooms and alcoves in the right wing provide for funeral chapels. In such chapels, a temporary altar is set up with a picture of the deceased surrounded by artificial flowers, candles, bowls of offerings, and colorful paper replicas of material possessions—automobiles, furniture, houses, airplanes, servants, money—that will be burned to provide the deceased person with all these comforts in the next life. Further to the right is a garden that winds around to the back of the temple.

The first hall of the main building, a rather small one located just beyond the entrance doors, has an altar on which are seated three gilded Buddhas. These are the Three Precious Buddhas of the Pure Realm of the Western Heaven (actually the three manifestations of the Buddha—Sakyamuni, the historical Buddha, in the center; Amitabha, the Buddha of the Western Paradise, on the left; and Maitreya, the Buddha of the future, on the right). On either side of this altar are open passages to the second hall. On the wall facing a small atrium in front of this hall, a painted relief depicts dragons coiling through clouds, and at the back of the hall, there is a second altar containing another Buddha identified as the Glorious and Universal Buddha, often called the Eternal Buddha or the God of Longevity. Again, passages to either side lead to the third and largest hall, which features a more substantial atrium with potted plants, incense burners, and coils of burning incense hanging from the rafters. On the left and right of the hall, behind glass cases, are eighteen seated Bodhisattvas, the principal "saints" of Buddhism, nine on each side. At the back, behind large altar tablets, sits the figure of Guan Yin, of "Supreme Compassion and Supreme Pity."[13] So heavily draped in embroidered robes and headdress that her features are indistinguishable, she is the object of one of the most pervasive Chinese cults, essentially autonomous from its Buddhist origins as the Indian Bodhisattva Avalokitesvara, the Compassionate Sovereign. She is found in virtually every Chinese temple in Macau, whoever its primary deity might be.

The ubiquitous presence of the cult of Guan Yin in Macau is echoed by the equally pervasive role of the cult of Maria. Numerous churches, pious institutions, schools, congregations, confraternities, legions, and festivals have been dedicated to the Virgin throughout Macau's history.[14] Like Guan Yin, she is venerated as a protectress (particularly of women), a patron of seafarers, a defender against enemies, and a goddess of remedies for sickness, disabilities, and infertility.[15] Indeed, it is probable that many devotees have trouble distinguishing between Guan Yin, Tian Hou, the Queen of Heaven, and the Virgin Mary, also Queen of Heaven.

Despite this confusion of identities, the Guan Yin temple, unlike many Chinese temples, is almost exclusively devoted to Buddhism. But its important function in Chinese funeral ceremonies testifies to the coexistence of traditional Confucian ancestral belief with Chinese Buddhism. The prevailing Buddhist iconography of the Guan Yin Tang does not differ greatly from that in Buddhist temples elsewhere in China. Other temples were devoted to more specifically local or regional cults, but the Guan Yin temple was clearly located in a national religious context. Impressive tablets hanging from the ceiling and pillars testify to the honors bestowed on the temple by successive emperors of the last dynasty from the Qianlong reign in the eighteenth century to the end of the nineteenth century. That visible official sanction, spanning the period of increasing Chinese settlement in the city, affirmed to the temple's patrons its affiliation with the rest of the Buddhist establishment throughout the empire.

In earlier times, a monastery was attached to the temple, and it was also a focus of activity and administration. Chinese local officials, visiting Macau in the course of their duties, would stay there since it was the most suitably dignified location, still uncompromised by the growing foreign settlement to the south of Wangxia across the fields and over the crest of Monte hill. In 1731, the temple became the headquarters of an assistant magistrate (*xiancheng*), who was appointed to Wangxia to supervise and administer justice to the growing Chinese population, as well as handle affairs relating to foreigners.[16] Thus, important temples like this one served both religious and secular functions, as they have continued to do to the present.

It was entirely appropriate, therefore, that the Treaty of Wangxia between the United States and China was signed in this temple in 1844 after the conclusion of the Opium War between the British and the Qing. A small, round stone table and stools and a tablet commemorating the event mark the spot in the garden where the Manchu commissioner Qiying and the U.S. negotiator Caleb Cushing signed the treaty. By that time, the British had acquired Hong Kong, but the Chinese were anxious to confine relations with the Western powers to their traditional venue on the South China coast and in Canton.

Toward the end of the sixteenth century (in 1592), as the early city approached the height of its prosperity due to the Japan trade, the Lianfeng Miao ("Lotus Peak Temple") was built at the northern base of Wangxia hill near the shore of the inner harbor. Sometimes called the "New Temple" to distinguish it from the older Guan Yin temple in Wangxia, it looked out over the narrow bar that connected the peninsula to the mainland. The Chinese saw in the shape of Macau a resemblance to a lotus flower, with the land bridge forming its stem and the peninsula itself the bud or flower. They called the bar the "Lotus Stem," and the rising summit of Wangxia hill just behind the temple was called "Lotus Peak," so the temple got its name from its location.

The Lianfeng temple may always have had, as it does now, a more eclectic function than the Guan Yin Tang, containing halls not only for Guan Yin but also for Tian Hou and two other, lesser goddesses who always appear together—the Goddess of Smallpox and the Protectress of Women.[17] The central entrance hall, actually a kind of atrium with a raised stone platform and stone railing surrounded by tall pillars, is the finest example of formal temple architecture in Macau.

From its beginning, the Lianfeng temple was important because of its location on the road running from Xiangshan, the district city on the mainland, through the subdistrict seat just to the north at Qianshan, across the "Lotus Stem," and on beyond Wangxia, along the Praia Patane to Macau. The temple virtually straddled the road in the narrow passage between the hill and the shore, so it was strategically located to control the route in and out of the peninsula. Along this road, all land traffic to and from the colony and especially all Chinese official traffic (which rarely went by sea) had to pass. It was also within easy reach of the barrier gate erected by the Chinese across the bar only two decades earlier, in 1573. The temple functioned, therefore, as an official way station and temporary headquarters for visiting officials. At the beginning of the Opium War, in 1839, it was a collection point for Chinese military forces, and when Imperial Commissioner Lin Zexu arrived in September to review operations, the temple was the scene of an elaborate ceremony and conference between the Chinese and the Portuguese, who were neutral in the war. A company of Portuguese troops, together with a military band, met the commissioner's procession at the barrier, and they proceeded together to the Lianfeng temple. There, surrounded by crowds of spectators, the commissioner, the provincial governor, and several subordinate local officials who were awaiting them met with the procurador of Macau. "Some presents,—consisting of silver, silk, teas, pigs, and bullocks with their horns decorated with scarlet ribbands,—were arranged before the middle door of the temple."[18] After refreshments were served and the conference with the procurador was completed, the procession set out for the city, passing around its entire perimeter from Praia Patane, under the Monte fort, which fired a twenty-one-gun salute, along the inner harbor, past the Ama temple at the point, back along the Praia Grande, and out across the Campo.[19] Following this visit, in January 1840, a military intendant was assigned to Macau and made the Lianfeng temple his residence.[20]

Lianfeng temple

South of Lotus Peak and Wangxia hill was a stream, Lotus Creek, that flowed out from the Campo into the inner harbor on the west where the road from the Lianfeng temple followed the shoreline south to the city. Not far from the bridge where the road crossed the creek, the Lianqi Xinmiao ("New Lotus Creek Temple") was built, probably in the seventeenth century. It is a complex building comprising four halls attached side by side but having only one entrance. Each hall has an antechamber and a larger hall behind. It is one of the most curious and interesting temples in Macau, an extreme example of the eclecticism of Chinese popular religion. Almost every imaginable deity makes its home here; there is a patron for every possible need and function—for fertility, for wealth and prosperity, and for protection from sickness and accidents. There is also an altar for victims of dog bites and another to repair marriages on the rocks, as well as a deity to ensure the birth of male children and another to guarantee many offspring.[21] Perhaps not surprisingly, contributions to the temple help support an associated hospital. In the central hall resides Bei Di, the Taoist God of the North, or the Pole Star, who is also more formally known as Xuan Tian Shang Di, the Supreme God of Mysterious Heaven. He is sometimes associated with Mazu, the Queen of Heaven, and like her, he is a particular protector of fishermen and commands a widespread following throughout the South China maritime region. He also protects against fires.[22] Ironically, in another hall is Hua Guang, the God of Fire. Also represented in various parts of this temple are Hua To, a third-century physician who became deified as the patron of physicians; Cai Shen, the God of Wealth; gods for each year of one's life; Guan Di, the God of War and patron of literature and scholars, also a deified historical figure of the third century; and Guan Yin, the Buddhist Goddess of Mercy.

In one of the antechambers, another quasi-historical figure and his mythical companions are found under an embroidered banner reading "The Holy Buddha Tripitaka of the Tang." In 629 A.D., during the Tang dynasty when Buddhism was spreading rapidly in China, Xuan Zang, a monk at the Tang capital at Changan, set out on a journey to India to seek Buddhist scriptures at their source. After an odyssey lasting fifteen years, he returned to Changan, where he settled down to translate his texts. His pious pilgrimage brought him not only fame but also veneration as a sort of saint. Later still, a satirical and whimsical novel, *Xiyu ji* ("Journey to the West"), loosely based on his journey, gave him imaginary companions and sent them off on a search for the Buddhist Western Paradise. In the novel, Xuan Zang is known as Tripitaka, the three holy treasures of Buddhism; he is accompanied by a monkey possessing supernatural powers, a clownlike pig, and another human companion. They are all found as small figures on the altar: Tripitaka is uppermost, but Monkey, who has assumed the role of a very popular minor deity in his own right, occupies the position of honor in the center. Monkey's popularity is perhaps best explained by his notorious power to cut through any obstacle on behalf of those he champions and by his irreverence toward the establishment, whether worldly or spiritual. On the left of the altar is Guan Di, and on the right is Bai Ma Jiangjun, "General White Horse," who is said to be the son of the Dragon King of the Western Seas transformed into a horse to carry Tripitaka and who appears separately and is widely venerated in many other temples.[23]

No easy or invariable sectarian rule allows us to identify Chinese temples or distinguish the purpose of one from another. The eight separate rooms or chapels of the Lotus Creek temple, for instance, could be considered as virtually distinct temples and the whole building a kind of condominium of divinities. Yet even so, any room may be shared by two or more unrelated deities, sometimes on the same altar. Guan Yin, who enjoys the supreme position in the Wangxia Guan Yin temple, here occupies a position subordinate to Bei Di, and she is placed in front of him on the same altar and is much smaller. In this case, however, she is dressed like Mazu, with whom, as we have observed, she is easily confused. Altogether, at least 19 distinct major divinities are represented in this temple; if one counts all the lesser deities, there are at least 123. Some appear in more than one location in different parts of the temple. In a general way, the Lotus Creek temple can be classified as Taoist, as the Wangxia Guan Yin temple is Buddhist, because its many deities are usually associated with popular Taoism. But in addition to the presence of Guan Yin, there are many traces of Buddhism here. And unless a very pantheistic definition of Taoism is adopted, other gods and goddesses, neither Taoist nor Buddhist, are identified with the vast spiritual substratum of Chinese popular religion: the local Earth God, the God of Wealth, the Year Gods, and so on. But it is also safe to say that the Lotus Creek temple exhibits a very different spiritual complexion now from what it did when it was constructed. The honorary tablets and signboards indicating official recognition of the temple all date from the late nineteenth and early twentieth centuries, when the Chinese population of the city greatly increased. What one sees now is the evidence of the slow accretion of a century or more of changes and modifications as the shifting interests and beliefs of the Chinese settlers of Macau, particularly the newcomers, were reflected by the temple. The complete reconstruction of temples, often on a new design and sometimes following destruction by fire, was not unusual. The original rustic setting of the temple, fancifully depicted on friezes along the eaves, has changed completely; it is now surrounded by a barrio of the city, and a movie theater is nearby. The creek and the bridge have long since disappeared. The memory of the old scene is preserved only in the names of the nearby streets: Travessa da Ponte, Rua Entre Campos, and Rua da Erva ("Grass Street").

Chinese temples exhibit a kind of symbolic archaeology of population movement and community formation, with "layers" of spiritual beings representing both popular religious cults and individual social needs juxtaposed and intermingled like the strata deposited by a physical settlement over time. In this sense, it is not the concrete presence of the temples themselves, as architectural artifacts, but their symbolic spiritual contents that provide a multidimensional map of the progress of the human settlement of Macau.

Protectors and Patrons of Special Interests: The New Urban Culture

The primordial Taoist deities were usually associated with natural forces or places, such as mountains, or with the rural occupations and concerns of farmers and fishermen. Few of them had specific historical origins. When the peninsula, with its rugged hills, was much wilder, before the settlement took over all of the open space, the deities' presence there was natural. The later influx of urban settlers brought diverse professions and urban crafts and occupations, together with the complexity of urban life, as well as interests in special popular patrons who had often started as historical figures and popular heroes.

Directly south from the Lotus Creek temple, across the fields and up against the hillside below Monte fort, is another cluster of temples. They are attached side by side as if they are parts of a single temple but are actually autonomous and distinct. This area was outside the walls of the old city, and it is not clear just when these temples were constructed and whether settlement had already begun there when they first appeared. They probably took their present form toward the end of the nineteenth century.[24] The site is not far from the location of the Santo Antonio gate, in the wall running down from Monte fort to Santo Antonio Church. Thus, the road crossing the Campo from Lotus Creek would have passed near that spot. Early Chinese settlers clustered along the hillside above the fields and near the city wall in a barrio named after the city gate as immigration increased in the late nineteenth and early twentieth centuries.

The temples there belong mainly to the Taoist tradition but are also shared with Buddhism. The main hall of the Bao Gong Miao, the temple on the left, houses the Taoist god Lord Bao (Bao Gong). Bao Gong is the God of Justice; he was originally a famous magistrate named Bao Cheng (also known as Bao Longtu), who lived from 999 to 1062 during the Northern Song dynasty in the capital of Kaifeng. Famous for his judiciousness and probity but betrayed by corrupt and jealous officials, he naturally became, in subsequent ages, a popular hero as a patron of justice.[25] In the temple, he is depicted seated and dressed as a high official, with a black face. But people go there especially to visit Tai Sui, the Year God, who presides in another hall over sixty subordinate deities, the Dangnian Tai Sui (Present Year Tai Sui), one for each year of the sixty-year cycle.[26] Beginning at birth and starting over again at age sixty, there is a god for each year of one's life—thirty figures in a row on each side of the hall. In another hall of the temple are figures especially concerned with women. Guan Yin, the Goddess of Mercy and protectress of women in childbirth, is seated on the altar at the back. At the front are the two Taoist goddesses Lady Jin Hua and Lady Dou Mu, the "Goddess of Smallpox," surrounded by eighteen smaller figures, most of them women, who ensure fertility and male children and protect women during pregnancy and child rearing. Some of these figures hold several infants and small children in their arms.

The central temple of this group, the Tai Sui Dian, is devoted almost exclusively to the Year God and his sixty subordinate gods of the sixty-year cycle, duplicating the temple on the left. Above the door leading from the small entry to the main hall is a portrait of Zhang Daoling, identified by his posthumous title Tianshi, or Heavenly Master, the first Taoist "pope." Zhang lived from 34 to 156 A.D.[27] He had mastered the basic texts of Taoism by the time he was seven years old. Abjuring an official career, he became a recluse in the mountains of central China, where he practiced alchemy. After discovering the elixir of immortality, it is said, he swallowed a pill and became an Immortal; he is considered one of the principal deified human protectors.[28] Steps at the end of the first room lead up to a moon gate, which gives entry to another room containing the altar of the chief year god, Lao Tai Sui, a sort of Father Time. A corridor to the left takes one up a flight of stairs to a temple at the back, higher up on the hillside, where a figure of the Reclining Buddha is found.

The temple on the right of this remarkable group consists of several rooms holding a plethora of figures, large and small, that are mainly identified with Taoism. Over the entrance is the sign "The Hostel of General Shi (*Shi Jiangjun Xingtai*). The Hall of the Immortal Ancestor Lu. In Front of the Hill." Lu Dongbin, with whom this place is identified, was a distinguished scholar and official of the eighth century from central China who became a recluse and sorcerer. He is said to have performed numerous miracles with a magic sword given to him by the fire dragon, and later he became the patron of druggists.[29] Hanging on either side of the entrance foyer are paired vertical inscriptions on carved wooden tablets, each comprising twelve cryptic

Year gods, Tai Sui Dian

characters that are actually complex combinations of words and names. They name the Eight Immortals of Taoism and the respective characteristics, powers, and accomplishments for which they are famous. Chief of the Immortals is Master Zhongli, who carries a fan with which he revives the dead. The sage Li Tieguai was able to leave his mortal body to seek the Tao. When he returned, he found his former body had been destroyed, and his spirit entered that of a disfigured beggar. Lu Dongbin, one of the Immortals and a disciple of Master Zhongli, rids the world of evil influences.[30] Some, like Lu, were once scholars or officials before they achieved immortality, and others were commoners; all are believed capable of magic feats and able to protect those who seek their help. The entrance foyer of the temple leads to the main chapel, where Lord Bao is seated on the central altar. He is flanked by Guan Di and the City God, Cheng Huang; all three are surrounded by many small figures, mostly of unspecified function, twenty-one of whom accompany Guan Di alone. Guan Di, perhaps due to his martial attributes, often functions, as he does here, as a guardian god in temples of local cults as well as in Buddhist temples. The function of Cheng Huang, also a god of city walls, is similar.

Other, smaller Taoist temples are hidden around the base of the hills, where they are obscured by the houses of the old Chinese districts. One of these is the tiny Old Temple of Na Cha on the south slope of Monte hill, built just under the fortress in 1850. Another, newer Na Cha temple was constructed in 1896 on the hill behind the ruins of São Paulo Church.[31] Na Cha, the Third Prince, is perhaps the most bizarre and implausible god of the Taoist pantheon. "Na Cha" is not really a name at all but the imitation of a sound, like a cry or an involuntary exclamation; it may be the transliteration of a Buddhist name. His legend maintains that he was a historical figure from the end of the second millennium B.C., the third son of a king. Born under supernatural circumstances, Na Cha was a monster as a child, over six feet tall. After numerous horrendous escapades, involving several potent deities, he so endangered his parents' lives that he committed suicide at age seven. From that point, he became an almost unpredictable god; riding fire wheels and wielding a spear, he engaged various foes without any clear cause or purpose as a guide. He is always depicted as a mischievous child.

Na Cha is a maverick; like Monkey, he is as much an agent of disturbance as of stability. It is probably for that reason that he is not often found in company with other deities in larger temples, yet he is nonetheless popular in Macau. If Na Cha fits uncomfortably into the stable hierarchy of gods and spirits, that may itself explain his popularity in Macau. One who has such a proclivity for shaking the system may seem to his followers to be a potent ally who must be appeased and whose support is worth enlisting if the other gods are unresponsive. The spiritual bureaucracy, like the worldly civil order, was sometimes afflicted by pomposity and rigidity. Surely, there are many who delight in Na Cha's ability to disrupt and bring ridicule to the establishment.

As the population of Macau grew, early temples were enveloped by the expanding city, although a few had been built in an urban setting from the start. Their architectural and social contexts changed accordingly. Larger numbers of worshippers meant more contributions, which, in turn, made possible the renovations and expansions that an increased volume of visitors demanded. Restoration almost always involved improvement and expansion. Through the late nineteenth and early twentieth centuries, many of Macau's existing temples were successively rebuilt: The Old Guan Yin temple in 1867, 1894, and 1908; the Old Guan Di temple in 1836 and 1893; and the Old Na Cha temple in 1898. The growing prosperity and importance of the Chinese city was reflected in the rich decoration lavished on renovations and on the recent temples. Though some reconstruction projects involved only the modest maintenance of older structures, more ambitious projects were recognized by the bestowing of impressive carved and gilt honorific tablets from Chinese officials and contributors. Bearing pious inscriptions, they are dated mainly from the second half of the nineteenth century, the heyday of temple construction.

Urban expansion did not always have a beneficial effect. In the district of Patane, which was once a little village on the north of the hillside formed by Camões's grotto and the garden surrounding it, there is an old temple dedicated to Tu Di, the Earth God. When it was built in the late eighteenth century, it must have looked out over the water toward Ilha Verde from an attractive natural setting shaded by trees. But as the Chinese population grew, land was reclaimed along the shoreline and built up densely with houses lining narrow streets, so that the temple has now lost its original character. It has gradually fallen into disuse and been partly converted to a private residence.

A few major temples were constructed in urban settings, where they were associated with markets. The oldest of these is the Old Guan Di temple in São Domingos market at the center of the city, in front of the Leal Senado. Built in 1750, it is a small temple of only two rooms. From its beginning, it was an important center of activity in the neighborhood, convenient to people going to and from the market. It also houses the Association of the Three Streets (*San Jie Hui Guan*), a beneficial organization of local merchants and residents centered on the Rua das Estalagens, a major shopping street in the heart of the old Chinese commercial district. On the wall beside the entrance is a painted sign announcing the services offered by the temple: *fengshui*, or geomancy, a method of determining the best location for buildings and gravesites in order to ensure good fortune and prosperity; *zheri*, or the selection of auspicious days for important events, such as weddings and funerals; *xiangming*, or physiognomy, the determination of a person's character (a prospective spouse, for instance) from physical features; and *qisi*, a similar technique involving complexions.

Facing an open square used as a market at the western end of the Rua das Estalagens is the Kang Zhenjun Miao ("Temple of Kang, the True Ruler").[32]

Like the Old Guan Di temple, it is a modest structure, with an entrance foyer and one large hall. The center of the altar is occupied by Kang Dazhenjun, the Great True Ruler Kang; on his left is Hong Sheng Long Wang, the Vast Holy Dragon King, who, it seems, is a god the sea; and on his right is Xishan Houwang, the Expectant King of the Western Mountain. These are obscure deities about which little can be discovered. The altars and the table in front of them are crowded with many smaller figures and objects. The date of construction for this temple is unclear, but from the evidence of inscriptions, it appears to date from at least the 1860s. There is only one other temple devoted to Kang in Macau; now closed, it is located in Wangxia.

Several other temples were erected in growing urban neighborhoods after the mid-nineteenth century. But these are the last new temples to be built, and they are usually smaller and less elaborate than the early temples, which had originally been less constrained by surrounding buildings.

The Spiritual Bureaucracy

The larger temples are only the summit of a hierarchy—several hierarchies, in fact—including shrines and smaller temples and the divinities who inhabit them. Chinese houses and shops and other businesses have small altars on the walls at the back of the main rooms, facing the front doors. These are most commonly dedicated to Guan Di or to Mazu. Guan Di is popularly known as the God of War, but the name is misleading: If his significance were not far broader than that, his cult as a patron of many diverse groups and professions would not be as prevalent as it is. Like so many other popular Chinese deities, Guan Di began as a historical person, Guan Yu, one of the greatest heroes in an age of heroism—the Three Kingdoms era of the third century. He was betrayed and executed by his enemies in 220 A.D. Shortly thereafter, a long process of apotheosis began under the imperial patronage of successive dynasties. In the late Ming, in 1594, the title Di, or "God," was conferred on him, and in the late Qing, at the time of the Taiping Rebellion, he was awarded the supreme title Guan Dafuzi, or "Guan the Great Sage and Teacher," equal to that of Confucius.[33] As a paragon of unwavering loyalty and martial virtue, Guan Di was thus co-opted by the state as a defender of order, especially the official order. Maverick gods like Monkey and Na Cha who shook up the established order were the analogues of popular heterodox movements. They could never be so favorably regarded by the state and consequently did not enjoy official patronage.[34]

Guan Di is always depicted as a formidable, red-faced figure with a long black beard; he is seated on a tiger skin and flanked on the left by his adopted son, Guan Ping, a bland-looking young man with a sack of money, and on the right by his bodyguard, Zhou Cang, a ferocious, swarthy fellow holding a battle-ax.[35] Depending on the elaborateness of the shrine, Guan Di may be painted or he may be represented by a single, carved figure, richly painted. He is usually placed in a boxlike altar, with a shelf in front to hold small offerings, an incense burner, and candleholders. Wax candles, which can only be burned briefly, have been replaced ubiquitously by electric "candles" with red bulbs that burn perpetually.

If the shrine is to Mazu, popular among seafarers, the goddess is represented by a carved figure wearing an elaborate headdress with a fringed veil. At a higher level, of course, both Guan Di and Mazu occupy small and large temples, which they share with other divinities.

A considerable local industry is devoted to manufacturing and supplying the paraphernalia of the various cults. Concentrated along the Rua da Madeira, the Rua da Tercena, and the Rua Nossa Senhora do Ampáro are the shops of the craftsmen who make the furnishings for household altars and shrines. Their shop windows display gilded and painted wooden figures; images of deities painted or printed on wooden, metal, or glass plaques; incense holders and candlesticks; electric altar candles and electric "incense" sticks; paper and cloth decorations for the gods; and even complete sets of altar furniture.

Outside the doors of Chinese houses, midway up on the walls to the right, are small votive tablets and holders for incense, inscribed with the name of the God of Wealth, Cai Shen. Except in larger neighborhood shrines and temples, he is rarely depicted in person; where he is, he holds an ingot of gold or sacks of money. Lowliest and most prevalent of all is Tu Di, the Earth God, who resides at the door of every house; he is situated in a shrine or tablet at ground level next to the threshold, with some means for holding incense sticks, perhaps only a cup molded out of the plaster of the wall.[36] He is referred to merely as Men Kou Tu Di, literally, the Earth God at the Door. Sometimes, the God of Wealth and the Earth God share the same tablet, as if they were two aspects of a single entity. At the doors of the large houses of wealthy people, his altar may take the form of a miniature temple set into the wall, with an ornamented roof; it is brightly decorated but has the same tablet inside.[37]

From this lowest level, the hierarchy extends upward through neighborhood shrines and small ward temples to the large temples, becoming more complex at each higher level. Neighborhood (*fang*) shrines dedicated to the Earth God and the God of Wealth and Prosperity are found where narrow alleys widen, at the entrances to patios and cul-de-sacs, or at the intersections of lanes. They may be only benchlike altars and niches in the walls, painted red. The most elaborate ones have a figure of the god covered by a miniature temple, but some may have only the name on a smooth, egg-shaped stone or two, painted red, to represent him. If they are of the larger kind, shrines for the Earth God are almost always called *Fu De Ci*, or "Shrine of Prosperity and Virtue." "Wang Ding She" identifies an altar of

Wall shrine   Shrine to the God of Wealth

the God of Wealth. Occasionally, an altar to Tai Shan, another god of the earth and the Taoist god of the Sacred Mountain of the East in North China near the birthplace of Confucius, protects against evil influences entering a neighborhood.

Slightly higher in this hierarchy are the first shrines dedicated to the City God, the guardian of walls and moats—Cheng Huang.[38] Beginning as a local Earth God, he was placed at the head of the empire-wide system of Tu Di with official sanction.[39] His altar is found in some of the larger temples; his own temple was once an official fixture of all traditional Chinese cities but was probably never as important in the quasi-European city of Macau, where it would have lacked direct official support. Cheng Huang's most prominent appearance in Macau is in the Old Guan Yin temple (Guan Yin Gu Miao), located near the larger Guan Yin Tang in Wangxia, where a large hall is devoted to him.

Deities like Tu Di and Cheng Huang are, in an important sense, not gods possessing distinct personalities but impersonal spiritual officials. Their names are really titles of bureaucratic offices, like the title for a district magistrate, and their spiritual functions are unrelated to the particular character of the "incumbent" in the office. Other deities, such as Mazu and Guan Di, however, do possess distinct personalities emanating from their purported origins as historical figures. Their spiritual powers have much to do with their individual characters and special competence. Thus, it is possible to distinguish between two classes of deities: impersonal officials, who preside over the same generalized administrative functions at the same level everywhere they appear, and personal heroes, sages, and saviors, who may offer special protection and assistance to individual supplicants.[40] Even so, to the degree that deities like Mazu or Guan Yin have become widely distributed in many localities, they have increasingly taken on the attributes of impersonal administrative functionaries.

In China, the state sometimes patronized popular religious cults as a means of co-opting their function of keeping order—in favor of the state rather than local society, where their autonomy might present a challenge to official authority. In Macau, however, Portuguese official patronage of popular religion was undeveloped relative to local Chinese patronage; it was vested, instead, in the Catholic Church. Nevertheless, Chinese official patronage, where it succeeded in crossing the barrier between the mainland and the city, may have helped to reinforce China's influence over the settlement's Chinese population. The late development of the Guan Di cult in Macau was a reflection not only of the growing Chinese urban culture but also of its continued attachment to the society from which it came.[41] Regardless of official patronage, imported deities such as Mazu provided a continued focus of identity to settlers from distant areas, defining a community across space and time.[42] The annual sharing of incense from the mother temple by subordinate temples is a common ritual recognizing this continuing link among members of a dispersed community. Within the locality, Tu Di, at the very bottom of the spiritual hierarchy of gods, though he is present in every neighborhood, is really nothing more than a rather anonymous replica of a single, generalized responsibility. As such, the Tu Di cult exerts a cohesive influence across communities and localities that are otherwise divided by local cultural, economic, and kinship differences.[43] Cults, then, are expressions of community structure and cohesion as much as or more than expressions of shared belief in a deity or supernatural power. The cult's myth anchors a community in a particular territory, even one that is actually the imaginary territory of a fragmented emigrant community.

Temples and shrines were part of the texture of daily life in a Chinese city, performing functions that were partly religious and partly secular, partly official and partly private. The largest temples enjoyed distinct official status, signified by flagpoles in their courtyards and honorary tablets bestowed by successive emperors and officials. The entire hierarchy of spirits, immortals,

Shrine to Tai Shan

divinities, and gods, from the lowest to the highest, was an analogue of the bureaucratic hierarchy of secular society—it was a kind of spiritual bureaucracy that mirrored the civil one, so that, in a sense, two parallel bureaucracies governed individuals' lives.[44] Just as there was a complex system of offices, functions, realms of competence, titles, and forms of address in the civil bureaucracy of the Chinese empire, so also was there a comparably complex order in the spiritual hierarchy.[45] Local gods and spirits, like local officials, presided over local affairs and assumed responsibility for the immediate welfare of the local inhabitants in specific matters, especially those over which the civil hierarchy had no control—such as good harvests and success in business or protection from natural disasters. People regularly reported to the local gods important events of their lives—births, marriages, deaths, misfortunes—much as they would to the local parish in the Catholic hierarchy or to the civil office responsible for maintaining vital statistics.[46]

Female divinities, however, have no counterpart in the secular bureaucratic hierarchy—there were no female officials in traditional China. But goddesses such as Mazu and Guan Yin, though they were, in this sense, anomalous, were nevertheless an analogue of a vital aspect of civil society. They represented the nurturing and reproductive functions of women in the family, which extended outward as a metaphor for compassion and nurture unserved by the official bureaucracy. As such, they could provide a counterpoise and even a point of opposition to both the official and the spiritual male-dominated bureaucracies.[47] To the extent that they were an underprivileged class in traditional Chinese society, women, who are the principal devotees of female divinities, were thus better served by this spiritual bureaucracy than by the real one.

More exalted divinities possess, like the higher officials of the bureaucratic world, more plenary powers over the general welfare of society. But the spiritual hierarchy, of course, is far less precisely defined and organized than the civil bureaucracy and is assumed to have far wider powers—to ensure fertility or the birth of male children or to protect from disease and all kinds of misfortunes. Thus, it fills the gaps left by the civil bureaucracy; it is not merely an alternative, parallel structure, it is also part of the order of life. Spiritual "officials" take up where human officials leave off.

Cultural Topography

If one plots the locations of the neighborhood shrines to Tu Di, the Earth God, Tai Shan, and the God of Wealth scattered through the streets and patios of Macau, one finds that they trace out the oldest areas of Chinese residence in the city.[48] These include the districts of mostly irregular, narrow streets that begin at the far end of the inner harbor between the Praia do Manduco and the top of Penha hill and extend in a band north through the center of the city to the southern flank of Monte fort, around the Camões Garden to the old district centered on Lotus Creek temple, and on to the north of Monte hill. Mainly older Chinese houses and hybrid Portuguese-Macanese row houses, small and crowded Chinese houses along the hillsides, and Chinese shops and businesses occupy these districts. On the other side of the hills, along the outer harbor and across the old Campo to Wangxia—where larger Macanese and European-style houses, churches, and official buildings, set in wide, more regular streets, predominate—one finds few or no shrines.

The spatial distribution of temples and shrines, along with their varied styles and functions, thus defines the pattern of Chinese settlement in Macau. The earliest and largest temples were located around the periphery, from the Mazu temple near the Barra fort at the point of the peninsula to the Lianfeng temple near the bar leading to the barrier gate. Others, such as the Guan Yin temple at Wangxia and the Lotus Creek temple, were located in open spaces near the small villages of the earliest Chinese settlers. They served the needs of the first Chinese inhabitants, the fishermen, the traders, a few farmers, and both the lower-status residents and the visiting Chinese officials. Later, temples were located inside this periphery, responding to the needs of a growing population of servants, merchants, shopkeepers, laborers, boatmen, and craftsmen, but they were constrained in size by their increasingly crowded environment. The plethora of deities represented in these temples, as well as those added later to the older temples, reflected the profusion of cults and popular traditions brought in by the new settlers, often from beyond the immediate neighboring coastal regions of China.

Modern city planning, with its regular grid pattern of wide streets and boulevards lined with trees, extends across the Campo north and east of Monte fort toward Wangxia and Guia hill; such planning was reserved for the areas of larger houses owned by Europeans and wealthy Europeanized Chinese and Macanese. The formal regularity and dominant European culture was hostile to the Chinese tradition of temple building and neighborhood shrines because it tended to exclude the people who patronized popular cults.

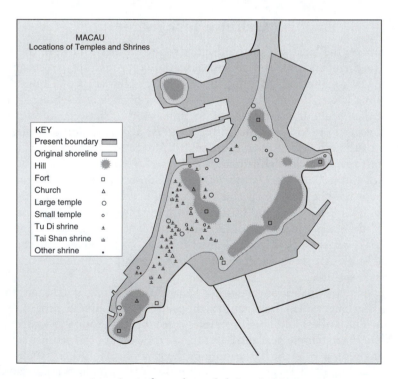

Locations of temples and shrines in Macau

Temples and shrines create a symbolic map of the spiritual geography of a place. (In the case of Macau, this map was very much compressed in a small area and made more complex by the diversity of cults coexisting in an emigrant community.) The territories marked by cults and their temples or shrines need not be mutually exclusive—they may overlap each other. In this sense, the Christian churches of Macau, linked to their own community territories, fit perfectly into the spiritual geography, whether their parishioners were aware of this fact or not. Christianity and Chinese popular religion could thus accommodate each other comfortably in Macau. And just as the churches linked the Catholic community of Europeans and their converts in

Statue of São Tiago, Fortaleza de Barra

a spiritual network to places remote from Macau (Europe, Goa, and Nagasaki, for instance), the temples of the various cults also linked the Chinese community to their places of origin elsewhere in China. The cult of Guan Di, officially sanctioned as a national cult, connected his followers to the nation from which they came. And the cult of Mazu linked her followers in places such as Macau to the larger seafaring population of the South China maritime region that transcended political boundaries.[49] So, on a larger scale, two spiritual maps, each tracing the migration of different peoples and cultures, overlapped in Macau.[50]

A visible and very real cultural frontier was thus established in Macau. It is easy to make too much of the mingling that occurred across that frontier; like the political and commercial worlds that also met there, different cultural traditions, Christian and Chinese, blended at some points but remained distinctly separate at others. Even the inscriptions on the facade of São Paulo Church that exhort the public in Chinese nevertheless express distinctly Christian sentiments.

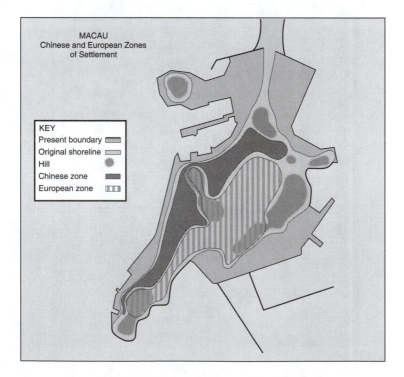

Chinese and European zones of settlement

天后聖母　為我等祈

The Virgin Mary with Jesus (painting in the chapel of São Francisco Xavier, Coloane)

With few exceptions, the European churches of Macau occupied the high ground of the peninsula—the slopes of the hills and the ridges connecting them. To the south is Penha Church, dominating the tip of the peninsula from the top of Penha hill; along the ridge north of there are São Laurenço and Santo Agostinho Churches. Further north is the cathedral, near the center of the city in front of the Leal Senado but standing on higher ground. São Domingos Church nearby is the only one that does not occupy a commanding location. Still further north on the ridge extending between Monte fort and Camões Garden are the ruins of São Paulo Church and Santo Antonio Church. São Francisco Church stood on the high point at the northern end of the curve of the Praia Grande. Finally, on the opposite slope of Monte hill toward Guia hill is São Lazaro Church.

Along an imaginary, irregular line connecting these churches and dividing Macau roughly into eastern and western segments, two very different cultural worlds met, like the confluence of two turbid streams carrying the evidence of very different headwaters.[51] The religious traditions of China and their popular manifestations in local shrines and temples were confined to the western side of this line. The churches seem to stand like sentinels guarding a defensive cultural frontier. Likewise, the spread of Chinese popular religious cults and their visible architectural manifestations—the neighborhood shrines and temples—served to define and contain, like boundary markers, the limits of Western cultural influence. But these contested divisions were never completely impermeable, especially to the least tangible cultural expressions. Thus, influences bled across the frontier, producing such infusions as the blurring of the images of Guan Yin or Mazu and the Virgin Mary.

The frontier was also a threshold. Just as Macau was the scene of a long process of cultural infusion from the West, planting Western cultural elements such as religion, architecture, language, and society on the edge of China, it was also the scene of Chinese acculturation. Religious themes and practices entered from both directions, and the closer proximity of Macau to China than to Europe did not lessen their significance. Macau was a threshold between two worlds, which some Europeans and Chinese succeeded in crossing and others did not. Even when they did not, they encountered people from across the threshold. In much the same way, though perhaps in a more figurative sense, deities like Mazu, the Goddess of Seafarers and Queen of Heaven, Guan Yin, the Compassionate and Merciful Sovereign, and the Virgin Mary, the Holy Mother Queen of Heaven, were representatives of their respective worlds who also encountered each other at this cultural juncture in Macau. Perhaps, then, the confusion of Mazu, Guan Yin, and Mary is appropriate. All of them, in varying degrees, spread beyond the parochial regions of their origins as powerful figures of devotion and protection.

conclusion

Illusions
Epilogue

Cities and Thrones and Powers
Stand in Time's eye,
Almost as long as flowers,
Which daily die:
But, as new buds put forth
To glad new men,
Out of the spent and unconsidered Earth
The Cities rise again.[1]

If you strain to look out to sea from above the Praia Grande, out beyond the bridge and past the breakwaters and buoys at the entrance to the outer harbor, out to the islands on the horizon to the east, you may catch the first glimpse of the plumes of spray from the arriving hydrofoils and jetfoils, still a half hour away from landing. At first, only undefined white blurs on the water, their silhouettes slowly grow larger as they approach. Now turning sharply around the outer buoy, they move swiftly into the outer harbor ferry terminal below Guia hill, passing the outbound boats whose plumes, in turn, disappear over the horizon toward Hong Kong. From early in the morning to late in the afternoon, they mark the hours of the day with their schedules. The larger, slower ferries come only two or three times a day. Once, they went around the Barra point to disembark their passengers at the inner harbor terminal. In those days, they had a more intimate connection with the place; now, they seem rather diffident and detached from the city that draws them there.

Occasionally, a patrol boat of the Macau Maritime Police cruises past on its way to its station in the waters surrounding Taipa and Coloane Islands; the crew watches for boat people from the coasts of South China and Vietnam to the west who are seeking refuge in Macau or Hong Kong, for illegal immigrants coming from the nearby islands, and for smugglers. At times, a fast, armed cruiser of the Chinese maritime customs fleet will sortie from across the inner harbor on some undetermined mission.

Day in and day out, with monotonous regularity, the boats come and go. At dawn, the small fishing junks and larger trawlers leave from their anchorage in the inner harbor, noisily chugging around the Barra point and under the bridge. From dusk to late in the evening, many of them return, some after several days at sea working the fishing areas in the estuary, among the islands, and out past Laowanshan. Following less regular routines, the cargo junks and coastal freighters and tugs towing laden barges bring in supplies and merchandise and carry out the cheap manufactured goods of Macau's small factories and processing plants. Most of them are bound for Hong Kong; they are small by the measure of international maritime trade, though they appear large in proximity to the other traffic in the channel.

At night, as the ships and boats pass through the harbor—with only the red and green navigation lights, the bright white beacons at the tops of their masts, and the deep throbbing of their engines locating them in the darkness—they seem strangely disembodied. Their wakes disturb the long, glimmering reflections cast in the water by the colored neon signs illuminating the Lisboa Casino and its brilliantly lit tower shaped like a huge roulette wheel. The dancing reflections mingle with the streetlights on the bridge and the red and white lights from the cars moving along the waterfront. High above the casino, the rotating beacon of the Guia lighthouse pierces the murky atmosphere.

Late into the night and in the early hours of the morning, when the streets are almost deserted, cars race along the Praia Grande with their tires squealing on the long curves, their drivers inspired to test their skills by the spectacle of the annual grand prix race through the streets around the Lisboa Hotel and the hydrofoil terminal.

In the darkness, another city emerges, defined by these sensations—a city of illusion and fantasy, more in company with the glittering world of the casinos than with the mundane life of the streets, markets, temples, and churches of the daylight world. Like the lights and sounds from the ships passing through the channel, this is a disembodied, phantom city. Yet in some ways, it is perhaps more real than the ghosts of the past cities of Macau, which now haunt this place, a graveyard of the monuments and memories of other times.

꙰   ꙰   ꙰

Macau was always a place apart. It was connected to the mainland by a single road through the barrier gate straddling the narrow bar of the isthmus.

Although this connection was not unimportant historically and has become more significant in recent times, the principal way to Macau was nonetheless the more tenuous sea route. When Hong Kong was established, it became the main route by which travelers and goods passed to and from Macau. But the shallow seas around Macau, increasingly silted up by the Pearl River, have limited traffic to ships of shallow draft.[2] Neither air routes nor rail lines yet link Macau to the rest of the world, and the great part of its commerce is borne by small ships and boats; the land bridge to the mainland has remained of secondary importance. Even the postal service and telegraph, which feebly connect Macau to the outside world, are routed through Hong Kong.

Not only in this geographical sense but in a historical sense, too, Macau was isolated. Its historical culture cut it off from the world as much as its marginal location did. Once, in the heyday of Portuguese maritime expansion when Portugal was counted among the major world powers, Macau, even if it was remote from the center of the empire, was at least a participant in the movements of people and the social and cultural influences that were altering the shape of the world. But its continuing link with Portugal after that nation's greatness waned and its Asian empire collapsed left Macau, like a piece of derelict driftwood, beached on a distant shore after the flood tide has receded.[3] The patina of Portuguese colonial culture gradually came to seem merely a fading image of a lost age, all the more so because its original source was so distant and no longer central to influences still emanating from the West. The physical presence of Portuguese administration preserved a kind of graceful charm no longer found in other former colonial outposts. But it was irrelevant. Macau's public landmarks, like its place-names, memorialize heroes and deeds associated with an era long past, their significance embedded in a history now recollected by only a few. And it was not Macau's colonial heritage alone that explained its peculiar isolation. Just as it was left stranded by the receding tide of the Western colonial era, the city was also left behind by the great modern upheavals of political revolution, colonial liberation, and economic modernization that have transformed the Chinese world. As a result, Macau is now the repository of cultural expressions long since obliterated from the mainland: a plethora of popular religious cults and fragments of an older lifestyle, in company with the flotsam and jetsam of a hybrid creole culture.

But the isolation of Macau is now only an illusion or at most a temporary condition that soon will finally pass. There is an odd inconsistency between the languid and increasingly irrelevant Portuguese presence and the expansive and frenetic development of the Chinese city, fueled by investment from Hong Kong, Taiwan, and Japan and employing the labor of the growing Chinese immigrant population.[4] An international airport and container port, under construction since 1989 on Taipa Island and open for service in late 1995, will effectively put an end to Macau's isolation. "With the airport

Macau will become open to the world."[5] These developments are expected
to transform the city into a major economic force in the Pearl River delta,
alongside Hong Kong and Canton.[6] In 1999, according to an agreement between China and Portugal, China will resume control of the territory, and at
that point, four and a half centuries of Portuguese administration will come
to an end.[7]

Even now, dumpy Chinese sight-seeing boats, overladen with gawking
mainland tourists, cruise close along the shore of the harbor, tantalizing their
passengers with views of the new office and apartment buildings and luxury
hotels rapidly altering the skyline. As cameras flash, the guides can be heard
on the loudspeakers pointing out the glittering attractions of the strange city
that soon will all be theirs. But when that time comes, it will no longer be the
place it once was.

The modernization of the hinterland just beyond the barrier gate is the
latest phase in the history of Macau's influence on the South China coastal
region. The differences between the settlement on the peninsula and the
mainland to the north of it, so obvious to every visitor until recent times, are
already rapidly disappearing.[8] Macau will cease to be a threshold between
two worlds, a place where two cultures and societies met and sometimes
mingled and across which each explored the other. In one sense, perhaps,
Macau will remain a bridge to a new world for those who are able to partici-
pate in its continuing development as a part of Zhuhai, one of the several
Special Economic Zones (SEZs) along the China coast. But it will then be no
different in that respect from any of the other enclaves of Western economic
development that have sprung up since treaty port days, fostered by the
sharing of finance and cheap labor that has characterized most of postcolo-
nial East and Southeast Asia in the late twentieth century.[9]

Macau's function as a cultural threshold between two worlds always depended on its marginality—a threshold by definition exists on the margins
of adjoining spaces. In allowing the Portuguese to settle on the peninsula in
the mid-1550s, the Ming authorities intended to isolate them on a virtually
uninhabited fringe of a peripheral district of China's southernmost coastal
province. There, any pernicious influences could be contained far from the
populous cities of the empire. At the same time, Macau's distance from the
centers of the Portuguese maritime empire at Goa and Lisbon left the settlement at the extreme horizon of European power. That eccentric location
helped to insulate it from the effects of abrupt political changes emanating
from both China and the West but not from the more slowly acting cultural
influences of the two worlds. Thus, it was a place of refuge for individuals
and groups alike—for European Jews and outcasts escaping the reach of the
Inquisition in Goa or conflicts with Portuguese authorities in the East; for
missionaries evading the capricious Ming decrees interdicting Christian
proselytism; for Japanese Christians fleeing persecution and martyrdom in

the 1630s and 1640s; for Chinese driven from the mainland by the Manchu conquest of South China and Canton in the 1650s; for Jesuit missionaries again escaping the proscription of Christianity by the Qing in the mid-seventeenth century; for European adventurers and expatriates abandoning their failures and avoiding their creditors;[10] and again for waves of Chinese fleeing the rebellions, wars, and revolutions of China and Southeast Asia in the nineteenth and twentieth centuries. It was Macau's isolation, its peripheral relation to both cultures, Western and Chinese, that defined its peculiar identity. It was very different in this respect from a place like Shanghai. Although "Shanghai was a place where two civilizations met and where neither prevailed," this queen of the treaty ports was located at the very nexus of the vast inland trading network of the Yangzi basin and Western maritime commerce with China.[11]

Cultural encounters are shaped by the places where they occur. Those that take place within the heart of one culture are mediated by the fully formed structure of one society, and the context can never be neutral. The experiences of Chinese and Japanese immigrants in the United States illustrate this point. Even in the still youthful frontier society of the American West in the nineteenth century, these people were surrounded by an expanding and dominant European culture, and they either had to come to terms with that culture or remain isolated from it. Those encounters that take place on the margins of cultures, however, are different. The cultural encounter that went on in Macau for more than four centuries was never perfectly symmetrical. It changed as the settlement changed and grew, reflecting the larger forces at work in the two worlds that met there. It was nonetheless significant for having occurred at the peripheries of these two worlds. In that sense, even the end of this encounter will mark the passage of those changes that have altered the relationship between the two worlds.

🕊 🕊 🕊

The sound of jackhammers chipping away at the rocks on the street below is a reminder that change is constant—Macau has always been rebuilding. If there were no jackhammers in the eighteenth century, even then they were tearing down the buildings of the previous decades and putting up new ones in their places. In cities like Macau, time, especially architectural time, never stands still. Cities are, in many ways, very fragile constructions, ephemeral creations that endure only through a process of perpetual change. Quite apart from intentional change wrought by the human proclivity for engineering, fires, floods, earthquakes, and typhoons have ravaged many cities. If nothing else, merely the waste of human habitation gradually fills them up, so that the strata of earlier growth succumb to the later development, sinking below the surface like the decomposing vegetation on a forest floor. Before the great earthquake of 1923, Tokyo, formerly known as Edo, was perhaps one of the most perishable of cities, with so much of its architecture built of wood. But although frequent fires (the "flowers of Edo") were an inherent part of the cycle of decay and growth of the city, Edo changed very slowly while remaining much the same.[12] A city like Edo can be destroyed piecemeal day after day and yet still retain its recognizable patterns—perhaps only the traveler, returning after a prolonged absence, would be struck by all that has changed; to the inhabitants, the changes are almost imperceptible. Catastrophic change could sometimes be viewed as a blessing and an opportunity. The great Tokyo earthquake interrupted a stagnant cycle and cleared the way for new and different growth, and the wartime bombing of the 1940s had a similar effect.[13]

Modern machines make changes more rapidly—and more ruthlessly—now, and in one sense, that is all that is different about the process of change for Macau. Yet never before was the human capacity to effect change so great that the past itself was endangered. Writing in the 1850s, William C. Hunter noted that Macau "has undergone no striking changes for many a year to the present day."[14] Now, the thread of historical continuity with the past cities of Macau has become attenuated almost to the breaking point. Will the past become a nostalgic illusion conjured only in memory by occasional, isolated, and lifeless fragments and glimpses of what once was?

Yet, as you wander through the streets of Macau, you can trace out the contours of the past in the patterns of the streets—like the curve of the Rua da Praia do Manduco, following what was once the shoreline of the harbor, or the rectilinear grid of the Campo. The past may be resurrected in the streets' names—Rua Entre Campos, the "Street Between the Fields," Rua Alfandega, "Customs House Street"—or in the different architectural styles and densities of the older buildings, in the locations of churches and temples, and by the occasional monument or fortress or building preserved as a relic of the most distant past. In this way, you can create in your mind's eye a historical map of the city or even several maps of the successive historical cities of Macau. What you have created, of course, is an illusion, an imaginary city, different in most respects from the present city of Macau but anchored to it at certain mysterious points.

☙   ☙   ☙

In late May 1985, Portugal and China jointly announced that discussions would soon begin to plan the return of Macau to Chinese sovereignty. Shortly after that announcement, I had talked with the Macanese proprietor of an antique shop on the Avenida Ribeiro, who was busily packing his stock in large crates for shipment to Portugal. He was about to leave Macau for good, he told me, and he talked with a mixture of anger and sadness about

Portugal's willingness to discuss the future of Macau with the Chinese and about the changes that had overcome the city. He seemed to feel that the Portuguese had not kept faith with the Macau Chinese, having abandoned them with such alacrity. Macau would hardly survive two years, he believed. For several days afterward, I felt an oppressive sense of loss—the loss of the old Macau that seemed to be disappearing everywhere before my eyes with the methodical demolition of the old buildings. In early June, after several days of light rain alternating with sunny spells, the weather turned fair and almost windless. The stillness made the air feel heavy. In the evening, a low, brooding mist settled over the water. Above it, far in the distance to the southeast, thunderstorms flashed silently, seeming to portend a change in the weather that never came. That night, I slept uncovered, with the tall windows of my room in the Bela Vista Hotel open to the veranda overlooking the bay.

> I found myself on the docks, which were rapidly becoming bare as people and goods were evacuated. Macau was being abandoned by its inhabitants forever, like a derelict ship. I could not make up my mind whether to stay or leave, but the act of abandonment seemed inevitable and matter-of-fact, done without passion. Then, somehow I was back in the abandoned city, but it seemed like the surface of the moon, gray and almost lifeless. There were several people wearing uniforms like spacesuits who appeared to be foreign, perhaps Chinese. We poked into some of the half-buried caverns and tunnels that had formerly been houses and streets. But we dared not go too far in, and no one remained there. When we finally came out and prepared to leave, I asked the men in uniform whether they thought Macau would ever be re-inhabited. In a rather indifferent and businesslike tone, one of them answered that it would not—the tunnels and passages were too narrow and dangerous and it was not worth exploring further.

His response made me cry out in desperation, and I awoke with a crushing sense of sadness and loss.

Notes

Abbreviations Used in the Notes

AMJL   Yin Guangren and Zhang Rulin, comps., *Aomen jilue.*
CR   Bridgman, Elijah Coleman, and S. Wells Williams, eds., *The Chinese Repository.*
DMB   L. Carrington Goodrich and Chaoying Fang, eds., *Dictionary of Ming Biography*
GDXY   Qu Dajun, *Guangdong xinyu.*
MS   Zhang Tingyu et al., eds., *Mingshi.*
PTY   Jie Zi, ed., *Putayao qinzhan Aomen shilue.*
QCYSDG   *Qingchao yeshi daguan.*

Introduction

1. Italo Calvino, *Invisible Cities* (San Diego: Harcourt Brace Jovanovich, 1972), 69.

2. Eugene Victor Walter, *Placeways: A Theory of the Human Environment* (Chapel Hill: University of North Carolina Press, 1988), 204.

3. See John E. Wills Jr., *Embassies and Illusions: Dutch and Portuguese Envoys to K'ang-hsi, 1666–1687* (Cambridge, Mass.: Harvard University Press, 1984), for a discussion of political approaches to China through Macau in the seventeenth century.

4. See, for examples, C. R. Boxer, *The Great Ship from Amacon: Annals of Macao and the Old Japan Trade, 1555–1640* (Lisbon: Centro de Estudos Historicos Ultramarinos, 1959); George Bryan Souza, *The Survival of Empire: Portuguese Trade and Society in China and the South China Sea, 1630–1754* (Cambridge: Cambridge University Press, 1986); T'ien-tse Chang, *Sino-Portuguese Trade from 1514 to 1644: A Synthesis of Portuguese and Chinese Sources* (Leyden: E. J. Brill, 1934); Michael Greenberg, *British Trade and the Opening of China, 1800–1842* (Cambridge: Cambridge University Press, 1951); John King Fairbank, *Trade and Diplomacy on the China Coast: The Opening of the Treaty Ports, 1842–1854* (Stanford: Stanford University Press, 1969); and Maurice Collis, *Foreign Mud: The Opium Imbroglio at Canton in the 1830's & the Anglo-Chinese War* (New York: W. W. Norton, 1968). The last is a popular account.

5. See George H. Dunne, *Generation of Giants: The Story of the Jesuits in China in the Last Decades of the Ming Dynasty* (Notre Dame, Ind.: University of Notre Dame Press, 1962), and Arnold H. Rowbotham, *Missionary and Mandarin: The Jesuits at the Court of China* (Berkeley: University of California Press, 1942).

6. For a collective effort of this kind, see Dilip K. Basu, ed., *The Rise and Growth of the Colonial Port Cities in Asia* (Berkeley: Center for South and Southeast Asia

Studies, University of California at Berkeley, 1985). This volume does not include a treatment of Macau. See also Rhoads Murphey, "Traditionalism and Colonialism: Changing Urban Roles in Asia," *Journal of Asian Studies* 29, no. 1 (November 1969), 67–84. On the typology of cities, see Max Weber, "The Nature of the City" (pp. 23–46), and Robert Redfield and Milton Singer, "The Cultural Role of Cities" (pp. 206–233), in Richard Sennett, ed., *Classic Essays on the Culture of Cities* (New York: Appleton-Century-Crofts, 1969).

7. Several more or less comprehensive histories of Macau already exist: C. A. Montalto de Jesus, *Historic Macao* (Hong Kong: Oxford University Press, 1984); C. R. Boxer, *Fidalgos in the Far East, 1550–1770* (Hong Kong: Oxford University Press, 1968); Austin Coates, *A Macao Narrative* (Hong Kong: Heinemann, 1978); and Cesar Guillen-Nuñez, *Macau* (Hong Kong: Oxford University Press, 1984). No work of which I am aware seeks to treat Macau from a cultural and social point of view over its more than four centuries of existence.

8. See Philip D. Curtin, *Cross-Cultural Trade in World History* (Cambridge: Cambridge University Press, 1984), 127–135.

9. See K. N. Chaudhuri, *Trade and Civilization in the Indian Ocean: An Economic History from the Rise of Islam to 1750* (Cambridge: Cambridge University Press, 1985), chaps. 5 and 8; Murphey, "Traditionalism and Colonialism," 70–74.

10. Jonathan Porter, "The Transformation of Macau," in *Pacific Affairs* 66, no. 1 (Spring 1993), 19. Cf. Murphey, "Traditionalism and Colonialism," 73–75.

11. James N. Anderson and Walter T. Vorster, "In Search of Melaka's Hinterlands: Beyond the Entrepôt," in Basu, ed., *The Rise and Growth of the Colonial Port Cities*, 1–6; Janet L. Abu-Lughod, *Before European Hegemony: The World System A.D. 1250–1350* (New York: Oxford University Press, 1989), 309–312; Curtin, *Cross-Cultural Trade*, 129–131; Chaudhuri, *Trade and Civilization*, 112.

12. Anderson and Vorster, "In Search of Melaka's Hinterlands"; Abu-Lughod, *Before European Hegemony*, 312.

13. Curtin, *Cross-Cultural Trade*, 166, 240–241.

14. Abu-Lughod, *Before European Hegemony*, 311.

15. Curtin, *Cross-Cultural Trade*, 242.

16. Rhoads Murphey, *Shanghai: Key to Modern China* (Cambridge, Mass.: Harvard University Press. 1953).

17. Walter, *Placeways*, 111.

18. Redfield and Singer, "The Cultural Role of Cities." Redfield and Singer distinguishes two contrasting cultural roles of cities, the orthogenetic and the heterogenetic. These roles describe the differing character of the cultural change in different types of cities. The orthogenetic city "is the place where religious, philosophical and literary specialists reflect, synthesize and create out of the traditional material new arrangements and developments that are felt by the people to be the outgrowths of the old" (p. 213). The heterogenetic city "is a place of conflict of differing traditions, a center of heresy, heterodoxy and dissent, of interruption and destruction of ancient tradition, of rootlessness and anomie" (p. 213). All cities are some combination of both types, and the combination may change with time. Macau would seem to belong largely to the heterogenetic type.

19. In addition to the usual secondary studies and writings on Macau, the documentary and textual foundation of this study comprises not only works in Por-

tuguese and English but also Chinese sources, including memoirs, descriptions, observations, and accounts by Chinese and European visitors.

20. Calvino, *Invisible Cities*, 67–68.

Chapter One

1. Luis Vaz de Camões, *Os Lusiadas,* Reis Brazil, ed. (Lisbon: Editorial Minerva, 1964), canto I, stanza 1.

2. Confucius, *The Great Learning*.

3. Of Henry's gathering of talent, one scholar says: "Henrique attracted to the Promontory many of the best geographers and mathematicians of his time, as well as cartographers, astronomers, and mariners. Besides Portuguese and Spaniards they included many brilliant Jews, as well as Germans, Genoese, Venetians, Moors, a Dane, Canary Islanders, and Syrians. With them he discussed the probability of existence of new lands and seas. Rather than a conventional 'school,' his retinue resembled a congress of experts in continuous session." William Freitas, *Camoens and His Epic: A Historic, Geographic and Cultural Survey* (Stanford: Institute of Hispanic American and Luso-Brazilian Studies, Stanford University, 1963), 24. Such characterizations of Henry's activities should be treated with considerable caution. The scope and significance of Henry's contribution to Atlantic exploration and Portuguese expansion has been the subject of much debate. From the fifteenth century onward, chroniclers and writers have tended to depict Henry in heroic proportions. For a more cautious assessment of Henry, see J.R.S. Phillips, *The Medieval Expansion of Europe* (Oxford: Oxford University Press, 1988), 232–233.

4. Henry's motivations, as well as the precise shape of his knowledge and his intellectual and material resources, of course, are subject to interpretation. To varying degrees, he has been idolized and idealized, as a prototypical Renaissance scientist, bent on expanding mankind's horizons. See J. M. Parry, *Europe and a Wider World, 1415–1715* (London: Hutchinson's University Library, 1949), 30; Edgar Prestage, *The Portuguese Pioneers* (London: A. & C. Black, 1933), 29–30; and H. V. Livermore, *Portugal: A Short History* (Edinburgh: Edinburgh University Press, 1973), 72. More cautious assessments portray him as a scholar and perhaps a "scientist," in the sense in which the word was understood at the time, but driven first and foremost by crusading and economic motives. See C. R. Boxer, *The Portuguese Seaborne Empire, 1415–1825* (New York: Alfred A. Knopf, 1969), 24, and A. H. de Oliveira Marques, *A History of Portugal,* 2d ed. (New York: Columbia University Press, 1976), vol. 1, 143–144.

5. Boxer, *The Portuguese Seaborne Empire*, 25–26; Marques, *A History of Portugal,* vol. 1, 149.

6. For an excellent description of the problems of navigation in the South Atlantic and the extraordinary achievement of da Gama's voyage, see Alfred W. Crosby, *Ecological Imperialism: The Biological Expansion of Europe, 900–1900* (Cambridge: Cambridge University Press, 1986), chap. 5.

7. Camões, *Os Lusiadas*, canto V, verse 18. For a discussion of the routes and itineraries, as well as the related hazards, of the Portuguese seaborne empire from the Atlantic to the East China Sea, see A.J.R. Russell-Wood, *A World on the Move: The*

Portuguese in Africa, Asia, and America, 1415–1808 (New York: St. Martin's Press, 1992), 30–40. In 1570, there were about twenty-seven carreiras.

8. Yung Wing [Rong Hong], *My Life in China and America* (New York: Henry Holt, 1909), 21.

9. Livermore, *Portugal: A Short History,* 72; Bailey Diffie, *Prelude to Empire: Portugal Overseas Before Henry the Navigator* (Lincoln: University of Nebraska Press, 1960), 39.

10. One must be cautious regarding Henry's motives and vision; nonetheless, his role as an heir to the Crusades seems secure. See Phillips, *The Medieval Expansion of Europe,* 249, 258.

11. Boxer, *The Portuguese Seaborne Empire,* 20–23.

12. Marques, *A History of Portugal,* vol. 1, 143.

13. Felipe Fernandez-Armesto, *Before Columbus: Exploration and Colonisation from the Mediterranean to the Atlantic, 1229–1492* (London: Macmillan Education, 1987), 140–148.

14. Charles Verlinden, *The Beginnings of Modern Colonization* (Ithaca: Cornell University Press, 1970), XII–XIII.

15. Fernandez-Armesto, *Before Columbus,* 67–69, 94–95.

16. Ibid., 118–119, 169–170; Phillips, *The Medieval Expansion of Europe,* 254–255. The question of the origins and continuities in European expansion is discussed at length by Verlinden, Phillips, and Fernandez-Armesto. Although these authors agree about the early origins of European expansion in the eastern Mediterranean and the trend of later developments in the western Mediterranean, they substantially differ regarding the degree of continuity between the Mediterranean and Atlantic patterns of colonization. See, in particular, Verlinden, *The Beginnings of Modern Colonization,* XVII, 3–13; Phillips, *The Medieval Expansion of Europe,* 227–228, 238–241; and Fernandez-Armesto, *Before Columbus,* 43, 169–170.

17. Bailey W. Diffie and George D. Winius, *Foundations of the Portuguese Empire, 1415–1580* (Minneapolis: University of Minnesota Press, 1977), 55; Parry, *Europe and a Wider World,* 11.

18. One hundred years after Ceuta, in the early 1500s, the Portuguese resumed their campaigns in North Africa. But it is clear that this activity was being financed by the revenues of the Estado da India, and although the campaigns were marginally more successful than the preceding offensive, they also reached a dead end. Diffie and Winius, *Foundations of the Portuguese Empire,* 278–280. See also Phillips, *The Medieval Expansion of Europe,* 238–239.

19. Diffie, *Prelude to Empire,* 13.

20. Marques, *A History of Portugal,* vol. 1, 3.

21. Ibid., 67–68, 89.

22. Ibid., 3, 89, 138; Livermore, *Portugal: A Short History,* 56.

23. Marques, *A History of Portugal,* vol. 1, 91; Livermore, *Portugal: A Short History,* 56.

24. Verlinden, *The Beginnings of Modern Colonization,* 12–13; Fernandez-Armesto, *Before Columbus,* 116–119.

25. Diffie and Winius, *Foundations of the Portuguese Empire,* 313; Diffie, *Prelude to Empire,* 12, 25–26, 44–45.

26. Diffie, *Prelude to Empire,* 68–69.

27. Ibid., 88; Marques, *A History of Portugal*, vol. 1, 94; Fernandez-Armesto, *Before Columbus*, 111–112.

28. Diffie and Winius, *Foundations of the Portuguese Empire*, 118–119; Phillips, *The Medieval Expansion of Europe*, 230, 234. A.J.R. Russell-Wood, *A World on the Move*, 28–29, offers a typology of vessels used by the Portuguese. Sizes varied from less than 100 tons to as much as 2,000 tons—the mammoth but cumbersome and fragile carracks. The mainstay of the Portuguese explorations in the fifteenth century, the caravel, was as small as 60 tons.

29. Boxer, *Fidalgos*, 13. "Between 1497 and 1612 no fewer than 806 ships were employed in the Indian trade; of which 425 returned to Europe, 285 remained permanently on Asiatic stations, and ninety-six were lost. Their ordinary size varied from 100 to 550 tons, armed with cannon, and fitted out for purposes of both freight and war. The ambition of the naval constructors of Portugal outran their technical skill, and ended in floating castles which could not stand the Indian voyage." Quoted from William Wilson Hunter, *A History of British India* (London: Longmans, Green, 1899), vol. 1, 165.

30. Livermore, *Portugal: A Short History*, 64; Marques, *A History of Portugal*, vol. 1, 109–110.

31. Marques, *A History of Portugal*, vol. 1, 130.

32. On the momentum of the crusade, see Phillips, *The Medieval Expansion of Europe*, 248–249.

33. The Cantonese "water world" of the South China coast is described in Dian H. Murray, *Pirates of the South China Coast, 1790–1810* (Stanford: Stanford University Press, 1987), chap. 1.

34. K. N. Chaudhuri, *Trade and Civilization in the Indian Ocean: An Economic History from the Rise of Islam to 1750* (Cambridge: Cambridge University Press, 1985), 50–52. J.J.L. Duyvendak, *China's Discovery of Africa* (London: Arthur Probsthain, 1949), 9–17, and Joseph Needham, *Science and Civilization in China* (Cambridge: Cambridge University Press, 1961–), vol. 4, pt. 3, 494–503, discuss the records of early Chinese maritime activity.

35. A biography of Zheng He and accounts of his voyages are found in Chang Kuei-sheng, "Cheng Ho," in L. Carrington Goodrich and Chaoying Fang, eds., *Dictionary of Ming Biography, 1368–1644* (hereafter cited as DMB) (New York: Columbia University Press, 1976), vol. 1, 194–200; Ma Huan, *Ying-Yai Sheng-Lan, "The Overall Survey of the Ocean's Shores,"* J.V.G. Mills, trans. (Cambridge: Cambridge University Press, 1970); Needham, *Science and Civilization in China*, vol. 4, pt. 3, 486–535; and William Willets, "The Maritime Adventures of Grand Eunuch Ho," *Journal of Southeast Asian History* 5 (September 1964), 2:27–42. These accounts are inconsistent in several respects, including the dates of the expeditions and their destinations. See also Duyvendak, *China's Discovery of Africa*, 27–35. For technical descriptions of Zheng He's ships, see Needham, *Science and Civilization in China*, vol. 4, pt. 3, 396–423, 479–486.

36. All of the expeditions but the last occurred under the Yongle reign. They were terminated by the fourth Ming emperor after the death of the Yongle emperor in 1424. The seventh expedition was launched by the Xuande emperor (1426–1436), the fifth emperor. Zheng He may have died either on the seventh voyage or soon after its return. Chang Kuei-sheng, "Cheng Ho," 198; cf. Ma Huan, *Ying-Yai Sheng-Lan*, 6.

37. Duyvendak, *China's Discovery of Africa*, 27–28.

38. Needham offers an extensive comparative discussion of both the motives and the consequences of the Chinese and Portuguese voyages. See Needham, *Science and Civilization in China*, vol. 4, pt. 3, 524–535.

39. Zheng He has been called, anachronistically, the "Vasco da Gama of China." For a recent comparison of a different kind from the one made here, see Robert Finlay, "Portuguese and Chinese Maritime Imperialism: Camões's *Lusiads* and Luo Maodong's *Voyage of the San Bao Eunuch*," in *Comparative Studies in Society and History* 34, no. 2 (April 1992), 225–241. Finlay uses the respective heroes of the two works, Vasco da Gama and Zheng He, as the basis for a comparison between Portuguese and Chinese attitudes toward maritime enterprise.

40. The Yongle emperor's probable motives are briefly sketched by J.V.G. Mills, in Ma Huan, *Ying-Yai Sheng-Lan*, 1.

41. Frederick W. Mote and Denis Twitchett, eds., *The Cambridge History of China*, vol. 7, *The Ming Dynasty 1368–1644, Part I* (Cambridge: Cambridge University Press, 1988), 223–224.

42. Chang Kuei-sheng, "Cheng Ho," 194–195; Ma Huan, *Ying-Yai Sheng-Lan*, 5–8.

43. F. W. Mote, "Chu Yün-wen" (pp. 397–404); Lienche Tu Fang, "Hu Ying" (p. 643); and Chang Kuei-sheng, "Cheng Ho" (p. 195), in Goodrich and Fang, eds., DMB, vol. 1; Duyvendak, *China's Discovery of Africa*, 27.

44. Marques, *A History of Portugal*, 166,

45. Livermore, *Portugal: A Short History*, 82, 90; Ray Huang, *1587—A Year of No Significance: The Ming Dynasty in Decline* (New Haven: Yale University Press, 1981), 147.

46. Marques, *A History of Portugal*, 180–181, 258–259. State control of all trade with the East was imposed in 1504, and certain valuable commodities fell under a state monopoly. After 1501, a royal office, the Casa da India (a successor to the Casa de Ceuta established at Lisbon in the early fifteenth century to manage African trade), received and sold merchandise and set customs duties. In contrast to the Portuguese experience, as J.V.G. Mills concludes, "the Ming court failed to grasp the possibilities of sea-power and lost interest in maritime expansion; so the great expeditions were not followed up but remained isolated *tours de force*, mere exploits; and an outstanding period of greatness in China's history came to an end." Quoted in Ma Huan, *Ying-Yai Sheng-Lan*, 34.

47. Marques, *A History of Portugal*, 170–171, 347. For a rather different assessment of the Portuguese and Chinese maritime enterprises, see Needham, *Science and Civilization in China*, vol. 4, pt. 3, 533–535.

48. See Andrew H. Plaks, *Archetype and Allegory in the "Dream of the Red Chamber"* (Princeton: Princeton University Press, 1976), 11; Luis Vaz de Camoens, *The Lusiads*, trans. by William C. Atkinson (Harmondsworth, England: Penguin Books, 1952), 7, 22. *Hong-lou meng* has been translated as *Dream of the Red Chamber* and *Story of the Stone*. Some may object to this comparison, observing that the two works are products of different times and different stages in the histories of their respective cultures. *Hong-lou meng* reflects society of the seventeenth and early eighteenth centuries, a plateau of cultural development. Does it also reflect the society of

the Ming? The *Lusiads*, completed in the late sixteenth century, looks back to the heroic age of Portuguese unification and expansion. Yet if both, in a sense, are reflections of the times in which they were written, those times are, after all, comparable. For Portugal, the sixteenth century during the reigns of Manuel I (1495–1521) and João III (1521–1557) was an age of mature self-confidence and cultural vitality. The "High Qing" of the late Kangxi and early Qianlong reigns from the 1680s to the 1760s stood in that same relationship to the Ming and early Qing. Both nations in these periods witnessed empire building, material affluence, the establishment of stable institutions, political strength and confidence, social integration, and flamboyant artistic and architectural styles.

49. *Os Lusiadas*, canto II, stanza 46.

50. Ibid., canto V, stanza 42.

51. Mary Helms, *Ulysses' Sail: An Ethnographic Odyssey of Power, Knowledge, and Geographical Distance* (Princeton: Princeton University Press, 1988), 259–260.

52. *Os Lusiadas*, canto VII, stanzas 2 and 3.

53. Cao Xueqin, *The Story of the Stone*, trans. by David Hawkes (Harmondsworth, England: Penguin Books, 1973), vol. 1, 31, 37–38. Cao Xueqin was the grandson of Cao Yin, a Chinese bond servant of the Manchus. He rose to a position of power as textile commissioner at Suzhou from 1690 to 1692 and then at Nanking, where his heirs continued in that position until 1728. He played host to the Kangxi emperor during the latter's southern tours and supplied him with confidential reports on conditions in the empire. The family suffered an abrupt decline after 1728 as a result of political reverses. Cao Xueqin died in 1763; *Hong-lou meng* appeared in a printed edition in 1792. An account of the family may be found in Jonathan D. Spence, *Ts'ao Yin and the K'ang-hsi Emperor, Bondservant and Master* (New Haven: Yale University Press, 1966).

54. Cao Xueqin, *The Story of the Stone*, vol. 1, 47.

55. Ibid., 51.

56. Ibid., 277.

57. Susan Naquin and Evelyn S. Rawski, *Chinese Society in the Eighteenth Century* (New Haven: Yale University Press, 1987), 34–35.

58. Cao Xueqin, *The Story of the Stone*, vol. 2, 473–474.

59. For example, see ibid., vol. 5, 76–78.

60. Laurence Sickman and Alexander Soper, *The Art and Architecture of China* (Baltimore: Penguin Books, 1956), 285. On Chinese gardens in general, see Maggie Keswick, *The Chinese Garden: History, Art & Architecture* (London: Academy Editions, 1978).

61. Cao Xueqin, *The Story of the Stone*, vol. 1, 346.

62. Huang, *1587—A Year of No Significance*, 117.

63. Reynaldo dos Santos, *L'Art Portugais: Architecture, Sculpture et Peinture* (Paris: Librairie Plon, 1953), 4, 16; Robert C. Smith, *The Art of Portugal, 1500–1800* (New York: Meredith Press, 1968), 50–51.

64. Marques, *A History of Portugal*, 202.

65. Smith, *The Art of Portugal*, 19.

66. See Charles Jencks, "The Meanings of the Chinese Garden," in Keswick, *The Chinese Garden*, 95–96.

67. Quoting *Yuan Ye,* by Ji Cheng, in William Willetts, *Chinese Art,* vol. 1 (New York: George Braziller, Inc., 1958), 686.

68. Helms, *Ulysses' Sail,* 20.

Chapter Two

1. Yin Guangren and Zhang Rulin, compilers, *Aomen jilue* (hereafter cited as AMJL) (Taipei: Ch'eng-Wen Publishing, reprint, 1968), 95.

2. Peng Qirui et al., *Xianggang yu Aomen* (Hong Kong: Shangwu yinshuguan, 1986), 245–246.

3. See Raquel Soeiro de Brito, "Achegas para a Geografia de Macau," in Adriano Moreira, ed., *Colóquios Sobre As Provincias do Oriente: Estudos de Ciencias Politicas e Sociais,* no. 81 (Lisbon: Junta de Investigações do Ultramar, Centro de Estudos Politicas e Sociais, 1968), 34–44.

4. On the typology of ships and boats on the South China coast, see Artur Leonel Barbosa Carmona, *Lorchas, Juncos e Outros Barcos Usados no Sul da China: A Pesca em Macau e Arredores,* 2d ed. (Macau: Imprensa Official de Macau, 1985).

5. See Jen Yu-wen, "The Southern Sung Stone-Engraving at North Fu-T'ang," *Journal of the Hong Kong Branch of the Royal Asiatic Society* 5 (1965), 65–68.

6. In the rammed earth walls constructed by the Portuguese for fortifications and buildings, in a construction method known as *taipa,* oyster shells were an important ingredient. Ground shells were used in plaster and mortar. See Chapter 3.

7. William C. Hunter, *The "Fan Kwae" at Canton Before Treaty Days, 1825–1844* (London: Kegan, Paul, Trench, 1882), 13–14. For a description of salt manufacturing processes, see Lin Su-yen, "Salt Manufacture in Hong Kong," *Journal of the Hong Branch of the Royal Asiatic Society* 7 (1967), 138–151.

8. Hunter, *The "Fan Kwae" at Canton,* 13–14.

9. "Xiangshan Ao," in *Qingqiao yeshi daguan* (Informal Overview of Qing History) (hereafter cited as QCYSDG) (Taibei: Zhonghua shuju, 1958), vol. 2, 123; Boxer, *Fidalgos,* 15–16.

10. The name of Xiangshan District is now Zhongshan, and the district capital has been called Shiqi since the revolution.

11. The birds included the *hwa-mei* (*Garrulux canorus*); white-eye (*Zosterops japonica*); great tit (*Parus major*); tree sparrow (*Passer montanus*); white wagtail (*Motacilla Alba*); blue rock thrush (*Monticola solitaria*); black kite (*Milvus migrans*); and black-headed gull (*Larus ridibundus*). See L. Barros, *Manual de Identificação das Aves de Macau* (Macau: Publicação da Direcção dos Serviços de Turismo de Macau, n.d.), and Clive Viney and Karen Phillips, *A Color Guide to Hong Kong Birds* (Hong Kong: Government Printer, 1979). These identifications are based on my personal observations.

12. AMJL, 72–73. At least fourteen places on the Guangdong coast, including Macau, are listed as having *Ao* in their names on maps of the mid-nineteenth century. Elijah Coleman Bridgman and S. Wells Williams, eds., *The Chinese Repository* (a periodical published by the American Board of Commissioners for Foreign Missions, 20 vols., 1832–1851) (hereafter cited as CR), vol. 12, no. 9 (September 1843), 477–485.

13. See "Xiangshan Ao" in QCYSDG, vol. 2, 122; AMJL, 69.

14. AMJL., 73–74.

15. On the origin of the Portuguese name for Macau, see, for instance, Nicola Trigault, *China in the Sixteenth Century: The Journals of Matthew Ricci, 1583–1610*, trans. Louis J. Gallagher (New York: Random House, 1953), 129; Boxer, *Fidalgos*, 3–4; and Manuel Teixeira, *The Story of Ma-Kok-Miu* (Macau: Information and Tourism Department, 1979), 7–8. Nothing has caused foreigners writing about Macau, down to the present, so much confusion as the origin and meaning of the name or names for the place. A recent example is the tortured attempt at explanation by Graciete Nogueira Batalha, "This Name of Macau . . . ," in *Review of Culture*, no. 1 (April–June 1987), 7–13. See also G (Luis G. Gomes), "Os Diversos Nomes de Macau," *Renascimento* 1, no. 1 (January 1943), 55–58. The confusion emanates from the fact that different people used different names at different times, that the same words are pronounced differently in different Chinese dialects (an entirely unnecessary semantic confusion), and that homophones in Chinese are often confused. For a Chinese treatment of this confusion, see Yuan Bangjian and Yuan Guixiu, *Aomen shilue*, 1–3.

16. Although both spellings, Macao and Macau, have been used historically by the Portuguese and other foreigners, I have chosen to use Macau, which is the current official spelling. See Chapter 6 for a further description and discussion of the Ama temple.

17. J. Dyer Ball, *Macao: The Holy City—the Gem of the Orient Earth* (Canton: China Baptist Publication Society, 1905), 28.

18. Hunter, *The "Fan Kwae" at Canton*, 82–85.

19. Zhang Renjun, *Guangdong yudi quantu* (Guangzhou: Shujingtang, 1897), map of Xiangshan District, 12a.

20. See William C. Hunter, *Bits of Old China* (Shanghai: Kelly and Walsh, 1911), 157–159, for a description of a pirate attack on a U.S. ship within sight of Macau in 1809.

21. Hunter, *The "Fan Kwae" at Canton*, 80–81.

22. CR, vol. 4, no. 4 (August 1835), 197. Severe damage by a typhoon that struck Macau on September 23, 1831, is described by Harriet Low. See "Harriet Low's Journal: 1829–1834," in Elma Loines, ed., *The China Trade Post-Bag of the Seth Low Family of Salem and New York, 1829–1873* (Manchester, Maine: Falmouth Publishing House, 1953), 143–144.

23. This account is based on eyewitness descriptions of the typhoon of 1874 found in Pedro Fragoso de Matos, *O Maior Tufão de Macau* (Lisbon: Anais do Clube Militar Naval, 1985), 8–15.

24. Ibid., 9–12, 22.

25. This description of Xiangshan (Zhongshan) District is based largely on personal observations made in 1988.

26. Huang Zuo and Shen Lianghan, comps., *Xiangshan xian zhi* (Gazetteer of Xiangshan District) (10 *juan*; 1750), 4:3b–8a.

27. Zhang Renjun, *Guangdong yudi quantu*, 12b.

28. AMJL, 165; Zhang Tingyu et al., eds., *Mingshi* (hereafter cited as MS) (Beijing: Zhonghua shuju, 1974), 8433.

29. Emma Helen Blair and James Alexander Robertson, eds., *The Philippine Islands, 1493–1898* (Cleveland: Arthur H. Clark, 1903–1909), vol. 19, 313. A vessel of 300 tons would pay about 3,000 to 4,000 taels.

30. Montalto, *Historic Macao,* 125.

31. AMJL, 165.

32. MS, 8433; Coates, *A Macao Narrative,* 30.

33. For several contemporary reports of alleged cannibalism by the Portuguese, see Jie Zi, ed., *Putaoya qinzhan Aomen shilue* (Historical Materials Relating to Portugal's Occupation of Macau) (hereafter cited as PTY) (Shanghai: Renmin chubanshe, 1961), 8–10, 19.

34. Montalto, *Historic Macao,* 3–10; José Maria Braga, *China Landfall 1513: Jorge Alvares' Voyage to China—A Compilation of Some Relevant Material* (Macau: Imprensa Nacional, 1955), 53–54.

35. MS, 8432–8433.

36. AMJL, 84–85; MS, 8433. AMJL mistakenly identifies the construction of Green Island as occurring in the Jiajing reign (1522–1566) rather than the Wanli reign (1573–1619).

37. PTY, 108. The six other villages were Longtian, Longhuan, Tashi, Zhenwang, Xinqiao, and Lidou.

38. See Kwan-wai So, *Japanese Piracy in Ming China During the 16th Century* (East Lansing: Michigan State University Press, 1975).

39. AMJL, 116–117.

40. Ibid., 122–123.

41. Ibid., 144.

42. MS, 8433.

43. Ibid., 8432.

44. Ibid., 8432. On Lin Fu, see DMB, vol. 1, 912–913.

45. PTY, 21. Zhang Xie (1574–1640) wrote *Dongxi yangkao,* a maritime geography of Southeast Asia, published in 1617. See DMB, vol. 1, 77–78.

46. William S. Atwell, "Notes on Silver, Foreign Trade, and the Late Ming Economy," *Ch'ing-shih wen-t'i* 3, 8 (December 1977), 1–8. For a discussion of the expansion of the trade in the early seventeenth century and its impact on the Ming, see Anthony Reid, "An 'Age of Commerce' in Southeast Asian History," in *Modern Asian Studies* 24, pt. 1 (February 1990), 1–30, especially 19–21.

47. Coates, *A Macao Narrative,* 33.

48. Atwell, "Notes," 15–22; William S. Atwell, "Some Observations on the 'Seventeenth-Century Crisis' in China and Japan," *Journal of Asian Studies* 45, no. 2 (February 1986), 229–233. For a good, brief discussion of the influence of the economic crisis on the late Ming, see Frederic Wakeman Jr., *The Great Enterprise: The Manchu Restoration of Imperial Order in Seventeenth-Century China* (Berkeley: University of California Press, 1985), vol. 1, 1–9.

49. PTY, 104–105.

50. CR, vol. 9, no. 8 (December 1840), 636.

51. Chun-hsi Wu, "Overseas Chinese," in Yuan-li Wu, ed., *China: A Handbook* (New York: Praeger Publishers, 1973), 415.

52. Ibid., 416–419.

53. "Chinese Abroad," in J. Dyer Ball, *Things Chinese, or, Notes Connected with China,* 5th ed., revised by E. Chalmers Werner (Shanghai: Kelly & Walsh, 1925), 127.

54. Yen Ching-Hwang, *Coolies and Mandarins: China's Protection of Overseas Chinese During the Late Ch'ing Period (1851–1911)* (Singapore: Singapore University Press, National University of Singapore, 1985), 256.

55. Wu, "Overseas Chinese," 427; also see 427–430.

56. Stephen Fitzgerald, *China and the Overseas Chinese: A Study of Peking's Changing Policy, 1949–1970* (Cambridge: Cambridge University Press, 1972), 50–51.

57. Chen Ta, *Emigrant Communities in South China: A Study of Overseas Migration & Its Influence on Standards of Living and Social Change*, edited by Bruno Lasker (New York: Institute of Pacific Relations, 1940), 100–113.

58. Wu, "Overseas Chinese," 414, 422–423.

59. Ibid., 423–426; Fitzgerald, *China and the Overseas Chinese*, app. D, 207–208.

60. The term *coolie* is popularly but mistakenly believed to derive from *ku-li* ("bitter labor") in Chinese. Actually, it is from the Tamil word meaning "hire, payment for occasional menial work." It probably came from an aboriginal tribe in Gujerat and was later carried to China by the Portuguese in the sixteenth century. See *Oxford English Dictionary* (1961), vol. 2, 960.

61. Yuan Bangjian and Yuan Guixiu, *Aomen shilue*, 145.

62. Yen, *Coolies and Mandarins*, 48, 54; Manuel Teixeira, *O Comércio de Escravos em Macau: The So Called Portuguese Slave Trade in Macao* (Macau: Imprensa Nacional, 1976), 78.

63. Yen, *Coolies and Mandarins*, 52–57.

64. Teixeira, *O Comércio de Escravos em Macau*, collects much information on the coolie trade. Yen Ching-Hwang cites figures of 15,000 to 20,000 coolies shipped annually from Macau between 1856 and 1864 and about 12,000 annually from 1868 to 1872. Yen, *Coolies and Mandarins*, 56–57. Teixeira gives lower figures, roughly 2,000 to 11,000 annually, for the early period; see *O Comércio de Escravos em Macau*, 79. Russell Herman Conwell, writing a few years before the traffic was suppressed in 1874, cited comparable numbers; see his *Why and How: Why the Chinese Emigrate, the Means They Adopt for the Purpose of Reaching America* (Boston: Lee & Shepard, 1871), 89.

65. Montalto, *Historic Macau*, 401–403.

66. Edward E. Fuller, manuscript journal, Macao, Sunday, December 2, 1866.

67. Yuan Bangjian and Yuan Guixiu, *Aomen shilue*, 146–147.

68. Persia Crawford Campbell, *Chinese Coolie Emigration to Countries Within the British Empire* (London: Frank Cass, 1971), 118; Yen, *Coolies and Mandarins*, 77; on brokers, see Yen, *Coolies and Mandarins*, 37–41.

69. Yen, *Coolies and Mandarins*, 62.

70. Campbell, *Chinese Coolie Emigration*, 156, n. 3.

71. Yen, *Coolies and Mandarins*, 117.

72. Yuan Bangjian and Yuan Guixiu, *Aomen shilue*, 148. A brief personal description of the coolie trade with Peru is found in Yung Wing, *My Life in China and America* (New York: Henry Holt, 1909), 191–196.

73. Yuan Bangjian and Yuan Guixiu, *Aomen shilue*, 147.

74. Montalto, *Historic Macao*, 410.

75. Coates, *A Macao Narrative*, 32.

76. See, for example, QCYSDG, vol. 2, 123–124. Chinese travelers to Macau tended to emphasize very much the same kinds of things that other Chinese travelers to Southeast Asia and India, including Chau Ju-kua (Zhao Rugua) in the twelfth and thirteenth centuries and Ma Huan in the fifteenth century, observed and recorded. If one compares these travel accounts, a fairly comprehensive list of common themes emerges, reflecting the dominant interests of the observers: appearance of foreigners

(dress, skin color, hairstyles); social customs (food, eating); moral customs (marriage, relation between sexes, religion); political and legal customs (laws, punishments); skills (prowess, unusual abilities); technology; trade and commerce (products, prices, practices); and flora and fauna. These categories, not surprisingly, embrace the more tangible features of foreign people and society, in particular the more obvious aspects of appearance, customs, behavior, material culture, and especially trade. See Friedrich Hirth and W. W. Rockhill, trans. and ed., *Chau Ju-Kua: His Work on the Chinese and Arab Trade in the Twelfth and Thirteenth Centuries, Entitled "Chu-fan-chi"* (Taipei: Ch'eng-Wen Publishing, reprint, 1967, originally published 1911), and Ma Huan, *Ying-Yai Sheng-Lan.*

77. Boxer, *Fidalgos*, 231; C. R. Boxer, *Portuguese Society in the Tropics: The Municipal Councils of Goa, Macao, Bahia, and Luanda, 1510–1800* (Madison and Milwaukee: University of Wisconsin Press, 1965), 65.

78. QCYSDG, vol. 2, 122.

79. CR, vol. 4, no. 9 (January 1836), 431.

80. CR, vol. 6, no. 6 (October 1837), 277–278.

81. AMJL, 142.

82. Helms, *Ulysses' Sail*, 28.

Chapter Three

1. Calvino, *Invisible Cities*, 30–31.

2. For a description of the Old Protestant Cemetery, see Manuel Teixeira, *The Protestant Cemeteries of Macau* (Macau: Direcção dos Serviços de Turismo de Macau, n.d.).

3. Montalto, *Historic Macao*, 2–3.

4. Braga, *China Landfall 1513*, 23–24, 30.

5. Ibid., 24, quoting Ruy de Buto Patalim.

6. AMJL, 87; Montalto, *Historic Macau*, 14–16; Boxer, *Fidalgos*, 2–3, 7–8.

7. AMJL, 112.

8. AMJL, 112; MS, 8433.

9. See Jorge Graça, *The Fortifications of Macau: Their Design and History*, 2d ed. (Macau: Direcção dos Serviços de Turismo de Macau, n.d.).

10. Boxer, *Fidalgos*, 231.

11. Ibid., 15–16; Blair and Robertson, eds., *The Philippine Islands*, vol. 19, 306–313.

12. C. R. Boxer, "Macao as a Religious and Commercial Entrepôt in the 16th and 17th Centuries," *Acta Asiatica*, no. 26 (1974), 70–71; William Lytle Schurz, *The Manila Galleon* (New York: E. P. Dutton, 1959), 132.

13. AMJL, 71–72.

14. Graça, *The Fortifications of Macau*, 29–30.

15. MS, 8433.

16. Boxer, *Portuguese Society in the Tropics*, 52. For Ricci's account, see Trigault, *China in the Sixteenth Century*, 482; for the Chinese account, see AMJL, 84–85.

17. Blair and Robertson, *The Philippine Islands*, vol. 20, 30.

18. Ball, *Macao: The Holy City*, 3–4.

19. Montalto, *Historic Macau*, 127–128, 148; CR, vol. 7, no. 11 (March 1839), 599, and vol. 8, no. 5 (September 1839), 268–269.

20. Ball, 6.

21. Graça, *The Fortifications of Macau*, 48–49.

22. Ball, *Macau: The Holy City*, 2–3. See Roderich Ptak, "The Demography of Old Macao, 1555–1640," *Ming Studies*, no. 15 (Fall 1982), 27–35, for a discussion of the early population of Macau. Montalto, *Historic Macau*, 41, 51–52.

23. Manuel Teixeira, *The Church of St. Paul in Macau* (Lisbon: Centro de Estudos Historicos Ultramarinos da Junta de Investigações Cientificas do Ultramar, 1979), 55.

24. Ibid., 57–58; Trigault, *China in the Sixteenth Century*, 134.

25. Boxer, "Macao as a Religious and Commercial Entrepôt," 67–69.

26. Teixeira, *Church of St. Paul*, 61; M. Hugo-Brunt, "An Architectural Survey of the Jesuit Seminary Church of St. Paul's, Macao," *Journal of Oriental Studies* 1, no. 1 (January 1954), 330.

27. Shann Davies, *Chronicles in Stone* (Macau: Department of Tourism, 1985), 81.

28. Teixeira, *Church of St. Paul*, 75; see also 69, 89.

29. Boxer, *The Great Ship from Amacon*, 39.

30. Teixeira, *Church of St. Paul*, 71; Hugo-Brunt, "An Architectural Survey," 332–333.

31. Peter Mundy, writing in 1637, in C. R. Boxer, *Seventeenth Century Macau in Contemporary Documents and Illustrations* (Hong Kong: Heinemann, 1984), 41–42.

32. QCYSDG, vol. 2, 122. Chinese were the principal workmen and craftsmen used in the construction of the church.

33. See C. Marreiros, "Traces of Chinese and Portuguese Architecture," in R. D. Cremer, ed., *Macau: City of Commerce and Culture* (Hong Kong: UEA Press, 1987), 99–100.

34. CR, vol. 3 (February 1835), 486.

35. For descriptions, see Teixeira, *Church of St. Paul*, 70–75; Davies, *Chronicles in Stone*, 129–132; and Hugo-Brunt, "An Architectural Survey."

36. Sanjay Subrahmanyam, *The Portuguese Empire in Asia: A Political and Economic History, 1500–1700* (London and New York: Longman, 1993), 225, 234; Coates, *A Macao Narrative*, 25; Diffie and Winius, *Foundations of the Portuguese Empire*, 391.

37. Boxer, *Portuguese Society in the Tropics*, 44–46.

38. Montalto, *Historic Macau*, 89–90.

39. Boxer, *Portuguese Society in the Tropics*, 54–56.

40. Boxer, *Fidalgos*, 217; Montalto, *Historic Macau*, 47.

41. Montalto, *Historic Macau*, 61–62.

42. Qu Dajun, *Guangdong xinyu* (hereafter cited as GDXY) (Macau: Wanyu shudian, reprint, n.d.; first published 1700), 24. See also "Xiangshan Ao," in QCYSDG, vol. 2, 122, and "Three Examples from Trading at Aomen," in QCYSDG, vol. 2, 123–124.

43. Schurz, *The Manila Galleon*, 134; Montalto, *Historic Macau*, 131.

44. João Marques Moreira, writing in 1644, in Boxer, *Seventeenth Century Macau*, 172.

45. Boxer, *Fidalgos*, 153–154.

46. Frederick Charles Danvers, *The Portuguese in India* (London: W. H. Allen, 1894), vol. 2, 292. The term *plague* is used loosely here. The precise nature of this

epidemic, which spread from north to south China during the Manchu conquest, is unknown, but it was one of the most lethal in Chinese history. See Mark Elvin, *The Pattern of the Chinese Past* (Stanford: Stanford University Press, 1973), 310–311.

47. Boxer, *Fidalgos*, 144.

48. Trigault, *China in the Sixteenth Century*, 129; Boxer, *Fidalgos*, 231; Montalto, *Historic Macau*, 61.

49. Boxer, *Fidalgos*, 144.

50. Boxer, *Portuguese Society in the Tropics*, 63.

51. AMJL, 75.

52. Subrahmanyam, *The Portuguese Empire in Asia*, 207–212.

53. For a definition of *casado*, see ibid., 72, 219–222.

54. Unlike many other Portuguese settlements in Asia, Macau resisted the authority of Goa, owing in part to the circumstances of its founding as a quasi-private entrepreneurial enterprise and the subsequent dominance of its *casado* population. See ibid., 207–211, 234.

55. Wong Shiu Kwan, *Macao Architecture: An Integrate of Chinese and Portuguese Influences* (Macau: Imprensa Nacional, 1970), 50–60.

56. Ball, *Macau: The Holy City*, 3.

57. Max Weber suggests a root definition of the city as a fusion of fortress and market but maintains that only in the Occidental city emerging in medieval times did the true urban community appear as a general phenomenon. Such a settlement is characterized by "1. a fortification; 2. a market; 3. a court of its own and at least partial autonomous law; 4. a related form of association; and 5. at least partial autonomy and autocephaly." Chinese cities did not meet these criteria for an autonomous urban community. The development of civic institutions was inhibited by the persistence of clan, tribal, and kinship associations, which tied residents to the rural communities from which they came, and by the absence of military autonomy, in the context of the state monopoly of military power. See Max Weber, *The City*, Don Martindale and Gertrud Neuwirth, trans. and ed. (Glencoe, Ill.: Free Press, 1958), 80 and 65–120. By the late eighteenth century, Macau would appear to have exhibited these characteristics.

58. Boxer, "Macau as an Entrepôt," 72–73.

59. Atwell, "Notes," 1–8; Coates, *A Macau Narrative*, 33; Wakeman, *The Great Enterprise*, vol. 1, 1–6. Wakeman suggests that as much as one-half of the precious metal mined in the United States may have reached China. Perhaps 60 percent of the total annual importation of silver came from Japan.

60. Atwell, "Notes," 13–22; Atwell, "Some Observations," 229–233.

61. Boxer, *Fidalgos*, 144.

62. Ball, *Macau: The Holy City*, 3.

63. AMJL, 73.

64. CR, vol. 7, no. 9 (January 1839), 503–504.

65. Ibid., vol. 11, no. 1 (January 1842), 59.

66. Ibid., vol. 9, no. 5 (September 1840), 328.

67. Ibid., vol. 12, no. 10 (October 1843), 555–556.

68. Ibid., vol. 15, no. 10 (October 1846), 526–527.

69. Ibid., vol. 18, no. 8 (August 1849), 448.

70. João Feliciano Marques Pereira, "Subsidios para o Estudo dos Dialectos Crioulos do Extremo Oriente," in J. F. Marques Pereira, ed., *Ta-Ssi-Yang-Kuo* (Lisbon: 1899–1900), vol. 1, 53–66; Graciete Nogueira Batalha, *Lingua de Macau* (Macau: Imprensa Nacional, 1974), 28; CR, vol. 4, no. 9 (January 1836), 431. The Chinese influence in the evolution of this pidgin dialect is most notable in its partial loss of the use of gender, number, and tense, also a characteristic of pidgin English. See Jorge Marais-Barbosa, "A Lingua Portuguesa de Macau," in Adriano Moreira, ed., *Colóquios Sobre As Provincias do Oriente* (Lisbon: Junta de Investigações do Ultramar, Centro de Estudos Politicas e Sociais, 1968), vol. 2, 147–157, and J.A.J., "The Macao Question," *The China Weekly Review*, November 24, 1928, 439.

71. Coates, *A Macau Narrative*, 33.

72. CR, vol. 3, no. 10 (February 1835), 485–486.

73. Ibid., vol. 4, no. 6 (October 1835), 292–293; vol. 9, no. 4 (August 1840), 237–239.

74. On the development of the opium trade, see Greenberg, *British Trade.*

75. Edward V. Gulik, *Peter Parker and the Opening of China* (Cambridge, Mass.: Harvard University Press, 1973), 26.

76. "Harriet Low's Journal: 1829–1834," in Loines, ed., *The China Trade Post-Bag,* 112, 122–123, 126, 140–141, 151.

77. Rodney Gilbert, "The Ancient Port of Macao," *The North-China Daily News,* December 8, 1923, 7.

78. Thomas R. Metcalf, *An Imperial Vision: Indian Architecture and Britain's Raj* (Berkeley: University of California Press, 1989), 176–177.

79. CR, vol. 10, no. 10 (October 1843), 555.

80. Edith Jorge De Martini, *The Wind Amongst the Ruins: A Childhood in Macau* (New York: Vantage Press, 1993), 54.

81. CR, vol. 4, no. 6 (October 1835), 293.

82. See Ball, *Macao: The Holy City,* 7.

83. CR, vol. 4, no. 6 (October 1835), 292–293; vol. 14, no. 1 (January 1845), 56; vol. 14, no. 2 (February 1845), 104; vol. 15, no. 6 (June 1846), 325.

84. Ibid., vol. 9, no. 1 (May 1840), 56.

85. A. Pinho, "Gambling in Macau," in Cremer, *Macau: City of Commerce,* 157; Fuller, manuscript journal. Fuller, explaining the origin of gambling, states that "some years ago a Portuguese procured a license from the municipal government to open a gambling house—provided that he would furnish an efficient police force for protection of the city and pay all expenses for maintenance of same."

86. See Harry A. Franck, *Roving Through Southern China* (New York and London: Century, 1925), 217.

87. For detailed descriptions of fan-tan in Macau, see Rodney Gilbert, "The Lotus Life of Macau," 408; Franck, *Roving Through Southern China,* 218; and Ian Fleming, *Thrilling Cities* (New York: New American Library, 1964), 28–29.

88. J.A.J., "The Macao Question," 438–439; J.A.J., "How Macao Lost Her Commercial Supremacy," *The China Weekly Review,* January 12, 1929, 287.

89. Hendrik De Leeuw, *Cities of Sin* (London: Noel Douglas, 1934), 146–147.

90. As late as 1988, there were reports of a North Korean spy nest appearing in the territory. See Nicholas D. Kristoff, "Macao Is Called North Korea Spy Site," *The*

New York Times, August 16, 1987, 10, and Simon Winchester, "Too Easy into Macao," *Manchester Guardian Weekly*, April 24, 1988, 22.

91. Portugal's refusal to sign the Bretton Woods Agreement in 1946 made Macau a center of a legal gold trade operated through a syndicate, which pays taxes to the government. John Clemens, compiler, *Discovering Macau: A Visitor's Guide* (Hong Kong: Macmillan, 1972), 56.

92. Pinho, "Gambling in Macau," 157, 162; Shann Davies, *An Illustrated Guide to Macau* (Hong Kong: The Guidebook Company, 1990), 25.

93. José Pereira Neto, "Comercio Externo," in Moreira, ed., *Coloquios Sobre As Provincias do Oriente*, vol. 1, 277–281; Macau Business Centre, *A Brief Guide to Macau Economy 1976* (Macau: Macau Business Centre, 1976), 21–22. In the decade from 1953 to 1963, the value of exports increased sixfold. Although imports also rose and subsequently exceeded exports in value, the two were approximately of equal value by 1976.

94. Macau Business Centre, *A Brief Guide*, 17.

95. Agencia-Geral do Ultramar, *Macau: Pequena Monografia* (Lisbon: Agencia-Geral do Ultramar, 1965), 16.

96. Wong, 31, *Macau Architecture*, 61.

Chapter Four

1. From "Macao," by Gerald Jollye, quoted in Manuel Teixeira, *Toponimia de Macau*, vol. 1, *Ruas com Nomes Genericos* (Macau: Imprensa Nacional, 1979), 338.

2. Manuel Teixeira, *Toponimia de Macau*, vol. 2, *Ruas com Nomes de Pessoas* (Macau: Imprensa Nacional, 1981), 318.

3. Ibid., vol. 2, 408.

4. Robin Hutcheon, *Chinnery: The Man and the Legend* (Hong Kong: South China Morning Post, 1981), 1–6.

5. Ibid., 4–16, 31–51, 53; Hunter, *Bits of Old China*, 271–272.

6. Hunter, *Bits of Old China*, 265–270.

7. Hutcheon, *Chinnery*, 63–67.

8. Hunter, *Bits of Old China*, 267, 269–270.

9. "Harriet Low's Journal: 1829–1834," in Loines, ed., *The China Trade Post-Bag*, 181.

10. Hutcheon, *Chinnery*, 67, 133–135.

11. Geoffrey Bonsall, "Introduction," in Hong Kong Museum of Art, *George Chinnery: His Pupils and Influence*, Exhibition Catalogue (Hong Kong: Hong Kong Urban Council, 1985), 6–9.

12. CR, vol. 4, no. 6 (October 1835), 293.

13. Hutcheon, *Chinnery*, 63–64.

14. Hunter, *Bits of Old China*, 73–75; CR, vol. 11, no. 1 (January 1842), 59. See Chapter 3 on Beale's death.

15. *Encyclopedia Britannica*, 11th ed., vol. 4, 101; Teixeira, *Toponimia de Macau*, vol. 2, 293–301.

16. Teixeira, *Toponimia de Macau*, vol. 2, 302–312.

17. Camoens, *The Lusiads*, 17–18; *Encyclopedia Britannica*, 11th ed., vol. 5, 117.

18. Montalto, *Historic Macao,* 36–37.

19. *Encyclopedia Britannica*, 11th ed., vol. 5, 116.

20. Kenneth Scott Latourette, *A History of Christian Missions in China* (Taipei: Ch'eng-wen Publishing, 1966), 91.

21. Ibid., 90.

22. Jonathan Spence, *The Memory Palace of Matteo Ricci* (New York: Viking Books, 1983), 192–193.

23. Trigault, *China in the Sixteenth Century,* 130.

24. Ibid., 117–118.

25. Ibid., 117.

26. Boxer, *Fidalgos,* 2–3; Trigault, *China in the Sixteenth Century*, 123–126.

27. Trigault, *China in the Sixteenth Century*, 131.

28. Rowbotham, *Missionary and Mandarin*, 48; *Encyclopedia Britannica*, 11th ed., vol. 28, 882–883.

29. Rowbotham, *Missionary and Mandarin*, 51; Pasquale M. d'Elia, *Galileo in China: Relations Through the Roman College Between Galileo and the Jesuit Scientist-Missionaries (1610–1640)*, trans. by Rufus Suter and Matthew Sciascia (Cambridge, Mass.: Harvard University Press, 1960), 4.

30. George H. Dunne, "Valignano, Alessandro," in DMB, 1334–1335; Joseph Franz Schutte, S.J., *Valignano's Mission Principles for Japan*, trans. by John J. Coyne (St. Louis: Institute of Jesuit Sources, 1980), vol. 1, pt. 1, 30, n. 106.

31. Diffie and Winius, *Foundations of the Portuguese Empire*, 198–201.

32. Trigault, *China in the Sixteenth Century*, 130–131.

33. Dunne, "Valignano, Alessandro," 1334–1335; George H. Dunne, *Generation of Giants: The Story of the Jesuits in China in the Last Decades of the Ming Dynasty* (Notre Dame, Ind.: University of Notre Dame Press, 1962), 19. The two attitudes toward conversion are concisely and cogently described by John W. Witek, S.J., "Understanding the Chinese: A Comparison of Matteo Ricci and the French Jesuit Mathematicians Sent by Louis XIV," in Charles E. Ronan and Bonnie B. C. Oh, eds., *East Meets West: The Jesuits in China, 1582–1773* (Chicago: Loyola University Press, 1988), 63–64. See also Joseph Sebes, S.J., "The Precursors of Ricci," in Ronan and Oh, eds., *East Meets West*, 32. Xavier believed the Chinese exhibited a *proclivity* for receiving the gospel, but it is a long way from this expectation to the policy of accommodation constructed by Valignano. Even if Xavier may have begun to see the need for some kind of cultural accommodation, there is no evidence he originated the new policy of evangelization, as Oh maintains in her introduction: "The Jesuit method of propagating Christianity through cultural accommodation was the brain child of Francis Xavier . . . , and was applied to China by Alessandro Valignano," Ronan and Oh, eds., *East Meets West,* XVII. There are other misleading aspects of Oh's introduction, including the change from a Buddhist to a Confucian approach by Matteo Ricci (see p. xx).

34. Spence, *Memory Palace*, 41–43. See also Jonathan Spence, "Matteo Ricci and the Ascent to Peking," in Ronan and Oh, eds., *East Meets West*, 5–8. In a similar series of changes in attitude, both Valignano and Ricci became successively disillusioned with India and Japan as prospective missionary fields.

35. George H. Dunne. "Ruggieri, Michele," in DMB, 1148–1149; Trigault, *China in the Sixteenth Century*, 134.

36. Dunne, *Generation of Giants*, 19.

37. Trigault, *China in the Sixteenth Century*, 134.

38. Sebes, "The Precursors of Ricci," 34; Witek, "Understanding the Chinese," 66.

39. Trigault, *China in the Sixteenth Century*, 135–137.

40. Ricci's "indigenization" approach was analyzed by Sebes, "The Precursors of Ricci," 42–53.

41. Witek, "Understanding the Chinese," 71.

42. Boxer, *The Great Ship from Amacon*, 39.

43. Spence, *Memory Palace*, 191.

44. Trigault, *China in the Sixteenth Century*, 295.

45. Ibid., 442.

46. Ibid., 478–480.

47. d'Elia, *Galileo in China*, 25. Trigault arrived in Macau in 1610 but did not reach Peking until 1611, after Ricci died. He left Macau for Europe in 1613, arriving in 1614. In translating Ricci's journal from Italian to Latin, Trigault made stylistic changes, deletions, and additions. See D. E. Mungello, *Curious Land: Jesuit Accommodation and the Origins of Sinology* (Honolulu: University of Hawaii Press, 1985), 46–49, for a discussion of Trigault's work on Ricci's journal. Although Mungello minimizes the differences between the versions, Jonathan Spence maintains that the Trigault version "is not a reliable reflection of Ricci's own views"; see Spence, *Memory Palace*, 271, n. 4.

48. B. H. Willeke, "Schall von Bell, Johann Adam," in DMB, 1153; Rachel Attwater, *Adam Schall: A Jesuit at the Court of China, 1592–1666*, adapted from the French of Joseph Duhr, S.J. (London: Geoffrey Chapman, 1963), 22–23.

49. Attwater, *Adam Schall*, 29.

50. Ibid., 37.

51. Ibid., 38–39; Boxer, *Fidalgos*, 84.

52. Attwater, *Adam Schall*, 43–44.

53. Jonathan Porter, "Bureaucracy and Science in Early Modern China: The Imperial Astronomical Bureau in the Ch'ing Period," *Journal of Oriental Studies* 18, nos. 1 and 2 (1980), 69–71.

54. Attwater, *Adam Schall*, 54.

55. Ibid., 55–56. Very early on, Ruggieri and Ricci had come to appreciate the value of gifts of European curiosities, books, clocks, and scientific instruments as a way of ingratiating themselves with the Chinese. See Spence, *Memory Palace*, 179–181.

56. Jacques Gernet, *China and the Christian Impact*, trans. by Janet Lloyd (Cambridge: Cambridge University Press, 1985), 19.

57. See Sebes, "The Precursors of Ricci," 44–45: "By presenting Christianity as morally persuasive as Confucianism, if not more so, he confucianized Christianity or christianized Confucianism."

58. Gernet, *China and the Christian Impact*, 47–57.

59. Dunne, *Generation of Giants*, 325, 347; Attwater, *Adam Schall*, 117, 120.

60. Attwater, *Adam Schall*, 118–119; Rowbotham, *Missionary and Mandarin*, 231–232.

61. For a detailed description of the crisis of 1662–1668, see John E. Wills Jr., *Embassies and Illusions: Dutch and Portuguese Envoys to K'ang-hsi, 1666–1687* (Cambridge, Mass.: Harvard University Press, 1984), 83–101.

62. Willeke, "Schall von Bell," 1155; Montalto, *Historic Macao*, 116–117.

63. See Porter, "Bureaucracy and Science"; John D. Young, "An Early Confucian Attack on Christianity: Yang Kuang-hsien and His *Pu-te-i*," *Journal of the Chinese University of Hong Kong* 3, no. 1 (1975), 159–186.

64. On the debate over the issue of rites in the accommodation policy, see Sebes, "The Precursors of Ricci," 47–51.

65. Dunne, *Generation of Giants*, 163, 300; Attwater, *Adam Schall*, 159–160.

66. Gernet, *China and the Christian Impact*, 23, 57–59.

67. Gernet succinctly summarizes the situation: "Just as some missionaries thought that the Chinese men of letters possessed a suitable disposition to receive their faith, there were some men of letters who judged that, once rid of their false notions, such as the belief in a creator God, the missionaries might have made quite good Confucians"; see Gernet, *China and the Christian Impact,* 39–40.

68. Trigault, *China in the Sixteenth Century*, 134–135.

69. Ibid., 298–299.

70. Fang Chao-ying, "Wu Li," in Arthur W. Hummel, ed., *Eminent Chinese of the Ch'ing Period (1644–1912)* (Taipei: Literature House, reprint, 1964), 875–876.

71. Ibid., 876.

72. Dunne, *Generation of Giants*, 149.

73. C. R. Boxer, "The Rise and Fall of Nicholas Iquan," *T'ien-hsia Monthly* 11 (1941), 411.

74. Earl Swisher, "Cheng Chih-lung," in Arthur W. Hummel, ed., *Eminent Chinese,* 110.

75. Boxer, "Iquan," 410–411.

76. Swisher, "Cheng Chih-lung," 110; Boxer, "Iquan," 412–413.

77. Boxer, "Iquan," 426–430; Swisher, "Cheng Chih-lung," 110.

78. Boxer, "Iquan," 438.

79. CR, vol. 3, no. 4 (August 1834), 180–181.

80. Ibid., vol. 1, no. 8 (December 1832), 319.

81. Ibid., vol. 11, no. 1 (January 1842), 48.

82. Ibid., vol. 5, no. 8 (December 1836), 373–374.

83. Yung Wing, *My Life in China,* 1–2; CR, vol. 6, no. 5 (September 1837), 231–232.

84. CR, vol. 7, no. 6 (October 1838), 306–307.

85. Yung Wing, *My Life in China,* 3–4.

86. Ibid., 8–11.

87. CR, vol. 7, no. 10 (August 1839), 530–531; vol. 10, no. 1 (January 1841), 53.

88. Ibid., vol. 10, no. 10 (October 1841), 565, 576–577.

89. Yung Wing, *My Life in China,* 13; CR, vol. 10, no. 1 (January 1841), 53.

90. CR, vol. 15, no. 12 (December 1844), 622–623; Yung Wing, *My Life in China,* 16.

91. Yung Wing, *My Life in China,* 23.

92. Ibid., 48.

93. Ibid., chaps. 7–12.

94. On Zeng Guofan's organization, see Jonathan Porter, *Tseng Kuo-fan's Private Bureaucracy* (Berkeley: University of California, Center for Chinese Studies, 1972). For Rong Hong's involvement with Zeng, see pp. 126–131.

95. Yung Wing, *My Life in China,* chaps. 13–16.

96. Ibid., chap. 19.

97. Ibid., 241–242.

Chapter Five

1. Samuel Taylor Coleridge, "Kubla Khan," in John Hayward, ed., *The Penguin Book of English Verse* (Harmondsworth, England: Penguin Books, 1956), 256.

2. Sadly, in 1995, the entire bay embraced by the Praia Grande was being filled in by a reclamation project on which luxury high-rise apartments and business and cultural centers will be built. Thus, the Praia Grande, probably Macau's most characteristic feature, will disappear forever.

3. Marco d'Avalo, writing in 1638, in Boxer, *Seventeenth Century Macau*, 80.

4. AMJL, 210.

5. Coates, *A Macao Narrative*, 100–101; Ball, *Macao: The Holy City*, 8.

6. Both Chinese and Western visitors left records of their observations of Macau and its people. It should be noted here that the Chinese records are far less abundant, and the two sides do not present evenly balanced accounts. What may have been noticed by one more often than not went unnoticed by the other. But the Chinese observations, though few, are frequently more precise and interesting because of the subjects they choose to describe.

7. "Quangdong Foreigners," in QCYSDG, vol. 2, 122; see also AMJL, 75; "Xiangshan Ao," in QCYSDG, vol. 2, 123.

8. Cf. AMJL, 201.

9. "Xiangshan Ao," in QCYSDG, vol. 2, 123; MS, 8434; GDXY, 24; AMJL, 183, 203.

10. AMJL, 205–207; "Xiangshan Ao," in QCYSDG, vol. 2, 123.

11. AMJL, 207, "Xiangshan Ao," in QCYSDG, vol. 2, 123; GDXY, 24.

12. Mundy, writing in 1637, in Boxer, *Seventeenth Century Macau*, 55.

13. AMJL. 203; GDXY, 24.

14. AMJL, 203; "Xiangshan Ao," in QCYSDG, vol. 2, 122.

15. Peter Mundy mentioned that there was only one Portuguese woman in Macau in 1637. See Mundy, writing in 1637, in Boxer, *Seventeenth Century Macau*, 55.

16. Boxer, *Portuguese Society in the Tropics*, 65–66; Trigault, *China in the Sixteenth Century*, 129; De Martini, *The Wind Amongst the Ruins*, 13–14.

17. "Guangdong Foreigners," in QCYSDG, vol. 2, 122; Mundy, writing in 1637, in Boxer, *Seventeenth Century Macau*, 57.

18. See CR, vol. 4, no. 6 (October 1835), 292–293; vol. 9, no. 4 (August 1840), 237–238.

19. Boxer, *Portuguese Society in the Tropics*, 63.

20. "Three Examples from Trading at Aomen," in QCYSDG, vol. 2, 124. See also GDXY, 24.

21. Samuel Shaw, *The Journals of Major Samuel Shaw, the First American Consul at Canton* (Boston: William Crosby & H. P. Nichols, 1847; reprint, Taipei: Ch'eng-Wen Publishing, 1968), 243, writing in 1787.

22. Yung Wing, *My Life in China*, 1–2, 7–8; CR, vol. 3, no. 4 (August 1834), 180–181, vol. 4, no. 5 (September 1839), 231–232, and vol. 11, no. 1 (January 1842), 48.

23. "Harriet Low's Journal: 1829–1834," in Loines, ed., *The China Trade Post-Bag*, 117.

24. Mundy, writing in 1637, in Boxer, *Seventeenth Century Macau*, 55, 58–59.

25. "Three Examples from Trading at Aomen," in QCYSDG, vol. 2, 124.

26. AMJL, 206–207; "Xiangshan Ao," in QCYSDG, vol. 2, 123; "Three Examples from Trading at Aomen," in QCYSDG, vol. 2, 124; GDXY, 24; Mundy, writing in 1637, in Boxer, *Seventeenth Century Macau*, 58–59. Some of those impressions, for instance, that women wore shawls and went barefoot—are confirmed by George Chinnery's sketches.

27. John Stuart Thomson, *The Chinese* (Indianapolis: Bobbs-Merrill, 1909), 82. See the drawing in AMJL, 27.

28. Thomson, *The Chinese*, 81. Harriet Low was most attentive to dress and fashion—with little else to do, it was one of the principal occupations of women in Macau: "The American ladies are said to be the best dressed of the place, because we are always neat; the clothes of many of the ladies, the gentlemen say, look as if they were thrown on with a pitchfork"; see "Harriet Low's Journal: 1829–1834," in Loines, ed., *The China Trade Post-Bag*, 184.

29. De Martini, *The Wind Amongst the Ruins*, 14–15.

30. "Guangdong Foreigners," in QCYSDG, vol. 2, 122; "Xiangshan Ao," in QCYSDG, vol. 2, 123.

31. "Xiangshan Ao," in QCYSDG, vol. 2, 123; "Three Examples from Trading at Aomen," in QCYSDG, vol. 2, 123–124; GDXY, 24.

32. "Three Examples from Trading at Aomen," in QCYSDG, vol. 2, 125.

33. Ibid.

34. C. R. Boxer, "The Cult of Mary and the Practice of Misogyny," in Boxer, *Mary and Misogyny: Women in Iberian Expansion Overseas, 1415–1815: Some Facts, Fancies and Personalities* (London: Gerald Duckworth, 1975), 97–112.

35. De Martini, *The Wind Amongst the Ruins*, 14.

36. GDXY, 24; AMJL, 204: "When seated, they all place their right hands below the cushion and do not use it [for eating]. They say this is because this hand is only for using in the privy and the left hand must be used for handling food." This report may be either an anomaly or a confusion perpetuated by an observer.

37. AMJL, 204.

38. GDXY, 24.

39. For a description of the similar English practice at Madras, see Percival Spear, *The Nabobs: A Study of the Social Life of the English in Eighteenth Century India* (London: Oxford University Press, 1963), 53–55.

40. Thomson, *The Chinese*, 80.

41. Mundy, writing in 1637, in Boxer, *Seventeenth Century Macau*, 50; see Jeri Bernadette Williams, "Namban Byobu of the Momoyama Period," *Journal of Asian Culture* 8 (1984), 33–60.

42. Antonio Bocarro, writing in 1635, in Boxer, *Seventeenth Century Macau*, 15; Mundy, writing in 1637, in Boxer, *Seventeenth Century Macau*, 50.

43. AMJL, 209–210.

44. Ibid., 205.

45. Ibid., 229. A similar variety of sedans existed in other parts of the Portuguese empire, particularly Brazil. See Russell-Wood, *A World on the Move*, 51–52.

46. CR, vol. 2, no. 5 (September 1853), 233–234, and vol. 5, no. 9 (January 1837), 403; "Harriet Low's Journal: 1829–1834," in Loines, ed., *The China Trade Post-Bag*, 111, 191–192. Harriet Low mentions what seems to have been a momentary enforce-

ment of the prohibition of Chinese sedan bearers in Macau by Chinese officials in August 1833; the women were thereby forced to walk (!) to a performance of an opera, which proved to be no great inconvenience; see "Harriet Low's Journal: 1829–1834," in Loines, ed., *The China Trade Post-Bag*, 193.

47. David Strand, *Rickshaw Beijing: City People and Politics in the 1920s* (Berkeley: University of California Press, 1989), 23–26. Strand notes that by the mid–1920s, there were approximately sixty thousand ricksha men in Beijing.

48. See ibid., 27–28.

49. In 1990, Macau had 32,992 registered motor vehicles, sharing 96 kilometers of roads. Of this total, 27,448 were private cars; see *South China Morning Post,* February 13, 1991, 3. The magnitude of the problem may be appreciated if one estimates that each vehicle is an average of 5 meters in length. Parked end to end, the vehicles would extend for 165 kilometers, 69 kilometers farther than the total length of the roads.

50. "Three Examples from Trading at Aomen," in QCYSDG, vol. 2, 124.

51. Mundy, writing in 1637, in Boxer, *Seventeenth Century Macau*, 50–51.

52. De Martini, *The Wind Amongst the Ruins*, 14–15.

53. Shaw, *The Journals of Major Samuel Shaw*, 242.

54. AMJL, 204–205.

55. Mundy, writing in 1637, in Boxer, *Seventeenth Century Macau*, 41, 47.

56. Ibid., 47.

57. Blair and Robertson, eds., *The Philippine Islands,* 312–313.

58. Maria Margarida Gomes, *A Cozinha Macaense* (Macau: Imprensa Nacional de Macau, 1984); Antonio Vicente Lopes, *Receitas da Cozinha Macaense* (Macau: Tipografia da Missão, 1977), 129–130; De Martini, *The Wind Amongst the Ruins*, 14.

59. Thomson, *The Chinese*, 77; De Martini, *The Wind Amongst the Ruins*, 14–15.

60. AMJL, 205.

61. "Xiangshan Ao," in QCYSDG, vol. 2, 122. Cf. AMJL, 249, for a similar description of this clock, which was installed on São Paulo Church.

62. GDXY, 24, 236; AMJL, 189, 250; "Xiangshan Ao," in QCYSDG, vol., 123.

63. David S. Landes, *Revolution in Time: Clocks and the Making of the Modern World* (Cambridge, Mass.: Harvard University Press, 1983), 37–42. See also Needham, *Science and Civilization in China*, vol. 4, pt. 2, 436–440.

64. GDXY, 24.

65. AMJL, 253–254.

66. GDXY, 236. Small arms are also described in AMJL, 250–251.

67. Landes, *Revolution in Time,* 44–48. Even in the case of artillery, which the Chinese had a more demonstrable need for in external and internal defense, the record of adaptation is uneven. See Carlo M. Cipolla, *Guns, Sails and Empires: Technological Innovation and the Early Phases of European Expansion, 1400–1700* (New York: Minerva Press, 1965), 116–122. Cipolla observes that "the Imperial Court never developed that kind of enthusiasm for cannon that inspired the more technically-minded and more warlike monarchs of the West. Fearing internal bandits no less than foreign enemies and internal uprisings no less than foreign invasion, the Imperial Court did its best to limit both the spread of the knowledge of gunnery and the proliferation of artisans versed in the art" (p. 117).

68. AMJL, 255–256.

69. Manuel Teixeira, *The Japanese in Macau* (Macau: Instituto Cultural de Macau, 1990), 15–16, 29, 30. The work of these Western-trained Japanese Christian artists is sometimes referred to as the "School of Macau." See Guillen-Nuñez, *Macau,* plates following pp. 6 and 22. Some of these paintings are now preserved in the Seminario de São José, Macau.

70. Teixeira, *The Japanese in Macau*, 19–23.

71. Ibid., 13; Hugo-Brunt, "An Architectural Survey," 335.

72. See Hugo-Brunt, "An Architectural Survey," 333.

73. AMJL, 266–267.

74. Hong Kong Museum of Art, *George Chinnery: His Pupils and Influence*, exhibition catalogue (Hong Kong: Urban Council, 1985); see also Leal Senado de Macau and Museu Luis de Camões, *George Chinnery: Macau*, exhibition catalogue (Macau: Museu Luis de Camões, 1985); Hutcheon, *Chinnery*.

75. Thomson, *The Chinese*, 81–82. See also "Harriet Low's Journal: 1829–1834," in Loines, ed., *The China Trade Post-Bag*, 112, 122–123, 126, for Harriet Low's descriptions of Catholic religious processions.

76. De Martini, *The Wind Amongst the Ruins*, 44–51.

77. Mundy, writing in 1637, in Boxer, *Seventeenth Century Macau*, 57, 61.

78. "Xiangshan Ao," in QCYSDG, vol. 2, 122; Mundy, writing in 1637, in Boxer, *Seventeenth Century Macau*, 51; Moreira, writing in 1644, in Boxer, *Seventeenth Century Macau*, 161, 165, 169,

79. GDXY, 24; "Xiangshan Ao," in QCYSDG, vol. 2, 122; Thomson, *The Chinese*, 80.

80. Shaw, *The Journals of Major Samuel Shaw*, 242; Thomson, *The Chinese*, 80; Ball, *Macao*, 8.

81. Mundy, writing in 1637, in Boxer, *Seventeenth Century Macau*, 61.

82. Ibid., 61.

83. Ibid., 56–57; Moreira, writing in 1644, in Boxer, *Seventeenth Century Macau*, 158.

84. "Harriet Low's Journal: 1829–1834," in Loines, ed., *The China Trade Post-Bag*, 112.

85. Pinho, "Gambling in Macau," 155–156; De Martini, *The Wind Amongst the Ruins*, 14, 49.

86. Franck, *Roving Through Southern China*, 217–218.

87. Gilbert, "The Lotus Life of Macao," 408. J.A.J., "The Macao Question," 438–439. Cf. Michael Weber, "Land of Saints and Sinners," *Geo*, September 1984, 82–93; Pinho, "Gambling in Macau."

88. See Thomson, *The Chinese*, 82–83.

89. See Rowe, *Hankow*, 201–206.

90. De Martini, *The Wind Amongst the Ruins*, 44–51.

91. For an extended description of these festivities, see Moreira, writing in 1644, in Boxer, *Seventeenth Century Macau*, 147–174.

92. Ibid., 161.

93. Ibid., 162–165.

94. Ibid., 172.

95. Sandra Lauderdale Graham, *House and Street: The Domestic World of Servants and Masters in Nineteenth Century Rio de Janeiro* (Cambridge: Cambridge University Press, 1988), 66–71.

96. Harriet Low observed one Chinese procession honoring the dedication of a temple and was rather mystified by the event. But so was she also by Catholic processions she witnessed. See "Harriet Low's Journal: 1829–1834," in Loines, ed., *The China Trade Post-Bag*, 128–129.

97. On temple fairs in China, see C. K. Yang, *Religion in Chinese Society* (Berkeley: University of California Press, 1967), 82–86.

98. Cf. Graham, *House and Street*, 68–69; Rowe, *Hankow*, 201–206.

99. Mundy, writing in 1637, in Boxer, *Seventeenth Century Macau*, 57.

100. GDXY, 273–274.

101. Ibid., 24; "Xiangshan Ao," in QCYSDG, vol. 2, 123.

102. GDXY, 286.

103. GDXY, 286.

104. Bocarro, writing in 1635, in Boxer, *Seventeenth Century Macau*, 15; Mundy, writing in 1637, in Boxer, *Seventeenth Century Macau*, 58, and 48–49. See note 6 on *manchuas*.

105. De Martini, *The Wind Amongst the Ruins*, 52.

106. "Harriet Low's Journal: 1829–1834," in Loines, ed., *The China Trade Post-Bag*, 153, and see also 116, 136, 161.

107. AMJL, 209; Mundy, writing in 1637, in Boxer, *Seventeenth Century Macau*, 42.

108. Mundy, writing in 1637, in Boxer, *Seventeenth Century Macau*, 57–58.

109. "Three Examples from Trading at Aomen," in QCYSDG, vol. 2, 124–125. The play referred to is based on the novel *Xi yu ji* ("Journey to the West").

110. Hunter, *Bits of Old China*, 73; "Three Examples from Trading at Aomen," QCYSDG, vol. 2, 124.

111. CR, vol. 11, no. 1 (January 1842), 59–60. See also Harriet Low's description of Beale's garden in "Harriet Low's Journal: 1829–1834," in Loines, ed., *The China Trade Post-Bag*, 114. That was one of the first visits she made after her arrival in Macau in 1829.

112. CR, vol. 6, no. 2 (June 1837), 66, and vol. 8, no. 11 (March 1839), 555–556.

113. "Harriet Low's Journal: 1829–1834," in Loines, ed., *The China Trade Post-Bag*, 113.

114. Shaw, *The Journals of Major Samuel Shaw*, 247; Manuel Teixeira, *A Gruta de Camões em Macau* (Macau: Imprensa Nacional, 1977), 33–41.

115. See Keswick, *The Chinese Garden*, 9–15; also Rhoads Murphey, "City and Countryside as Ideological Issues: India and China," *Comparative Studies in Society and History* 14, no. 3 (June 1972), 253–254.

116. Trigault, *China in the Sixteenth Century*, 19, 21–22, 61–65.

117. Ibid., chap. 9.

118. Arthur H. Smith, *Chinese Characteristics*, 3d ed., rev. (New York: Fleming H. Revell, 1894); J. MacGowan, *Sidelights on Chinese Life* (Philadelphia: J. B. Lippincott, 1908), 2–20, 112–125.

Chapter Six

1. From W. H. Auden, "Macao," in *The Collected Poetry of W. H. Auden* (New York: Random House, 1945), 18–19. The juxtaposition of religious zeal or devotion and personal greed—the one seen in the prevalence of religious activity in Macau

throughout its history, the other in the pursuit of wealth through trade and later gambling—has always been one of Macau's remarkable and peculiar characteristics.

2. See AMJL, 73–74. This was not the first time Mazu saved mariners in such a fashion. See Duyvendak, *China's Discovery of Africa,* 29. Tian Hou (the Queen of Heaven) is variously known as Mazu (Mother Ancestor), Ama (the prefix "A" is honorific), Tian Fei (Heavenly Maiden), and Niangma (Queen Mother or, merely, Mother).

3. AMJL, 72–73; Trigault, *China in the Sixteenth Century,* 129. Cf. Braga, *China Landfall,* 47.

4. E.T.C. Werner, *A Dictionary of Chinese Mythology* (New York: Julian Press, 1961), 503; Clarence Burton Day, *Chinese Peasant Cults,* 2d ed. (Taipei: Ch'eng-wen Publishing, 1969), 83–84. James L. Watson accepted the standard account of the tenth-century Fujian origin of the cult; see his "Standardizing the Gods: The Promotion of T'ien Hou ('Empress of Heaven') Along the South China Coast, 960–1960," in David Johnson et al., eds., *Popular Culture in Late Imperial China* (Berkeley: University of California Press, 1985), 295–296.

5. Watson, "Standardizing the Gods," passim. The cult is very popular and active today in Taiwan. See P. Steven Sangren, "History and Rhetoric of Legitimacy: The Ma Tsu Cult of Taiwan," *Comparative Studies in Society and History* 30, no. 4 (October 1988), 674–697.

6. Duyvendak, *China's Discovery of Africa,* 28–30.

7. See Watson, "Standardizing the Gods," 299–310. It is worth noting that the title Tian Hou is associated with the state-sponsored cult; among those who were less influenced by the process of state patronage, as in Taiwan where the cult is extremely popular, the more personal and unofficial name for the deity, Mazu, is preferred.

8. See, for example, CR, vol. 1, no. 2 (June 1832), 58.

9. Jonathan Chamberlain, *Chinese Gods* (Hong Kong: Long Island Publishers, 1983), 104–107.

10. Manuel Teixeira, *O Culto de Maria em Macau: Macau e a Sua Diocese,* vol. 9 (Macau: Tipografia da Missão do Padroado, 1969), 7–63; see also Boxer, *Mary and Misogyny.*

11. Teixeira, *O Culto de Maria em Macau,* 168–169, 191–198.

12. Braga, *China Landfall,* 47; J. M. Braga, "Picturesque Macao," in *Renascimento: Revista Mensal* 1, no. 2 (February 1943), 221.

13. See Manuel Teixeira, *Pagodes de Macau* (Macau: Direcção dos Serviços de Educação e Cultura, 1982), 75–100.

14. Teixeira, *O Culto de Maria em Macau.*

15. Ibid., 191–212.

16. AMJL, 122–123. The assistant magistrate was under the command of the assistant prefect for coast defense with military and civil authority (often called the *junminfu*) stationed just beyond the barrier at Qianshan military post (Casa Branca). The latter position was created in 1730. J. M. Braga, who apparently confused the assistant magistrate with the assistant prefect, gave 1739 as the date when an official was first stationed at Wangxia; see his "Picturesque Macao," 222–223. See also CR, vol. 9, no. 4 (August 1840), 237–238.

17. These are Dou-mu fu-ren or Dou-mu niang-niang, the Goddess of Smallpox, and Jin-hu fu-ren (literally, "Ennobled Lady"), the Protectress of Women.

18. CR, vol. 8, no. 5 (September 1839), 268.

19. CR, vol. 7, no. 11 (March 1839), 599, and vol. 8, no. 5 (September 1839), 268–269.

20. Ibid., vol. 9, no. 4 (August 1840), 238.

21. The multiple functionality of Chinese temples and cults is well documented by C. K. Yang, *Religion in Chinese Society* (Berkeley: University of California Press, 1967), 7–16.

22. Although it is not always reliable, Jonathan Chamberlain's work, *Chinese Gods* (Hong Kong: Long Island Publishers, 1983), offers stories and characteristics of the various gods of the Chinese pantheon.

23. See Werner, *Dictionary of Chinese Mythology*, 462.

24. See Teixeira, *Pagodes de Macau*, 155.

25. Herbert A. Giles, *A Chinese Biographical Dictionary* (Taipei: Literature House, 1962), vol. 2, 618.

26. See Day, *Chinese Peasant Cults*, 77.

27. Zhang Daoling is also known as Zhang Ling. For further details, see Holmes Welch, *Taoism: The Parting of the Way* (Boston: Beacon Press, 1957), 115.

28. Day, *Chinese Peasant Cults*, 49–52; Giles, *A Chinese Biographical Dictionary*, vol. 1, 43.

29. Day, *Chinese Peasant Cults*, 111.

30. R. de Rohan Barondes, *China: Lore, Legend and Lyrics* (New York: Philosophical Library, 1960), 17–21; Day, *Chinese Peasant Cults*, 139.

31. Teixeira, *Pagodes de Macau*, 142–146.

32. This temple is colloquially known as Hong Kong Miu, but the name has nothing to do with the port of Hong Kong and actually represents different characters in Chinese.

33. Edwin D. Harvey, *The Mind of China* (New Haven: Yale University Press, 1933), 263–265.

34. See Prasenjit Duara, *Culture, Power, and the State: Rural North China, 1900–1942* (Stanford: Stanford University Press, 1988), 141–143.

35. Day, *Chinese Peasant Cults*, 52–54. Many authors erroneously identify Guan Di's companions as his colleagues of the Three Kingdoms era, Zhang Fei and Liu Bei; see Chamberlain, *Chinese Gods*, 62.

36. On the general significance of Tu Di in Chinese society, see Yang, *Religion in Chinese Society*, 96–98.

37. On the origin and development of the Earth God cult, see Day, *Chinese Peasant Cults*, 59–67.

38. On the uses and significance of the cult of the City God, see Stephen Feuchtwang, "School-Temple and City God," in G. William Skinner, ed., *The City in Late Imperial China* (Stanford: Stanford University Press, 1977), 581–608.

39. Day, *Chinese Peasant Cults*, 67–68.

40. Cf. Arthur P. Wolf, "Gods, Ghosts, and Ancestors," in Arthur P. Wolf, ed., *Religion and Ritual in Chinese Society* (Stanford: Stanford University Press, 1974), 140–141. On generalized deities as distinct from deified personalities, see also Yang, *Religion in Chinese Society*, 11–13.

41. See Duara, *Culture, Power, and the State*, 146: "Cults like those of Guandi were responsible for integrating the village with the larger society not only symbolically but organizationally."

42. Sangren, "History and Rhetoric of Legitimacy," 687.

43. Wolf, "Ghosts, Gods, and Ancestors," 134–137; Yang, *Religion in Chinese Society*, 96–99.

44. See Wolf, "Ghosts, Gods, and Ancestors," 133–145; Lloyd E. Eastman, *Family, Field, and Ancestors: Constancy and Change in China's Social and Economic History, 1550–1949* (New York: Oxford University Press, 1988), 43–44; Welch, *Taoism*, 137–139; Feuchtwang, "School-Temple and City God," 583–592; and David K. Jordan, *Gods, Ghosts, and Ancestors: The Folk Religion of a Taiwanese Village* (Berkeley: University of California Press, 1972), 40–41.

45. Day, *Chinese Peasant Cults*, 61–70; Yang, *Religion in Chinese Society*, 145–150.

46. Harvey, *The Mind of China*, 19–22.

47. Robert P. Weller, *Unities and Diversities in Chinese Religion* (Seattle: University of Washington Press, 1987), 50–51.

48. The locations of shrines on the map on p. 182 are based on extensive, direct personal observations during more than ten visits to Macau from 1967 to the present. Even so, this survey is by no means exhaustive, since new construction is constantly changing the cultural topography of the city, and I may have overlooked many shrines. Every visit yields new discoveries. At best, the map depicts a minimum.

49. See Duara, *Culture, Power, and the State*, 146, and Watson, "Standardizing the Gods," 301–303, 322–324.

50. For the conception of a spiritual map of a place defined by a cult, I am indebted to the intriguing and provocative discussion by Brigitte Berthier on "The Usage of the Myth of Lin Shui Furen," delivered at the annual meeting of the Association for Asian Studies, Washington, D.C., March 17, 1989.

51. The impression of two faces of Macau, divided by the line of churches, is noted in travelers' descriptions. See, for instances, Gilbert, "The Lotus Life of Macao," 408–409; Michael Weber, "Land of Saints and Sinners," *Geo* 6 (September 1984), 90–92.

Chapter Seven

1. Rudyard Kipling, "Cities and Thrones and Powers," in John Hayward, ed., *The Penguin Book of English Verse* (Harmondsworth, England: Penguin Books, 1956), 402.

2. Rodney Gilbert, "The Ancient Port of Macao," *North-China Daily News*, December 8, 1923, 7.

3. J.A.J., "The Macao Question," 438.

4. "Money," *South China Morning Post*, August 5, 1990, 7.

5. Luis Vasconcelos, assistant secretary for public works and transportation, quoted (p. 36) in "Aeroporto já Descolou," *Macau,* no. 19 (January 1990), 33–35.

6. "Macau Tipped to Become Economic Force," *South China Morning Post*, January 16, 1991; see also "Monitor" (p. 10) in the same issue.

7. "Macao to Revert to China in 1999," *New York Times*, March 24, 1987.

8. See Ball, *Macao: The Holy City*, 6–7.

9. This transformation, though long delayed, was anticipated as early as the 1920s: "When this [adequate connection with the interior] is a *fait accompli* much that is picturesque and attractive, in Macao, chiefly because of its native wickedness, will

disappear; but the recompense will be a rich new field for commercial endeavor which will very quickly find ways of compensating the sentimentalist"; see Gilbert, "The Ancient Port of Macao," 7. See also Gilbert, "The Lotus Life of Macao," 408–409.

10. Hunter, *Bits of Old China*, 272.

11. Murphey, *Shanghai: Key to Modern China*, 9.

12. Edward Seidensticker, *Low City, High City: Tokyo from Edo to the Earthquake* (New York: Alfred A. Knopf, 1983), 62–67.

13. Ibid., 14–16.

14. Hunter, *Bits of Old China*, 149. See also Gilbert, "The Lotus Life of Macao," 407.

Bibliography

Abu-Lughod, Janet L. *Before European Hegemony: The World System* A.D. *1250–1350*. New York: Oxford University Press, 1989.

Agencia-Geral do Ultramar. *Macau: Pequena Monografia*. Lisbon: Agencia-Geral do Ultramar, 1965.

Attwater, Rachel. *Adam Schall: A Jesuit at the Court of China, 1592–1666*. Adapted from the French of Joseph Duhr. S. J. London: Geoffrey Chapman, 1963.

Atwell, William S. "Notes on Silver, Foreign Trade, and the Late Ming Economy," *Ch'ing-shih wen-t'i* 3, no. 8 (1977), 1–33.

Atwell, William S. "Some Observations on the 'Seventeenth-Century Crisis' in China and Japan." *Journal of Asian Studies* 5, no. 2 (1986), 223–244.

Ball, J. Dyer. *Macao: The Holy City—the Gem of the Orient Earth*. Canton: China Baptist Publication Society, 1905.

Ball, J. Dyer. *Things Chinese, or, Notes Connected with China*. 5th ed., rev. by E. Chalmers Werner. Shanghai: Kelly & Walsh, 1925.

Barondes, R. de Rohan. *China: Lore, Legend and Lyrics*. New York: Philosophical Library, 1960.

Barros, L. *Manual de Identificação das Aves de Macau*. Macau: Publicação da Direcção dos Serviços de Tourismo de Macau, n.d.

Basu, Dilip K., ed. *The Rise and Growth of the Colonial Port Cities in Asia*. Berkeley: University of California, Center for South and Southeast Asian Studies, 1985.

Batalha, Graciete Nogueira. *Lingua de Macau*. Macau: Imprensa Nacional, 1974.

Batalha, Graciete Nogueira. "This Name of Macau . . ." *Review of Culture*, no. 1 (April–June 1987), 7–13.

Bentley, Jerry H. *Old World Encounters: Cross-Cultural Contacts and Exchanges in Pre-Modern Times*. New York: Oxford University Press, 1993.

Blair, Emma Helen, and James Alexander Robertson, eds. *The Philippine Islands, 1493–1898*. 55 vols. Cleveland: Arthur H. Clark, 1903–1909.

Boorman, Howard L., ed. *Biographical Dictionary of Republican China*. 5 vols. New York: Columbia University Press, 1967.

Boorstin, Daniel J. *The Discoverers*. New York: Vintage Books, 1985.

Boxer, C. R. *Fidalgos in the Far East, 1550–1770*. Hong Kong: Oxford University Press, 1968.

Boxer, C. R. *The Great Ship from Amacon: Annals of Macao and the Old Japan Trade, 1555–1640*. Lisbon: Centro de Estudos Historicos Ultramarinos, 1959.

Boxer, C. R. "Macao as a Religious and Commercial Entrepôt in the 16th and 17th Centuries," *Acta Asiatica*, no. 26 (1974), 64–90.

Boxer, C. R. *Mary and Misogyny: Women in Iberian Expansion Overseas, 1415–1815: Some Facts, Fancies and Personalities*. London: Gerald Duckworth, 1975.

Boxer, C. R. *The Portuguese Seaborne Empire, 1415–1825*. New York: Alfred A. Knopf, 1969.

Boxer, C. R. *Portuguese Society in the Tropics: The Municipal Councils of Goa, Macao, Bahia, and Luanda, 1510–1800*. Madison and Milwaukee: University of Wisconsin Press, 1965.

Boxer, C. R. "The Rise and Fall of Nicholas Iquan," *T'ien-hsia Monthly* 11 (1941), 401–439.

Boxer, C. R. *Seventeenth Century Macau in Contemporary Documents and Illustrations*. Hong Kong: Heinemann, 1984.

Braga, J. M. "The Panegyric of Alexander Valignano, S.J. (Reproduced from an Old Portuguese Codex) With an Introduction and Notes," *Monumenta Nipponica* 5 (1942), 523–535.

Braga, J. M. "Picturesque Macao," *Renascimento: Revista Mensal* 1, no. 2 (February 1943), 220–226.

Braga, José Maria. *China Landfall 1513: Jorge Alvares' Voyage to China, a Compilation of Some Relevant Material*. Macau: Imprensa Nacional, 1955.

Braga, José Maria. "Notes on the Lingua Franca of the East," *Renascimento: Revista Mensal* 1, no. 4 (April 1943), 404–412.

Bridgman, Elijah Coleman, and S. Wells Williams, eds. *The Chinese Repository* (a periodical published by the American Board of Commissioners for Foreign Missions). 20 vols. 1832–1851.

Brito, Raquel Soeiro de. "Achegas para a Geografia de Macau," in Adriano Moreira, ed., *Colóquios Sobre As Provincias do Oriente*. Lisbon: Junta de Investigações do Ultramar, Centro de Estudos Politicas e Sociais, 1968, vol. 2, 25–48.

Calvino, Italo. *Invisible Cities*. Translated by William Weaver. San Diego: Harcourt Brace Jovanovich, 1972.

Camoens, Luis Vaz de. *The Lusiads*. Translated by William C. Atkinson. Harmondsworth, England: Penguin Books, 1952.

Camões, Luis de. *Os Lusiadas*. Edited by Reis Brazil. Lisbon: Editorial Minerva, 1964.

Campbell, Persia Crawford. *Chinese Coolie Emigration to Countries Within the British Empire*. London: Frank Cass, 1971.

Cao Xueqin. *The Story of the Stone*. Translated by David Hawkes. 5 vols. Harmondsworth, England: Penguin Books, 1973.

Carmona, Artur Leonel Barbosa. *Lorchas, Juncos e Outros Barcos Usados no Sul da China: A Pesca em Macau e Arredores*. 2d ed. Macau: Imprensa Official de Macau, 1985.

Chamberlain, Jonathan. *Chinese Gods*. Hong Kong: Long Island Publishers, 1983.

Chang, T'ien-tse. *Sino-Portuguese Trade from 1514 to 1644: A Synthesis of Portuguese and Chinese Sources*. Leyden, The Netherlands: E. J. Brill, 1934.

Chaudhuri, K. N. *Trade and Civilization in the Indian Ocean: An Economic History from the Rise of Islam to 1750*. Cambridge: Cambridge University Press, 1985.

Chen Ta. *Emigrant Communities in South China: A Study of Overseas Migration & Its Influence on Standards of Living and Social Change*. Edited by Bruno Lasker. New York: Institute of Pacific Relations, 1940.

Cipolla, Carlo M. *Guns, Sails and Empires: Technological Innovation and the Early Phases of European Expansion, 1400–1700*. New York: Minerva Press, 1965.

Clemens, John, comp. *Discovering Macau: A Visitor's Guide*. Hong Kong: Macmillan, 1972.

Coates, Austin. *City of Broken Promises*. Hong Kong: Heinemann, 1977.

Coates, Austin. *A Macao Narrative*. Hong Kong: Heinemann, 1978.

Coelho, R. Beltrão. *Album: Macau, 1844–1974*. 2d ed. Macau: Fundação Oriente, 1990.

Collis, Maurice. *Foreign Mud: The Opium Imbroglio at Canton in the 1830s & the Anglo-Chinese War*. New York: W. W. Norton, 1968.

Conwell, Russell Herman. *Why and How: Why the Chinese Emigrate, the Means They Adopt for the Purpose of Reaching America*. Boston: Lee & Shepard, 1871.

Cremer, R. D., ed. *Macau: City of Commerce and Culture*. Hong Kong: UEA Press, 1987.

Crosby, Alfred W. *Ecological Imperialism: The Biological Expansion of Europe, 900–1900*. Cambridge: Cambridge University Press, 1986.

Curtin, Phillip D. *Cross-Cultural Trade in World History*. Cambridge: Cambridge University Press, 1984.

Danvers, Charles Frederick. *The Portuguese in India: Being a History of the Rise and Decline of Their Eastern Empire*. 2 vols. London: W. H. Allen, 1894.

Davies, Shann. *Chronicles in Stone*. Macau: Department of Tourism, 1985.

Davies, Shann. *An Illustrated Guide to Macau*. Hong Kong: Guidebook Company, 1990.

Day, Clarence Burton. *Chinese Peasant Cults: Being a Study of Chinese Paper Gods*. 2d ed. Taipei: Ch'eng Wen Publishing, 1969.

De Leeuw, Hendrik. *Cities of Sin*. London: Noel Douglas, 1934.

De Martini, Edith Jorge. *The Wind Amongst the Ruins: A Childhood in Macao*. New York: Vantage Press, 1993.

Diffie, Bailey. *Prelude to Empire: Portugal Overseas Before Henry the Navigator*. Lincoln: University of Nebraska Press, 1960.

Diffie, Bailey W., and George D. Winius. *Foundations of the Portuguese Empire, 1415–1580*. Minneapolis: University of Minnesota Press, 1977.

Dodge, Earnest S. *Islands and Empires: Western Impact on the Pacific and East Asia*. Minneapolis: University of Minnesota Press, 1976.

Duara, Prasenjit. *Culture, Power, and the State: Rural North China, 1900–1942*. Stanford: Stanford University Press, 1988.

Dunne, George H. *Generation of Giants: The Story of the Jesuits in China in the Last Decades of the Ming Dynasty*. Notre Dame, Ind.: University of Notre Dame Press, 1962.

Duyvendak, J.J.L. *China's Discovery of Africa*. London: Arthur Probsthain, 1949.

Duyvendak, J.J.L. "The True Dates of the Chinese Maritime Expeditions in the Early Fifteenth Century," *T'oung Pao* 34 (1939), 341–412.

Eastman, Lloyd E. *Family, Fields, and Ancestors: Constancy and Change in China's Social and Economic History, 1550–1949*. New York: Oxford University Press, 1988.

Edmonds, Richard Louis. "Land Use in Macau: Changes Between 1972 and 1983," *Land Use Policy*, January 1986, 47–63.

Elia, Pasquale d'. *Galileo in China: Relations Through the Roman College Between Galileo and the Jesuit Scientist-Missionaries (1610–1640)*. Translated by Rufus Suter and Matthew Sciascia. Cambridge, Mass.: Harvard University Press, 1960.

Elvin, Mark. *The Pattern of the Chinese Past*. Stanford: Stanford University Press, 1973.

Fairbank, John King. *Trade and Diplomacy on the China Coast: The Opening of the Treaty Ports, 1842–1854*. Cambridge, Mass.: Harvard University Press, 1953.

Fernandez-Armesto, Felipe. *Before Columbus: Exploration and Colonization from the Mediterranean to the Atlantic 1229–1492*. London: Macmillan Education, 1987.

Feuchtwang, Stephen. "School-Temple and City God." In G. William Skinner, ed., *The City in Late Imperial China*. Stanford: Stanford University Press, 1977, 581–608.

Finlay, Robert. "Portuguese and Chinese Maritime Imperialism: Camões's *Lusiads* and Luo Maodong's *Voyage of the San Bao Eunuch*," *Comparative Studies in Society and History* 34, no. 2 (April 1992), 225–241.

Fitzgerald, Stephen. *China and the Overseas Chinese: A Study of Peking's Changing Policy 1949–1970*. Cambridge: Cambridge University Press, 1972.

Fleming, Ian. *Thrilling Cities*. New York: New American Library, 1964.

Franck, Harry A. *Roving Through Southern China*. New York and London: Century, 1925.

Freitas, William. *Camoens and His Epic: A Historic, Geographic and Cultural Survey*. Stanford: Institute of Hispanic American and Luso-Brazilian Studies, Stanford University, 1963.

Fuller, Edward E. Manuscript journal, 1866–1867.

Gernet, Jacques. *China and the Christian Impact: A Conflict of Cultures*. Translated by Janet Lloyd. Cambridge: Cambridge University Press, 1985.

Gilbert, Rodney. "The Ancient Port of Macao," *The North-China Daily News*, December 8, 1923, 7.

Gilbert, Rodney. "The Lotus Life of Macao," *The North-China Herald*, May 6, 1922, 407–409.

Giles, Herbert A. *A Chinese Biographical Dictionary*. 2 vols. Taipei: Literature House, 1962.

Gomes, Luis G. *Bibliographia Macaense*. Macau: Imprensa Nacional, 1973.

Gomes, Luis G. "Os Diversos Nomes de Macau," *Renascimento* 1, no. 1 (January 1943), 55–58.

Gomes, Maria Magarida. *A Cozinha Macaense*. Macau: Imprensa Nacional de Macau, 1984.

Goodrich, L. Carrington, and Chaoying Fang, eds. *Dictionary of Ming Biography, 1368–1644*. 2 vols. New York: Columbia University Press, 1976.

Graça, Jorge. *The Fortifications of Macau: Their Design and History*. 2d ed. Macau: Direcção dos Serviços de Tourismo de Macau, n.d.

Greenberg, Michael. *British Trade and the Opening of China, 1800–1842*. Cambridge: Cambridge University Press, 1951.

Groot, J.J.M. de. *The Religious System of China*. 6 vols. Taipei: Literature House, 1964.

Guillen-Nuñez, Cesar. *Macau*. Hong Kong: Oxford University Press, 1984.

Gulik, Edward V. *Peter Parker and the Opening of China*. Cambridge, Mass.: Harvard University Press, 1973.

Harvey, Edwin D. *The Mind of China*. New Haven: Yale University Press, 1933.

Helms, Mary W. *Ulysses' Sail: An Ethnographic Odyssey of Power, Knowledge, and Geographical Distance*. Princeton: Princeton University Press, 1988.

Hong Kong Museum of Art. *George Chinnery: His Pupils and Influence*. Exhibition catalogue. Hong Kong: Urban Council, 1985.

Huang, Ray. *1587: A Year of No Significance—The Ming Dynasty in Decline*. New Haven: Yale University Press, 1981.

Huang Zuo and Shen Lianghan, comps. *Xiangshan xian zhi* (Gazetteer of Xiangshan District). 10 *juan*. 1750.

Hugo-Brunt, M. "An Architectural Survey of the Jesuit Seminary Church of St. Paul's, Macao," *Journal of Oriental Studies* 1, no. 1 (January 1954), 327–344.

Hummel, Arthur W., ed. *Eminent Chinese of the Ch'ing Period (1644–1912)*. Taipei: Literature House, 1964.

Hummel, Arthur W. "The Journal of Harriet Low," *Quarterly Journal of Current Acquisitions* 2, nos. 3 and 4 (January–June 1945), 45–60. Reprinted in Ping-kuen Yu, comp. *Chinese Collections in the Library of Congress*. Vol. 3. Washington, D.C.: Center for Chinese Research Materials, 974–989.

Hunter, William C. *Bits of Old China*. Shanghai: Kelly and Walsh, 1911.

Hunter, William C. *The "Fan Kwae" at Canton Before Treaty Days, 1825–1844*. London: Kegan, Paul, Trench, 1882.

Hunter, William Wilson. *A History of British India*. 2 vols. London: Longmans, Green, 1899.

Hutcheon, Robin. *Chinnery, the Man and the Legend*. Hong Kong: South China Morning Post, 1981.

Instrução para o Bispo de Pequim, e Outros Documentos para a Historia de Macau. Preface by Manuel Múrias. Lisbon: Agencia Geral das Colonias, 1943.

J.A.J. "How Macao Lost Her Commercial Supremacy," *China Weekly Review*, January 12, 1929, 280–281, 287.

J.A.J. "The Macao Question," *China Weekly Review*, November 24, 1928, 437–439.

Jen Yu-wen. "The Southern Sung Stone-Engraving at North Fu-T'ang," *Journal of the Hong Kong Branch of the Royal Asiatic Society* 5 (1965), 65–68.

Jie Zi, ed. *Putaoya qinzhan Aomen shilue* (Historical Materials Relating to Portugal's Occupation of Macau). Shanghai: Renmin chuban she, 1961.

Jordan, David K. *Gods, Ghosts, and Ancestors: The Folk Religion of a Taiwanese Village*. Berkeley: University of California Press, 1972.

Keswick, Maggie. *The Chinese Garden: History, Art & Architecture*. London: Academy Editions, 1978.

Knoerle, Jeanne. *The Dream of the Red Chamber: A Critical Study*. Bloomington: Indiana University Press, 1972.

Kostof, Spiro. *The City Shaped: Urban Patterns and Meanings Through History*. Boston: Little, Brown, 1991.

Landes, David S. *Revolution in Time: Clocks and the Making of the Modern World*. Cambridge, Mass.: Harvard University Press, 1983.

Latourette, Kenneth Scott. *A History of Christian Missions in China*. Taipei: Ch'eng-wen Publishing, 1966.

Li Shijin, ed. *Xiangshan xian zhi xubian* (Gazetteer of Xiangshan District, Supplementary Edition). 16 *juan*. 1920.

Lin Su-yen. "Salt Manufacture in Hong Kong," *Journal of the Hong Kong Branch of the Royal Asiatic Society* 7 (1967), 138–151.

Livermore, H. V. *Portugal, A Short History*. Edinburgh: Edinburgh University Press, 1973.

Lopes, Antonio Vicente. *Receitas da Cozinha Macaense*. Macau: Tipografia da Missão, 1977.

Low, Harriet. "Harriet Low's Journal: 1829–1834." In Elma Loines, ed., *The China Trade Post-Bag of the Seth Low Family of Salem and New York, 1829–1873*. Manchester, Maine: Falmouth Publishing, 1953, 100–234.

Ljungstedt, Anders. *An Historical Sketch of the Portuguese Settlements in China; and the Roman Catholic Church and Missions in China*. Hong Kong: Viking Hong Kong Publications, 1992 (reprint of 1836 edition).

Ma Huan. *Ying-yai Sheng-lan: "The Overall Survey of the Ocean's Shores."* Translated and edited by J.V.G. Mills. Cambridge: Cambridge University Press, 1970.

Macau Business Centre. *A Brief Guide to Macau Economy 1976*. Macau: Macau Business Centre, 1976.

Macau. Gabinete de Commincação Social do Governo de Macau, no. 1 (May 1987), no. 42 (December 1991/January 1992).

Macau, Leal Senado de, and Museu Luis de Camões. *George Chinnery: Macau*. Exhibition catalogue. Macau: Museu Luis de Camões, 1985.

Macau, Leal Senado de, and Museu Luis de Camões. *Macau: Anos 40: George Vitalievich Smirnoff*. Macau: Museu Luis de Camões, 1985.

MacGowan, J. *Sidelights on Chinese Life*. Philadelphia: J. B. Lippincott, 1908.

Marais-Barbosa, Jorge. "A Lingua Portuguesa de Macau." In Adriano Moreira, ed., *Colóquios Sobre As Provincias do Oriente*. Lisbon: Junta de Investigações do Ultramar, Centro de Estudos Politicas e Sociais, 1968, vol. 2, 147–157.

Marques, A. H. de Oliveira. *A History of Portugal*. 2d ed. 2 vols. New York: Columbia University Press, 1976.

Matos, Pedro Fragoso de. *O Maior Tufão de Macau*. Lisbon: Anais do Clube Militar Naval, 1985.

Metcalf, Thomas R. *An Imperial Vision: Indian Architecture and Britain's Raj*. Berkeley: University of California Press, 1989.

Montalto de Jesus, C. A. *Historic Macao*. Hong Kong: Oxford University Press, 1984.

Mote, Frederick W., and Denis Twitchett, eds. *The Cambridge History of China*. Vol. 7, *The Ming Dynasty, 1368–1644, Part I*. Cambridge: Cambridge University Press, 1988.

Mungello, D. E. *Curious Land: Jesuit Accommodation and the Origins of Sinology*. Honolulu: University of Hawaii Press, 1985.

Murphey, Rhoads. "City and Countryside as Ideological Issues: India and China," *Comparative Studies in Society and History* 14, no. 3 (June 1972), 250–267.

Murphey, Rhoads. *Shanghai: Key to Modern China*. Cambridge, Mass.: Harvard University Press, 1953.

Murphey, Rhoads. "Traditionalism and Colonialism: Changing Urban Roles in Asia," *Journal of Asian Studies* 29, no. 1 (November 1969), 67–84.

Murray, Dian H. *Pirates of the South China Coast, 1790–1810*. Stanford: Stanford University Press, 1987.

Naquin, Susan, and Evelyn Rawski. *Chinese Society in the Eighteenth Century*. New Haven: Yale University Press, 1987.

Needham, Joseph. *Science and Civilization in China*. 7 volumes projected. Cambridge: Cambridge University Press, 1961– .

Neto, José Pereira. "Comercio Externo." In Adriano Moreira, ed., *Colóquios Sobre As Provincias do Oriente*. Lisbon: Junta de Investigações do Ultramar, Centro de Estudos Politicas e Sociais, 1968, vol. 1, 267–343.

Parry, J. M. *Europe and a Wider World, 1415–1715*. London: Hutchinson's University Library, 1949.

Peng Qiri et al. *Xianggang yu Aomen* (Hong Kong and Macau). Hong Kong: Shangwu yinshuguan, 1986.

Pereira, João Feliciano Marques. "Susidios para o Estudo dos Dialectos Crioulos do Extremo Oriente." In J. F. Marques Pereira, ed., *Ta-Ssi-Yang-Kuo*. Lisbon: 1899–1900, vol. 1, 53–66.

Phillips, J.R.S. *The Medieval Expansion of Europe*. Oxford: Oxford University Press, 1988.

Plaks, Andrew H. *Archetype and Allegory in the Dream of the Red Chamber*. Princeton: Princeton University Press, 1976.

Porter, Jonathan. "Bureaucracy and Science in Early Modern China: The Imperial Astronomical Bureau in the Ch'ing Period," *Journal of Oriental Studies* 18, nos. 1 and 2 (1980), 61–76.

Porter, Jonathan. "The Transformation of Macau," *Pacific Affairs* 66, no. 1 (Spring 1993), 7–20.

Porter, Jonathan. *Tseng Kuo-fan's Private Bureaucracy*. Berkeley: University of California, Center for Chinese Studies, 1972.

Prestage, Edgar. *The Portuguese Pioneers*. London: A. & C. Black, 1933.

Ptak, Roderick. "The Demography of Old Macao, 1555–1640," *Ming Studies*, no. 15 (Fall 1982), 27–35.

Qingchao yeshi daguan (Informal Overview of Qing History). 6 vols. Taibei: Zhonghua shuju, 1958 (reprint of original undated edition).

Qu Dajun. *Guangdong xinyu* (The Latest Word on Guangdong). Macau: Wanyu shudian, reprint, n.d.; first published in 1700.

Reid, Anthony. "An 'Age of Commerce' in Southeast Asian History," *Modern Asian Studies* 24, pt. 1 (February 1990), 1–30.

Ride, Lindsay. "The Old Protestant Cemetery in Macao," *Journal of the Hong Kong Branch of the Royal Asiatic Society* 3 (1963), 9–35.

Ronan, Charles E., and Bonnie B. C. Oh, eds. *East Meets West: The Jesuits in China, 1582–1773*. Chicago: Loyola University Press, 1988.

Rowbotham, Arnold H. *Missionary and Mandarin: The Jesuits at the Court of China*. Berkeley: University of California Press, 1942.

Rowe, William T. *Hankow: Conflict and Community in a Chinese City, 1796–1895*. Stanford: Stanford University Press, 1989.

Russell-Wood, A.J.R. *A World on the Move: The Portuguese in Africa, Asia, and America*. New York: St. Martin's Press, 1992.

Sá Nogueira, A. C. de. *Catalogo Descritivo de 380 Especies Botanicas da Colonia de Macau*. 2d ed. Macau: Serviços Florestias e Agricolas de Macau, 1984.

Sangren, P. Steven. "History and Rhetoric of Legitimacy: The Ma Tsu Cult of Taiwan," *Comparative Studies in Society and History* 30, no. 4 (October 1988), 674–697.

Santos, Reynaldo dos. *L'Art Portugais: Architecture, Sculpture et Peinture*. Paris: Librairie Plon, 1953.

Schurz, William Lytle. *The Manila Galleon*. New York: E. P. Dutton, 1959.

Schutte, Franz Joseph. *Valignano's Mission Principles for Japan*. 2 vols. Translated by John J. Coyne. St. Louis: Institute of Jesuit Sources, 1980.

Seidensticker, Edward. *Low City, High City: Tokyo from Edo to the Earthquake*. New York: Alfred A. Knopf, 1983.

Sennett, Richard, ed. *Classic Essays in the Culture of Cities*. New York: Appleton-Century Crofts, 1969.

Shaw, Samuel. *The Journals of Samuel Shaw, the First American Consul at Canton*. Boston: William Crosby & H. P. Nichols, 1847 (reprint, Taipei: Ch'eng-Wen Publishing, 1968).

Sickman, Laurence, and Alexander Soper. *The Art and Architecture of China*. Baltimore: Penguin Books, 1956.

Smith, Arthur H. *Chinese Characteristics*. 3d ed., rev. New York: Fleming H. Revell, 1894.

Smith, Robert C. *The Art of Portugal, 1500–1800*. New York: Meredith Press, 1968.

So, Kwan-wai. *Japanese Piracy in Ming China During the Sixteenth Century*. East Lansing: Michigan State University Press, 1975.

South China Morning Post. Hong Kong, 1980–1991.

Souza, George Bryan. *The Survival of Empire: Portuguese Trade and Society in China and the South China Sea, 1630–1754*. Cambridge: Cambridge University Press, 1986.

Spear, Percival. *The Nabobs: A Study of the Social Life of the English in Eighteenth Century India*. London: Oxford University Press, 1963.

Spence, Jonathan D. *The Memory Palace of Matteo Ricci*. New York: Viking Books, 1981.

Spence, Jonathan D. *Ts'ao Yin and the K'ang-hsi Emperor, Bondservant and Master*. New Haven: Yale University Press, 1966.

Strand, David. *Rickshaw Beijing: City People and Politics in the 1920s*. Berkeley: University of California Press, 1989.

Struve, Lynn. *The Southern Ming, 1644–1662*. New Haven: Yale University Press, 1984.

Subrahmanyam, Sanjay. *The Portuguese Empire in Asia, 1500–1700: A Political and Economic History*. London: Longman, 1993.

Tcheong-Ü-Lâm [Zhang Rulin] and Ian-Kuong-Iâm [Yin Guangren], comps. Translated by Luis G. Gomes. *Ou-Mun Kei-Leok [Aomen jilue]: Monografia de Macau*. Lisbon: Edição da Quinzena de Macau, 1979.

Teixeira, Manuel. *The Church of St. Paul in Macau*. Lisbon: Centro de Estudos Historicos Ultramarinos de Junta de Investigações Cientificas do Ultramar, 1979.

Teixeira, Manuel. *O Comércio de Escravos em Macau: The So Called Slave Trade in Macao*. Macau: Imprensa Nacional, 1976.

Teixeira, Manuel. *O Culto de Maria em Macau: Macau e a sua Diocese*. Vol. 9. Macau: Tipografia da Missão do Padroada, 1969.

Teixeira, Manuel. *George Chinnery, no Bicentenario do seu Nascimento, 1774–1974.* Macau: Imprensa Nacional, 1974.

Teixeira, Manuel. *A Gruta de Camões em Macau.* Macau: Imprensa Nacional, 1977.

Teixeira, Manuel. *The Japanese in Macau.* Macau: Instituto Cultural de Macau, 1990.

Teixeira, Manuel. *Pagodes de Macau.* Macau: Direcção dos Serviços de Educação e Cultura, 1982.

Teixeira, Manuel. *The Protestant Cemeteries of Macau.* Macau: Direcção dos Serviços de Tourismo de Macau, n.d.

Teixeira, Manuel. *The Story of Ma-Kok-Miu.* Macau: Information and Tourism Department, 1979.

Teixeira, Manuel. *Toponimia de Macau.* Vol. 1, *Ruas com Nomes Genericos.* Macau: Imprensa Nacional, 1979.

Teixeira, Manuel. *Toponimia de Macau.* Vol. 2, *Ruas com Nomes de Pessoas.* Macau: Imprensa Nacional, 1981.

Thomson, John Stuart. *The Chinese.* Indianapolis: Bobbs-Merrill, 1909.

Trigault, Nicola. *China in the Sixteenth Century: The Journals of Matthew Ricci: 1583–1610.* Translated by Louis J. Gallagher. New York: Random House, 1953.

Verlinden, Charles. *The Beginnings of Modern Colonization.* Translated by Yvonne Freccero. Ithaca: Cornell University Press, 1970.

Viney, Clive, and Karen Phillips. *A Color Guide to Hong Kong Birds.* Hong Kong: Government Printer, 1979.

Wakeman, Frederic Jr. *The Great Enterprise: The Manchu Restoration of Imperial Order in Seventeenth-Century China.* 2 vols. Berkeley: University of California Press, 1985.

Walter, Eugene Victor. *Placeways: A Theory of the Human Environment.* Chapel Hill: University of North Carolina Press, 1988.

Watson, James L. "Standardizing the Gods: The Promotion of T'ien Hou ('Empress of Heaven') Along the South China Coast, 960–1060." In David Johnson et al., eds., *Popular Culture in Late Imperial China.* Berkeley: University of California Press, 1985.

Weber, Max. *The City.* Translated and edited by Don Martindale and Gertrud Neuwirth. Glencoe, Ill.: Free Press, 1958.

Weber, Michael. "Land of Saints and Sinners," in *Geo* 6 (September 1984), 81–93.

Welch, Holmes. *Taoism: The Parting of the Way.* Rev. ed. Boston: Beacon Press, 1966.

Weller, Robert P. *Unities and Diversities in Chinese Religion.* Seattle: University of Washington Press, 1987.

Werner, E.T.C. *A Dictionary of Chinese Mythology.* New York: Julian Press, 1961.

Werner, E.T.C. *Myths and Legends of China.* New York: Farrar & Rinehart, c. 1922.

Willetts, William. *Chinese Art.* Vol. 1. New York: George Braziller, 1958.

Willetts, William. "The Maritime Adventures of Grand Eunuch Ho," in *Journal of Southeast Asian History* 5, no. 2 (September 1964), 25–42.

Williams, Jeri Bernadette. "Namban Byobu of the Momoyama Period," *Journal of Asian Culture* 8 (1984), 33–60.

Wills, John E., Jr. *Embassies and Illusions: Dutch and Portuguese Envoys to K'ang-hsi, 1666–1687.* Cambridge, Mass.: Harvard University Press, 1984.

Wolf, Arthur P. "Gods, Ghosts, and Ancestors." In Arthur P. Wolf, ed., *Religion and Ritual in Chinese Society.* Stanford: Stanford University Press, 1974, 131–182.

Wong Shui Kwan. *Macao Architecture: An Integrate of Chinese and Portuguese Influences*. Macau: Imprensa Nacional, 1970.

Wu, Chun-hsi. "Overseas Chinese." In Yuan-li Wu, ed., *China: A Handbook*. New York: Praeger Publishers, 1973, 413–442.

Yang, C. K. *Religion in Chinese Society*. Berkeley: University of California Press, 1967.

Yen Ching-Hwang. *Coolies and Mandarins: China's Protection of Overseas Chinese During the Late Ch'ing Period (1851–1911)*. Singapore: Singapore University Press, National University of Singapore, 1985.

Yin Guangren and Zhang Rulin, comps. *Aomen jilue* (Gazetteer of Aomen). Taipei: Ch'eng-wen Publishing, 1968 (originally published in 1751).

Young, John D. "An Early Confucian Attack on Christianity: Yang Kuang-hsien and His *Pu-te-i*," *Journal of the Chinese University of Hong Kong* 3, no. 1 (1975), 159–186.

Yuan Bangjian and Yuan Guixiu. *Aomen shilue* (History of Macau). Hong Kong: Zhongliu chubanshe, 1988.

Yung Wing. *My Life in China and America*. New York: Henry Holt, 1909.

Zhang Renjun. *Guangdong yudi quantu* (Atlas of Guangdong). Guangzhou: Shujingtang, 1897.

Zhang Tingyu et al., eds. *Mingshi* (History of the Ming). 28 vols. Beijing: Zhonghua shuju, 1974.

Zhao Rugua. *Chau Ju-Kua: His Work on the Chinese and Arab Trade in the Twelfth and Thirteenth Centuries, Entitled Chu-fan-chi* (Record of Foreign Nations). Translated by Friedrich Hirth and W. W. Rockhill. Taipei: Ch'eng-wen Publishing, 1967.

Zhu Huai and Xu Naiji, comps. *Xiangshan xian zhi xinxiu* (Gazetteer of Xiangshan District, Revised). 8 *juan*. Xiangshan, 1827.

About the Book and Author

"For many people who have encountered it, Macau makes a deep impression on the imagination, as if the city were not entirely real or, rather, not of the real world. Macau often seems dreamlike, as though it were sustained by the effort of some powerful imagination."

In this evocative essay on the cultural and social history of a unique and fragile city, Jonathan Porter examines Macau as an enduring but ever-changing threshold between East and West. Founded by the Portuguese in 1557, Macau emerged as a vibrant commercial and cultural hub in the early seventeenth century. The city then gradually evolved, flourishing first as a Eurasian community in the eighteenth century and then as an increasingly Chinese city in the nineteenth century. Macau became a modern manufacturing center in the late twentieth century and is now destined for reversion to the People's Republic of China in 1999.

The city was the meeting ground for many cultures, but central to this fascinating story is the encounter between an expansive, seaborne Portuguese empire and the introspective, closed world of imperial China. Unlike the other great colonial port cities of Asia, Macau did not provide natural access to the hinterland, and this geographical and historical isolation has fostered a unique balance of cultural influences that survives to this day. Poised on the periphery of two worlds, an isolated but global crossroads, Macau is a unique cultural and social melange that illuminates crucial issues of cross-cultural exchange in world history.

Establishing Portugal and China as distinct cultural archetypes, Porter then examines the subsequent encounters of East and West in Macau from the sixteenth to the twentieth century. Avoiding the traditional linear chronological approach, Porter instead looks at a series of images from the city's history and culture, including its place in the geographical context of the South China coast; the architecture of Macau, which reflects the memories of its historical passages; the variety of people who crossed the threshold of Macau; the material culture of everyday life; and the spiritual topography resulting from the encounters of popular religious movements in Macau.

Jonathan Porter concludes his literary journey by reflecting on the character and meaning of the many cultural and social influences that have met and mingled in Macau. His words and photographs eloquently capture the essence of a place that seems too ephemeral to be real, too captivating to be anything but an imaginary city.

Jonathan Porter is professor of history at the University of New Mexico and author of *All Under Heaven: The Chinese World.*

Index

New Perspectives on Asian History

Series Editors
Ainslie Embree and Edward Farmer

MACAU: THE IMAGINARY CITY
Culture and Society, 1557 to the Present,
Jonathan Porter

Learning to Be Modern: Japanese
Political Discourse on Education,
Byron K. Marshall

Merchants and Faith: Muslim Commerce and
Culture in the Indian Ocean,
Patricia Risso

FORTHCOMING

The Making of Early Modern Asia:
A Polycentric Approach,
Sanjay Subrahmanyam

The Environmental History of China,
Mark Elvin